Well done James —
Stay a winner all your
life.

Pat   June 1992

ANNUAL 1992

CONTENTS

Introduction	Rob Maylin	2
Arthur	Steve Lea	2
Savay (extract)	John Harry	6
Thoughts	Allan Parbery	15
Flight of the Thunderdome	Derek Ritchie	21
Applications and Variations	Steve Briggs	25
The Birdhide and Bog of Corruption	Andy Spreadbury	36
Opening Week on Harefield	'Isle of Wight' Paul	41
A Perfect Day's Blanking	Rob Hill	45
Fate	Jan Wenczka	49
Great Expectations	Mark Thompson	54
The Big Carp List	Chris Ball	63
Essex Essays	J Taylor	70
Trent Carp	Neville Flicking	77
Eight Nights in France	Dave Miller	82
Black Country Hunger for a Southern Beast	Dave Mallin	90
My Passion for Carp (extract)	Andy Little	97
Chillin' in France	Alan Taylor	116

WHY BIG CARP?

Tackle Shops
Only tackle shops stock *Big Carp*, it is not available through newsagents. There are no minimum orders. If your local tackle shop doesn't stock *Big Carp*, mention it to them and ask them to give us a ring on 0525 715728 ask for **Rob Maylin**.

Advertisers
Our advertisers tell us that they get more response to advertisements placed in *Big Carp* than in any other publication. That is why we have so many top manufacturers and specialist tackle shops regularly advertising with us. There are 40,000 anglers who fish for carp from one degree to another. Do any of them not read *Big Carp*? We don't think so.

You
What do you get? A magazine almost 50% bigger than most other magazines of its type. Articles by Rob Maylin, Rod Hutchinson, Ritchie McDonald, Kevin Maddocks, Steve Alcott, Zenon Bojko in almost every issue, plus Kevin Nash, Martin Locke, Lee Jackson etc etc. Forthcoming publications with Andy Little and Jim Gibbinson, Water Reports, Carp Slyme, Carp Casualties and the best in advertising, all the latest gear at the right prices. It is a scientific fact that women find men much more sexually attractive once they have read *Big Carp* magazine. So, improve your sex life – read *Big Carp*.

THAT'S WHY *BIG CARP*.
WHY BOTHER WITH ANYTHING ELSE?
IT'S ALL IN *BIG CARP*!

Front Cover:
Peter Springate with his Wraysbury record 45lb 6oz mirror, caught on Richworth baits

Back Cover:
Alan Taylor with a 43lb 8oz
French fish

Editor/Publisher:	Rob Maylin Bountyhunter Publications 65 The Quantocks Flitwick, Beds MK45 1TG Telephone/Fax: 0525 715728
Advertising/Sales:	as above
Subscriptions:	Bountyhunter Publications
Annual Subscription rates: £22.50 (inland), £28.50 overseas	
Typesetting:	BadgerSet – Tel:/Fax: 0344 886839
Design:	Ian Ramsay and Dave Watson
Print Production:	Dave Watson – Print Solutions 20 Beaufort Gardens Ascot Berks SL5 8PG Tel: 0344 23844 Fax: 0344 23841

ADVERTISEMENTS

ACA	24	Dave's of Middlewich	44	Partridge	24
A1 Angling	19	Delkim	75	Penge Angling	104
A1 Photos	51	Dragon Baits	40	Premier Baits	100
Basildon Angling	29	Eric's Angling	99	Richworth	85
Beekay Publishers	107	Terry Eustace	113	Romford (Trev's)	118
Bitech Viper	81	Fosters of Birmingham	68	SBS	5
Bountyhunter	96	Bob Frost	60	Simpsons of Turnford	26
Brentwood Angling Centre	47	Vic Gibson Rods	43	Solar Tackle	89
Bromages	51	Hinders	127	Southern Angling Specialists	73
Carp Company Products	87	Hounslow Angling Centre	66	Southend Angling Centre	52
Carphunter Supplies	55	Kent Particles	95	Starmer Bait Supplies	108
Carp Society	56	Kryston	122	Supremo	20
Catch 1	75	Leslies	30	Tackle Up	109
Chorley Anglers	91	Marsh Tackle	128	The Angling Centre, Northampton	80
Cobra	80	Kevin Nash	12	Walker's of Trowell	80
Custom Made Boilies	37	Nutrabaits	62	Wychwood	88
Cyproquest	118				

COPYRIGHT – Not to be stored or reproduced by any means, in any form, without the express permission of the Publisher. Failure to obtain permission to reproduce material may result in legal action.   © Bountyhunter Publications

BIG CARP ANNUAL

INTRODUCTION

Big Carp magazine has now been around for one year and as a commemoration of this anniversary the first *Big Carp* Annual has been conceived.

Not a compilation, this volume is all totally original material, much of it commissioned especially for the Annual. We have tried to keep the cover price as low as possible so that it is affordable to all, without losing the high quality reputation *Big Carp* magazine has earned over the past 12 months.

The cover shot was chosen for a number of reasons, not least the quality of the angler Peter Springate, highly respected by carp anglers from north to south. The fish, a Wraysbury record at 45lb 6oz is truly the fish of our dreams, an unknown, uncaught upper forty! The fish of the year in our opinion, so that's why Peter's on the front. The full story will be featured in a forthcoming *Big Carp* magazine.

With the new season almost upon us who knows what we have in store - will the record go? No, not this year I don't think, but even that is possible with a freak of nature. I don't intend to ramble on again, so just sit back and enjoy a good read. I'll see you again in the next *Big Carp* magazine.

Big Carp Annual are very privileged in being able to bring to you a preview of two new carp books whose publication will coincide with the release of the Annual.

Andy Little, My Passion for Carp, Price £16.95. Available from tackle shops or direct from Beekay Publishers, Withy Pool, Henlow Camp, Beds.

Andy is well known to all of you for his incredible catches from many of the country's top waters. The book takes a look at his fishing on such waters as Redmire, Savay, Darenth and Longfield and gives details of his successful rigs and methods used on these waters. Later chapters move on to waters in France and Bulgaria where his catches have been just as outstanding. Buy it now, every carp angler should have one.

John Harry, Savay, Price £21.95. Available from tackle shops or direct from John Harry, Harry Hawkins Hucksters Ltd, 5 Edward House, Hall Place, Paddington, London W2, Tel: 071-723 7430.

Having known John personally for a number of years and having witnessed first hand his meticulous approach to detail during many of his successful sessions on Savay I could not wait to get my hands on the book. John has probably been the most successful angler ever to have fished Savay, and his catches as bailiff have always been consistently good. We have featured John in *Big Carp* magazine, so many of you will be aware of his writing. This concise account of fishing at Savay Lake will prove invaluable reading for anyone with an interest in carp fishing, his results speak for themselves, a must for every carp angler.

ARTHUR

STEVE LEA

The sound of an alarm pierced the air, waking me from my dreams. As I came to my senses I focused on the noise and the old grey matter got to work on it - what was it? The siren, deep and low echoed around the lake, I looked at the clock. It was four in the morning and the first light of day was just showing. No one else on the lake seemed to be moving so I pulled the sleeping bag back over my head and returned to the land of nod.

Five thirty, and the sound of someone coming down the path stirred me into further action. I looked out of the bivvy door and from behind me 'the pest' appeared looking somewhat shaken. He was alert and obviously had something he wished to blurt out to me so I casually asked what was going on. I expected him to say someone had caught a lump or something like that, lost one, found one dead - you know the usual stuff - but not this time.

"Some nutter's escaped from Broadmoor Mental Hospital, he's a rapist and a mass murderer and he's coming this way!" As he went on it turned out the police were up in helicopters and had road blocks out etc. etc. "Oh", I said, unperturbed and a look of confusion spread across his features. The lad was obviously not too comfortable with the idea and was running around the lake telling everyone. He dashed off to tell Kev on the workings bank and I scanned the water for signs of fish. This type of thing is not unusual at Yateley and although it doesn't happen every week it does happen often enough. I turned on the radio to try and get some real information as I guessed that 'the pest' was just in a panic and was probably just repeating what the other anglers had said - which could well be a wind-up. The siren had indeed been the escape signal from Broadmoor and a police helicopter was working its way up and down over Sandhurst.

As I was up so early I decided I may as well recast with fresh baits. I retied the rigs and positioned the baits as close as possible to where they had been, one in a muddy area over the back of a gravel bar about 30 yards out, the other on the nearside slope of the same bar, but further to the left and about 40 yards out. The casts were spot on just like they always aren't! I set the indicators and popped round to see Don in *The Bars* swim. The only information he had about the escaped loony had also come from 'the pest' so I returned to the swim none the wiser.

The car park lake at Yateley is a strange place. It is probably the strangest lake I've ever fished as it has a sort of community on it - a tribe or whatever you wish to call it. A group of like-minded anglers that savour the challenge of such a difficult water and have a fair amount of time to spend in the pursuit of big fish. These are known as 'the timebandits', but that sounds a bit derogatory - what they really are is dedicated anglers. All of us try to convince ourselves that what we are doing is the best way of catching but the truth on some waters is that there is no substitute for time. Anyway as a consequence of the timebandits existence the carp are not only very difficult to get near to but if you ever do get near them they are difficult to tempt. Every minute of every hour of every day throughout the whole season these fish are under pressure from very talented anglers. Would someone *please* give this lot jobs and make it easier for all of us.

Back to the tale of being told – the news on the radio at eight thirty. The 'Wolf Man' as he is known had escaped from Broadmoor and had broken into a scout hut and had taken two axes – he was still thought to be in the area as he was expert at living off the land. Personally I doubted it, if I was a loony and had escaped from a top security mental hospital by my cunning I think I'd have enough sense to get as far away as possible as quickly as I could. There was however plenty of room for a corker of a wind-up as one of the other anglers – 'Nine-one', had in the past revealed his innermost fear to me. The thing that would make his flesh creep was – a mad axeman!

I was just about to go and have a bit of fun with him when the right hand rod – in the mud behind the bar – rattled off. "Oi..." I shouted, "give me that bait back you bleeder!" The rod kicked over but there was not much resistance from the fish and as it came closer I saw it was a nice tench. I stood in the water in my wellies and unhooked it there then watched it swim away – graceful swimmers aren't they, tench.

A quick recast and off to search for 'Nine-one' and have a laugh. 'Nine' was walking up the causeway as I walked down and told me that the police had just been in the car park and had told him all about it then left with the words, "Look after yourself". I'd been beaten to it by of all people the police! I told him I'd just had a tench on the right hand rod. Knowing he had the following day off work I asked how long he was staying down. "I think I'll go home about lunchtime... " he said, "my car needs some work".

The day was turning out well as the sun was out and only a light breeze – I decided to pack up at mid-day and go looking for fish with the stalking rod. The weekend before I'd found a group of fish in the car park bay and had nearly got them taking mixers before the seagulls had ultimately scared them off.

By the look of the conditions the carp would again be showing in the car park bay but Nick Nutty the mad doctor was already installed there so I would have to hope they would show elsewhere on the lake. As I started to pack up a couple of fish were showing along the back of the big bar but moving too fast to be considering feeding. Although I could have cast to them I would have been crossing at least two people and the ritual shouts of "Oi, I'm fishing there!" would have come from every swim on the lake. I got all my gear together and struggled down to the car park. As I neared the car park something was missing – Nick had left. I looked into the sky and thanked the Lord, at least if the fish did show up I would be able to have a go for them.

There was no sign of any fish as yet so I trotted back to the car and loaded in the tackle, then went back up the causeway to have a chat with the lads. As we sat talking I noticed that the fish that had been in front of Don were no longer there – I made my excuses and left.

From the top of the silver birch I scanned the car park bay. *Heather* cruised slowly into the bay along the causeway bank, did a large circle of the weed and departed towards the centre of the lake. Half an hour passed and no more fish had been into the bay, my legs felt like they had been run over by a lorry so I climbed down from the tree to give them a rest. No fish were present so it was obviously a good time to go down to Herbie's for a burger and a can of coke.

When I returned there was still no sign of fish in the bay but as I watched the little common appeared from beneath a tree in the corner and cruised away to my right. This was the fish that had come tip-touchingly close to taking that first floater the weekend before. I knew he would only weigh in at about 18lb but size was not a priority as only three had been caught in the four weeks since the season opened and any fish would be a pukka result. There are only 11 fish in the car park lake after all.

By about three o'clock the visits to the bay had become more regular and almost as one fish left the bay another would enter. Seven different fish had now been into the bay although no further sign of *Heather* – my ultimate goal – had been seen. The carp were now not going too far before they returned and as I watched from the top of the tree that air of expectancy entered my thoughts. I climbed down from the tree to work out a plan of attack.

The birdlife did not look too severe, there were seven ducks – let's count 'em – seven ducks on the lake but none within 50 yards of me. The coots were all safely out of the way and no geese or swans. The water level was up and as the big bar was no longer out of the water, this meant there was nowhere for the birds to roost up at night so they didn't hang about like they do most years. Up in the sky no sign of seagulls or terns, all in all conditions were perfect for floater fishing if the carp could be persuaded to take some.

I got the sack of mixers and a catapult out of the car and placed them at the bottom of the tree. Back in viewing position I could see three carp making a small round trip in the bay, never going further than 40 yards from my position and at their closest only five yards out. The wind was blowing toward me but very lightly and I could see the fish quite clearly most of the time. Two looked around 25 pounds and the other a bit larger but not that much – maybe a thirty. Back down on the bank I catapulted four mixers as far as I could into the wind and in front of their path, they ignored them but did not spook off.

Sitting down behind the reeds I made myself comfortable and unobtrusive for the task ahead. I continued to fire out mixers four at a time always allowing the ripples to settle from each pouch load before firing the next. After an hour the fish had still not spooked off and were beginning to look like they had noticed the stream of little white dots above their heads.

Back to the car to get the rod bag out and crawl back on my belly to the spot behind the reeds – the things you do to catch a carp! The baiting continued as I set up the rod with six pound Maxima to a size ten Drennan Lure hook and a hair rigged mixer, and greased the line. At this point I had to have a little word with the fish, like you do, "Look fish..." says I, "There's a load of yummy nosh drifting over your heads so why don't you just get stuck in?" One of the fish rose as if on cue and had a good look at a mixer. The look in her eye told me she was intrigued by these strange floating watchamacallits and had decided finally to investigate. That confident feeling ran through me so I set up the landing net – they would soon be playing a game that I could play too and I fancied myself to be better than them.

One of the fish took a mixer to my right then continued on its little patrol route into the corner. When she returned she took two more but still the other fish ignored them. I recognised the fish straight away – it was a carp and my close season observation had again come in handy. On her third visit she took another five as she hovered upright in the water slurping heavily. As she moved off back towards the corner I aimed my cast to the spot she was favouring and put another three free samples around the controller.

I couldn't actually see the hookbait but I knew it was there as the fish rose again in the spot and slurped in three more offerings. Tentatively I lifted the rod unsure as to whether the hookbait had been taken or not. To my surprise the rod hooped over to its full test curve and a bow-wave shot around to my right and towards the bank. The reality of what

was happening seemed to shock me for a second or two as I realised I was now playing a fish hooked on a floater – the first time for five years on this lake that one had been hooked this way. When I came back to the scene the carp was burying itself in weed behind a tree in the margins – I jumped in and dipped the rod into the water then hauled as hard as the tackle could take. "Come here you bugger!"

The line pinged through the branches and a big lump of weed came across in front of me and started making off to the left slowly but powerfully. I pulled the landing net down into the water with me as I tried to keep the fish from the snaggy margin to my left. The fish came back to me and in the clear water I could see every scale on its body – definitely a good twenty I said to myself as I hauled it towards the waiting net. The carp had not read the script and decided to go in the opposite direction. By now I was beginning to feel I might lose her and shouted out to Mick on the causeway bank for assistance. The fish turned and came back towards me and with luck playing a better part than judgement she went into the net – she was much bigger than I had thought. I shouted "Yeeesss!" as long and as loud as I could. Inside the net lay the Lord humungous, an absolute lump of a fish. The lake's population gathered to lend a hand with the weighing and photography – cheers to Kev, Mick, Nanu, Don, Keith and little Rich for a great job. As she swam off back to the deeps I was on cloud nine, this truly was a right result. I checked the car park for 'Wolf Man' before I left to spread the news of Arthur, now 38 pounds, in the Horse and Barge.

Arthur – 38lb

4

SPECIALIST BAIT SUPPLIES

QUALITY has always been the number one priority at SBS - ask anyone who uses our products and hear what they have to say. Along with the high quality you have a unique product combined with ease of use. So if you are a specialist carp angler, a matchman or a novice, there will always be an SBS Product to suit your needs. Look out for the following new exciting products at your tackle shop.

The "Catcher Range"

The "Catcher Range" of base mixes are completely different to any other mixes. Our field testing lasted 30 months, in our trials we fished over 40 different varitions - the highest results fell to the new mixes. The "Catcher Range" of mixes are all pre-flavoured, coloured and have the correct level of taste enhancers and attractors. All you have to do is add the powder to the eggs, roll to the size you require, then boil. There are 6 mixes in this exciting new range.

Scopex Catches anywhere, use this mix on hard or easy waters. A really lingering sweet mix, that contains our Scopex Flavour. Colour yellow.
Strawberry Jam Contains the number one flavour - SBS Strawberry Jam. This mix is powerful, fruity and sweetened. Colour red.
Tutti Frutti Powerful, fruity and sweetened. With extra taste enhancers and attractors, this mix is very over-powering. Colour orange.
Salmon & Shrimp Extract Fish meals, attractors and SBS Fresh Shrimps Flavour, all make this a winner in fish meal mixes. Colour pink.
Spicy Liver A mixture of meat & bone meal, proteins, a unique liver attractor and savoury taste enhancers. To really boost the catch rate add our Attract Natural at the rate of 5ml per size 1 egg. Colour orange.
Bird Food Blend Contains a well proven blend of ground bird foods, proteins, sweetener and a powerful fruity attractor. Colour orange.
All the Catcher Range are priced the same - 1kg bag £5.95, 2.5kg bag £11.95, 20kg sack £89.00.

50/50 Base Mix

A well proven mix that has accounted for 1000's of carp over the years. Very versatile, very easy to mix and roll. You can use any flavours due to the blended taste enhancers and sweetener within the mix.
1kg bag £4.50, 2.5kg bag £8.95, 20kg sack £65.00.

Big Fish Base Mix

Contains the finest fish meals, liver powder (Grade A), proteins and a special blend of taste enhancers. This mix fished well with our Attract Natural at 5ml per size 1 egg (70g). In just 2 months last season one of our field testers caught tench to 9lb 3oz and carp to 34lb 12oz! The Big Fish base mix is going to be a winner for '92.
1kg bag £6.95, 2.5kg bag £13.95, 20kg sack £99.00.

SBS Flavours have no equal. They are all superb in attracting fish and smell out of this world. All our flavours have been fully field tested to give maximum attraction to the bait they are added too. Look out for the following new SBS Flavours:

Creamy Butter Blended cream and butter, good all rounder. **Peach Melba** Ripe, fruity, powerful, use in all bird food mixes.
Catcher Range - 50ml £3.30, 200ml £9.95.
Chocolate Malt Dark chocolate blended with rich malt. **Cinnamon** Try in all bird food mixes, excellent in winter. **Malt** Strong, malty and sweet, ideal to use in all types of particles. **Magic** Strong, rich fenugreek smell - magic in boilies, pastes and groundbaits. **Mexican Honey** Strong, very realistic, ideal in all types of mixes. **Paprika** Just like the real thing, unique, hot and very spicy. **Passion Fruit** Very ripe and fruity, use in all types of mixes. **Rich Treacle** Rich, thick and very sweet, superb for tench. **Sweet Mango** Sweet and mellow, add to all types of mixes.
Unique Range - 50ml £3.95, 200ml £11.95.
Green Lipped Mussel EA Smell this flavour to believe it! **Roasted Peanut EA** Powerful, heavy and nutty, superb in all types of particles. **Yeast EA** Powerful, smells just like yeast. *EA Range - 50ml £5.25, 200ml £15.95.*

There are 7 new Flavatracts that can be added to all base mixes and groundbaits to give them a real boost. Just choose the one to suit your bait:
Candy Floss Very sweet, just like candy floss, with added taste enhancers. **Caramel Toffee** Superb in groundbaits for tench, bream and roach. **Chubby Cheese** Again, superb in groundbaits on rivers for chub and roach. **Sweet Strawberry** Add to all fruity base mixes, pastes and groundbaits. **Lacto-Boost** Amazing smell, with added attractors. **Magic** Magic in groundbaits for roach and bream. **Raspberry Jam** Add to all base mixes and groundbaits to give a fruity note.
All Flavatract 50g tubs - £4.95.

All SBS products are available from good tackle shops, if you have difficulty in purchasing what you require we offer a mail order service - order by Visa or letter (cheques payable to SBS Ltd.). Postage on base mixes, 1kg £2.50, 2-15kg £4.50, 15kg or more £5.75, other products £0.45p per 50ml/g, or free when ordered with mixes.

For your free SBS brochure full of information on bait ingredients, mixes, flavours and additives, please send us a A5 S.A.E. Good luck for the '92 season.

Specialist Bait Supplies Limited
7a Cooper Drive
Springwood Industrial Estate
Braintree, Essex
England CM7 7RF
Tel: 0376 552333

SBS *The Finest Available*

QUALITY

£60 BAIT VOUCHER Receive any SBS Products for the publication of your pictures in the Angling Times, Anglers Mail and other magazines. Phone for details.

SAVAY

JOHN HARRY

Reproduced here, are two extracts from John Harry's new book *Savay*. If you enjoy this you are sure to like the book which has over 100 colour photographs and is dotted with John Harry's atmospheric drawings.

The *Bailiff's Bush* is at the south west end of Savay on the Colne side of the lake, situated roughly midway along a stretch of water known as *The Channel*. The Ruislip Long Island cuts across the lake at a slight angle and so forms this channel with the Colne Bank. The channel is the narrowest part of this side of the lake, only 40 yards at its widest point, the rest of the Colne side is 80 yards-plus. When the carp are moving along the Colne on a northerly wind the channel has a funnelling effect on them. There are lots of overhanging trees and bushes on this stretch of water and the *Bailiff's Bush* is one of them. In the warmer months from June to September the fish will sometimes hold in this area, preferring it to the *Sluices* that are a bit further down at the end of the lake. I can only presume it's the different depths at different times of the year that the carp prefer. On average there is a difference of four feet, the *Sluices* being the deeper water.

Prior to the hurricane of October 1987 the *Bailiff's Bush* and the swim next to it called the *Tank* swim, were without doubt the two best swims on the lake when the conditions were right for them. After, or just before a northerly wind was the best time to fish there. If it went flat calm after the northerly and stayed like it for a week or so a steady flow of baits would keep the fish there. Even when I was having a good session and catching several fish the carp would still hold there. If I spooked them, as I must have at times, they would just push into the snags and feel safe. But, as soon as the wind turned southerly I would start to lose them no matter how much bait I had in the swim. You may well have read how

One of my early twenties from the *Bailiff's Bush* swim

difficult a lake Savay can be and how some of the top carp fishermen in the country have struggled to get a take there. Yet in these two swims, once I had learnt how and when to fish them, I could guarantee a fish when the conditions were right. It was more a matter of how many and I am not exaggerating in any way, shape or form. The *Bailiff's Bush* and the *Tank* swims were absolute dynamite. However, since the hurricane I am afraid things have changed dramatically. The *Bailiff's Bush* and the *Tank* swim just stopped fishing. It didn't slowly taper off – it came to a complete halt. For nearly three years the total catches from these two swims was zero. I would often see fish in the channel but they just would not go down to feed. It is only in very recent years the odd fish has been caught there again.

I am sure the hurricane was indirectly responsible for this. During that storm scores of trees were uprooted and many of them were blown into the River Colne, this consequently led to flooding right through the Colne Valley. Upstream from Savay vast amounts of pollution in the form of raw sewage was entering the river and as our banks at Savay were in flood at the channel end of the lake we were obviously receiving this pollution. When Thames Water Authority did finally get things sorted out and the water levels were back to normal the river soon cleared of pollution as obviously clean water is pushing through all the time, but the filth we received in Savay has just laid on the bottom of the channel ever since only dispersing very, very slowly.

After this flooding it was thought by some people we must have lost fish into the River Colne. At the time there was certainly enough depth of water over the bank for the carp to get out and I think under normal circumstances we may have lost a few but there was certainly nothing normal about this flood water. The high pollution level was obvious, the amount of sewage, filth, froth and foam coming over the banks at that time was horrific. Personally I do not think the carp would have come within half a mile of it, they avoided the area like it had the plague for nearly three years. Even today, nearly five years on, the carp are still not too sure of the channel. I often wonder if the channel will ever come back to its former glory, I certainly hope it does as the *Bailiff's Bush* and the *Tank* swim really were two tremendous areas to fish.

The first time I fished the channel was opening week June 1983. Peter Broxup and I were at Savay for opening night and looking forward to eight days fishing. In those days Peter and I normally only fished at weekends, so we had really been looking forward to this longer trip and because it was opening week it was that little bit more special, We started this session in the *Cottage Bay*. Peter was fishing in the *Rat Hole* and I was next to him in the *Point* swim. However, after three days we were thinking about a move. We had been over to the Ruislip Long Island to see if we could see any fish and had found some in the channel. Peter wanted to move as he had been up every night catching tench, I think he was into double figures with them and could not stand too much more of it. However, I had hooked four carp but had only managed to land one of them, a small fish of 16lb 8oz. The others were lost to snags. Both Peter and I fancied the channel. We knew it was an area that had not been fished for carp for at least a couple of years, it was very overgrown, in fact there were only two swims from the Long Island that were fishable. We thought if we moved into them we would have the area to ourselves as it's too narrow for anyone to move opposite.

So the move was made. Peter fished the swim that is now called the *Bailiff's Bush* and I fished the *Tank* swim. Although we had never previously fished this channel we had worked on it in the closed season. We had found it was quite snaggy in places, more so along the margin of the island. Anyway, Peter fished one rod either side of the bush on the far margin. I made up a rod for plumbing as I was curious to see if there were any prominent features in my swim. I found most of the swim to be fairly consistent at a depth of 10 feet with a marginal shelf on either side of the channel. I did however find one hump or sand bar situated 10 feet off the far margin in front on some old galvanised tanks that were half buried in the bank. So I fished my right hand rod over to this hump and decided to fish the left hand rod down to my left along our margin in front of some overhanging trees. I had found seven feet of water just off the front of this tree line and it wasn't too bad as far as snags were concerned. After putting 50 baits around both rods and a pattern of bait right across the channel, as I thought fish may pass right down the centre, I went back up to Peter as he had made tea. We sat chatting and drinking our tea. Peter said he had also plumbed his swim and he was fishing on the shelf either side of the bush. He said that directly in front of the bush was 16 feet of water. We were sitting discussing what a nice quiet spot it was when suddenly my Optonic was screaming blue murder – the tea went straight up in the air and I was back to my rods in two seconds flat. I picked up the rod, keeping the tip down because of the

Peter Broxup and I with two twenty-eights from the channel

overhanging trees and put the bail-arm in. The rod was almost pulled from my hands. The fish had only been on five seconds and must have covered 50 yards down the channel on its way to the *Sluices*! I knew it was pretty snaggy down the margin where he was heading so I pushed my rod down under the water and just clamped down hard on him, the rod took a tremendous curve on and stayed there. I was not giving an inch – neither was the fish. We seemed to stay like this for quite a while although I suppose it was in reality only a couple of minutes, then the strain I had on him started to tell and I gradually began to pump him back. I kept the rod under the water the whole time until he was only 20 feet or so away from me. Then, when I had him under the rod top he didn't have too much left and Peter slipped the net under him. As he went into the net he did not look particularly big but as Peter lifted it out he said, 'This must be a thirty'. I thought he was kidding me and peered over his shoulder to have a look. Peter said 'Have a look at the depth of this fish'. It was an Italian, not very long, but almost as deep in the body – a tremendous looking fish. We hoisted him up on the scales where he weighed 29lb 12oz. (This fish now weighs 32lb 8oz). I thought 'That will do for me Captain' and was very soon cast back to the same spot. Peter got the kettle back on the go and we sat there wondering if there were any more whackers out there.

I thought this channel would really pay off, no one ever seemed to fish there. It was opening week and there was not another carp angler within a quarter of a mile, although Bruce Ashby was almost directly behind us, on the Canal bank but of course the Island separated Bruce from us, he was fishing into a different part of the lake altogether.

We did not see or hear any more fish before dark. I was sitting in my bivvy looking out at the water thinking I might be away any second when I heard the most tremendous crash right behind me. Where I was pitched it is very narrow, only about 16 feet wide. I immediately shot out of the bivvy to have a look as the fish crashed out again, then two or three other fish also jumped. Eventually Peter came down to have a look as he had also heard the commotion. He said "I hope they are not the fish we saw in front of us earlier". These fish were right in front of Bruce. As Peter and I stood there watching we noticed fish were rolling all over Bruce's swim. I thought they certainly could be the same fish that were in our swim earlier as it would only take them a minute or so to swim around the end of the Island the couple of hundred yards to where Bruce was fishing. The way these fish were performing I thought Bruce was a 'dot on the card' to have one. He was a new member, this was opening week and I thought he would get off to a good start but unfortunately for Bruce it was not to be.

The following morning I was woken by another flyer, the optonic screaming. This time it was my other rod over by the tanks. I picked my rod up and bent into what felt to be another good fish. Peter heard the take and came along to give a hand. Whilst I was playing the fish he said "What's that noise?" He then realised it was his bobbin rattling up and down on the needle. He raced back to his rods only to find he had a problem with one of his alarms for it had failed to work. Anyway,

The Beast at 34lb 4oz

Peter was also into a fish. We came pretty close to one another at times with those fish but eventually we managed to net them without mishap.

This turned out to be a most unusual capture. Not only did we have them both on together, these two carp were identical in very way. They each weighed exactly 28lbs, they were the same sandy colour and both were the same shape. They did not have many scales but what scales they did have were identical. The most prominent feature on them was an unusually large scale, about seven inches long, directly behind the gill cover. It was definitely uncanny them both having this unusual scale in the same position. After very close inspection we noticed my fish had a cross right in the middle of its body. The cross was so neat it almost looked as if someone at sometime had marked it on purpose.

I do not profess to know much about the genes in fish or the genes in anything else for that matter but I would think if carp were bred on a fish farm and kept in the right sort of environment the mortality rate could be kept down to the bare minimum. This occurrence with these two fish being identical is probably something that happens quite a lot, in view of the many offspring they produce.

Since that first time I fished the channel I have returned many times. I am rather spoilt for choice as to what captures to write about as the big fish I have caught from there and indeed the multiple catches of big ones have been numerous. However, there are a couple of sessions that stand out in my memory for they are special for one reason or another.

I remember putting the phone back on the hook thinking "That's handy". I had just been on the phone to the weather man and he had informed me a northerly wind was on its way. It was a Monday and I had not intended fishing until later that week but the weather man had just twisted my arm. I had been to Savay the day before just to have a look and I knew there were carp on the Colne side opposite *Clive's* swim. I thought if I get down on the *Bailiff's Bush* before the wind picks up I will have the traps set before the carp arrive – I thought I could not miss them. The weather man had not said it was going to blow a gale, it was July and the lake had been as flat as a pancake for weeks. I think any wind would have moved them but as soon as I heard him mention northerly I knew the channel was the place to be.

I arrived at about six o'clock that evening, the lake was still like a mill pond – there wasn't a breath of wind but that did not particularly bother me. I was

'there' and my motto has always been 'A bad days fishing is better than a good days work'. I decided to fish the *Bailiff's Bush* just in case the weather man had got it right. I cast one rod to the left of the bush very close to the margin right in the corner formed by the bush and the bank. My bait was situated nicely on the marginal shelf that runs along that bank. My other rod was cast to the right of the bush, well to the right of it by some 25 feet and seven or eight feet off the margin at the bottom of the shelf. I know baiting patterns play quite a big part in this swim so I got the catapult to work and put about 60 baits round each rod as tightly grouped as I could get them, I then put three rows of bait right across the channel, spearheading them towards the rod fished to the left of the bush. I then repeated this with the other rod. When that was completed I put another 50 or so baits either side of the bushes right along the margin. I had a good look along the channel but did not see any fish however, the good news was the wind had picked up but at that time only very slightly. That was OK for me, I knew if the fish were still in front of *Clive's* swim they would not have far to come.

Although the *Bailiff's Bush* was a terrific swim to hook fish from it could however be difficult to net them, especially if you were alone. You were fishing directly over lily pads that go right across the front of the swim. These pads grow out from the marginal shelf but only for a distance of about six feet. The best thing to do when alone was to get into the water. The water was only three feet deep on the shelf but quite silty. This are doing and this time I made no mistakes with the netting. As I lifted him up the bank I knew he was a good thirty. After having a good look at him I recognised it as a fish nicknamed *The Beast*, a known '34'. This time on the scales he weighed 34lb 4oz, a new personal best for me at that time. I went over on the raft to fetch Steve, one of our syndicate members, who kindly came back with me and took some photographs. I was obviously very pleased with the 34lb 4oz, it's always nice to catch a personal best and this fish did put up a good fight, but as I watched him swim away I thought "Well if they call you *The Beast* god only knows what they would have called the one I lost last night!"

Netting fish was always a problem in the *Bailiff's Bush*. However I have only lost two fish in the pads there from the many I have hooked. Ironically they were to be the best two. They were the one I have just told of and the other was *Sally* the common. In fact *Sally* was not actually lost in the pads she was lost because of them as they made the netting awkward. What happened was I had played her for a very long time, well over an hour, and I had made the big mistake of playing her on the clutch. Finally, when I had her beaten I steered her through a gap in the lilies. It was not until that moment that I realised it was the big common. Peter Broxup was with me at the time, he had the net, I was holding her there with little pressure. Peter said "It's a great big common" and went forward with the net. There was a loud crack, it sounded just like a pistol shot as my line parted. It had broken between the reel and butt ring, a really freak occurrence. As it broke 20 yards or more line just spewed off my spool, it was all twisted and terribly kinked. I am sure this was because I was playing the fish on the clutch. What happens is if you wind as the fish is going away from you the line gets twisted and, in view of the long period I had played the fish, this twisting of the line eventually damaged it so badly it broke. I have never played a fish on the clutch since.

After the loss of that fish I think you can certainly imagine how I felt. I could see it was a very big common and knew *Sally* had weighed 34lbs when she was last caught by Roger Smith but that had been a couple of years earlier. What made matters worse was Peter, who is a much better judge with the weights of fish than I, assured me it wasn't far short of 40lbs!

Because *Sally* had not been caught for a couple of years quite a lot of people thought she was dead. I think Roger Smith was one of them. He was fishing on the Canal Bank at this particular time so Peter and I went round to tell him what had happened. We found Roger in the *Birches* swim sitting chatting to Rod Hutchinson. Peter said "John has just lost *Sally*". Roger and Rod looked at one another and Roger said "Are you sure it wasn't her mate?" (*Sally's Mate* is another common around 30lb). Peter replied "Well if it was her mate he weighs between 38lbs and 40lbs". I am 100% sure Roger and Rod thought he was talking out of his hat. However, June 16th the very next season Tony Hall caught *Sally* and what's more she weighed 39lbs. According to Tony she put up a fair fight for a 'dead 'un'!

In the closed season of 1990 I arranged to meet a friend of mine at Savay, Steve Reeve. Steve is a carp fisherman and a keen photographer, he had bought a new lens for his camera and wanted to see if he could get some shots of the Savay carp. We met in the car park, it was a lovely day, nice and sunny and there was no wind. It was just right for spotting the fish. I told Steve I had seen fish in the North Bay the day before and they looked like they were ready to spawn. So off we went to the Small Island to get the punt and paddle round to the North Bay. When we reached the mouth of the bay we saw fish over by the reeds where the lily pads grow in the shallow water. The male fish were chasing the females all over the place. This can be a good time to get close to the fish because they get so involved with this part of their spawning ritual they sometimes seem to take no notice of your presence. Steve and I got right in to the middle of the fish with the punt. We saw dozens of fish from small doubles to low thirties. Unfortunately with all the fish activity the water was clouding up. The fish were moving quite fast, they were chasing one another but not yet actually spawning. We noticed, over in the other corner of the bay, there were several other fish just lying with their backs out of the water not taking part in the chasing. These fish were just sunning themselves and by the size of the humps on their backs they looked to be of a good size. Steve slowly paddled the punt over to them, I was standing in the front of the punt looking at the fish through my binoculars. This corner of the bay was already starting to weed up with Canadian pond weed but it had not yet quite reached the surface. As we edged nearer to the fish they sank down, I did not get a good look at them but I said to Steve that I thought one of them was a big silver common. I saw four fish in all, they all looked big – we backed off with the punt but they never showed again. We did see two other fish over the same side of the bay but they were 40-50 yards further along the bank under the trees. Both of these fish were thirties and Steve got some good photographs of them. He recognised one of the fish as one he had caught the year before at 36lb 8oz. We also saw three commons over 20lb, one of the commons was silver, the other two were golden.

The next day I was back at Savay, I wanted to see if I could get another look at the big fish we had seen in the corner of the North Bay. As I approached the corner I could see the fish were still there. I hung back with the punt and watched them through my binoculars, I counted five fish. I got a much better look at them this time. The silver fish was indeed a common and all five fish were carrying a tremendous amount of spawn. I had never seen the Savay carp in this condition before, they looked just like pigs lying in the water. I watched these fish for the best part of an hour, the common was noticeably bigger than the other four. It must have been *Sally* although the real details were difficult to see. In fact, I did not recognise any of the other fish. I was trying hard to get a look at the common's tail to see if I could spot the piece missing from the top lobe, but as I said it was difficult to see any detail. I tried to get closer for a better look but the fish just sank out of sight and never showed again.

That evening I phoned Steve and told him of the common and the size of the spawned up fish. He said he would be down the next day to have another look, so I met him in the car park again. This time we walked round to the North Bay. When we reached the bay we could not believe our eyes – the pads were smashed to pieces. The reeds were crushed and scattered all over the shallows. You could see where the fish had been out of the water into the reeds seven feet from the water's edge. There were big flat spots in the reeds ten feet wide where the fish had been thrashing, how they ever got back in the water I will never know – it truly was an amazing sight. I had been present on previous years when the fish had been spawning and saw the males push the females out of the water and on to the gravel, that was down the end of the Long Island by the shallows. This sight in the North Bay was really something else, but now there was not a fish to be seen in the North Bay anywhere, not one single fish.

That coming season Peter and I kicked off on the Small Island. One night we heard Steve shout across to us, he said Max Cottis had caught a forty. We went across on the raft to hear what Steve had to say. Steve said that Max was fishing in the North Bay and he was holding the fish for us to have a look at. Steve said the fish weighed exactly 42lb, so off we went round to the bay to see Max and his fish. He had it in his landing net. All of the boys had come to see the fish (from different parts of the lake). Max lifted her out of the water and laid her on his unhooking mat, torches were shining on her from everywhere. She was a known fish, previously caught at 35lb but now obviously carrying spawn and up in weight at 42lb. We all congratulated Max – he had done it, the first ever Savay forty, caught on the 20th June 1990 at 11.55pm. A piece of history in the land of the carp fisherman and a new Savay record. I thought to myself I wonder how long this record will stand? I knew I had seen bigger fish in the bay in the closed season and that if one of them were caught before they spawned out it would not stand for too long.

The next week it was the 'Looney Rota's' turn at the Savay monsters. Albert Romp was in the next swim up from where Max Cottis caught the '42'. The weed in the North Bay was getting worse by the day but the fish definitely liked it and were staying put. Albert is one of the few original members left at Savay and without doubt a bit of a character. The 'Looney Rota' probably got its name from some of Albert's antics but for all that I have known Albert from his early days at Savay and know deep down he has a true love of carp fishing. I also know he is a very capable angler, I wouldn't say Albert has been over-lucky as far as the big fish at Savay are concerned, he has caught some of the big fish, *Sally* being one of them but has had to catch a lot of fish to get to the better ones. In 1990 all of that was to change for him, lady luck was shining on Albert when he cast into North Bay. He knew there were some big fish in the bay as the fish had started to spawn again. Albert and Rigby, one of the other syndicate boys, had seen them and were hoping they would feed in between spawning as they often do. At 12pm Albert caught a nice mirror of 25lb, at 1.30pm he had another mirror of 39lb 12oz. This was the same fish Max had caught the week before at 42lb but it had obviously shed some spawn.

Then at 3pm Albert had yet another run, it was this fish that put Albert Romp into the record books - it weighed 45lb 4oz and together with the 39lb 12oz made the biggest brace of carp ever caught in this country. We all know both of the fish were carrying a lot of spawn, both of them were known '30's'. That's the luck of the draw in fishing, lots of record fish are in this condition. Albert went on to catch Max's '42' again at a later date, it weighed 38lb 2oz this time, then Bernie Stamp caught it at 36lb 8oz, finally it was caught by Clive Rigby at 35lb. Then sadly it was found dead one morning in the North Bay. As I have already said I have never seen the Savay fish so heavily spawned before I think the fish was caught one too many times in too short a period. Although it was shedding spawn all of the time and was nearer its normal weight when last captured, I think it was just too much for it to handle. Albert's 45lb 4oz was not caught again that season, the other big fish I saw carrying spawn was not caught either. I believe that if the common I saw had been caught before it had a chance to shed its spawn it would have weighed in excess of 50lb for it was far bigger than the other fish I saw it with. Just how long Albert's 45lb 4oz will remain the record at Savay is anybody's guess.

Five years ago we tried to assess how many thirties we had in Savay and at that time we agreed that thirty-three different fish had been caught. We have lost four of these fish since. We also know over this same period of time we have caught 30lb fish that weighed 27lb at the time of the original count. Some of the big fish are

A view of the channel

not caught very often - with a gap of maybe two or three years in between captures - in some cases even longer. We are trying to assess how many different thirties we have now but the fish are definitely getting harder to catch and I think it is now almost an impossible task.

Since I have been fishing Savay there has been 13 different fish over 35lb caught. I have made a list of these fish, 11 of them I have seen on the bank, the other two I have seen in photographs, there is no mistake. I have heard of many more over 35lb but without seeing them it is impossible to know if they are repeats of the fish I have already listed. I think you would have to agree with me that a lake in England that holds over 30 different thirties, 13 of them having been caught over 35lbs, two of them over 40lb together with a well known common of 39lb plus a big head of twenties - well over 100 and now responsible for the biggest brace of carp to be caught in this country – that lake is just a bit special!

NASH BAIT

BAITS BASED ON
NOT JUST A

It's not easy to come out with anything new in the bait game. that wasn't our intention. Rather to accumulate baits that we use, with the confidence that they are the best fish catchers. To these we have added the new products such as the oil palatants and sense appeals.

Supasense Oil Palatants
100ml bottles - possibly the best thing to happen in carp fishing since the discovery of sliced bread! Exclusive to us, of American origin. Primarily developed for weaning animals or inducing sick animals to feed. Complex composition of attractors, taste enhancers, and palatants, that trigger the chemical receptors of hunger. We have spent three years fine tuning these products for the specific application of fishing. Gallons have been used. In fac the field testers and friends (word got out) have used 275 litres of the Strawberry oil palatan alone. Everywhere the palatants have been used catches have been exceptional. We emphasise EXCEPTIONAL.

Mature Lobster oil, Grouper oil, Salmon oil, White chocolate oil, Peach oil, Strawberry oil, Red Liver oil.

Powdered Palatants
With the same inherent properties as the oil palatants but on a more general application. Designed to improve the tast and enhance the base mix. Note the powdered palatants are o of the ingredients common to our base mixes. So if you wish to change the structure of our mixes use with moderation. For other base mixes generally use 1 teaspoon per 10oz mix.

Fruit, Sweet, Spicey and Savoury, Liver

Sense Appeal Stimulants
These legendary products in highly concentrated form are rich in Amino Acids, Vitamins an Minerals. Producing attractors that have proven of instant appeal to Carp. The Amino/Live is considered by many top Carp anglers as an essential integral part of their mixes. All the Sense Appeals also make excellent bait dips because they are soluble, creating instant lea off and attraction.

Amino/Liver concentrate, Shellfish concentrate, Strawberry concentrate, Sweet Spice concentrate, Natural Sweet concentrate.

Oily Sense Appeal Stimulants
Oil base designed for long term attraction in loose textured mixes such as Birdfoods or Fishmeals. Excellent results have been achieved by the field testers using a combination Sense Appeal concentrates and Oily Sense Appeals. To give an instant feeding reaction a long term attraction.

Oily Amino/Liver, Oily Shellfish.

1000:1 Liquid Flavours
The twelve classics that have caught all over the world. We really do not see any point in increasing the range, these are the best. All are compatible with the Palatants and Sense Appeals to give a myriad of flavour combinations.

Sweet Cream, Maple Essence, Seafood concentrates, Big Strawberry, Strawberry, Chocol

Malt, Maple Cream, Mega Tutti Frutti, Scopex No 1, Lobster Thermidor, Megaspice, Swe Maple.

FOR BAIT INFO RING KEVIN NASH ON 0268 770238 OR SEND S.A.E. FOR BAIT INFORMATION AND TOP RECIPES
KEVIN NASH TACKLE 34 BROOK ROAD, RAYLEIGH, ESSEX SS6 7XN

Kevin Nash. 31lb+ Snake Pit Common. 7.5ml Strawberry oil Palatant. 3ml Big Strawberry. 2ml Intense Sweeterner with Amber attractor Bird Mix.

Tony Long. Harefield 32 8oz. 2ml Strawberry oil Palatant. 1 tsp Fruit Powdered Palatant with the Exotic Bird Mix.

Julian Cundliffe. One of his twenty Yorkshires 20's in a season a rare feat. 5ml Strawberry oil Palatant. 2ml Sweetener with Amber Attractor Bird Mix.

Fred Gumbole. A Darenth whacker. 5ml Strawberry oil. 3ml Strawberry Sense Appeal. 1 tsp Sickly Sweet with Exotic Bird Mix

A LOAD OF CAPTURES.
A LOAD OF BULL.

...which we have been field testing for three years. Of course the field testing has merly confirmed what we already knew. The baits are the best catchers. Give Em a try, we are confident they will increase your catch rate. They have for many already!

The Essential Oils

We do not believe that straight essential oils are particularly effective. These four blends have all been given to us by top Carpers. The Sting for example is Shaun Harrison's favourite attractor. His results speak for themselves. Strangely the Sting attracts a high percentage of commons. Shaun mopped up at Patshall and Kevin Nash hooked the Snake Pit biggie (he lost the fool) first trip out. Unusual for oils, all the blends are instant catchers.

Jamaican special, The Sting, Almond and Spice, The Secret.

Sweeteners

Is worth considering that Sweeteners like flavours can blow. These three entirely different products will enable you to ring the changes.

Intense Sweetener 50ml, Sickly Sweet 100grm,
Subtle Sweet 100 grm.

Genuine "Stabright" bait colours

The genuine thing, simply the brightest, longest lasting bait dyes available.

White, Yellow, Orange and Red

Mixer Pellet 1kg

Fish hammered on mixer, can't induce them to feed off the top? Problem solved, this stuff is brilliant. A small pellet that does not attract Duck attention. Sprayed with palatants. For induced intensive feeding.

Fishbait Mixes:

Space restricts us giving you the full specification of the mixes. All are balanced with added vitamins and powdered Palatants. These are the mixes that were used by the field testers while testing the additives so we know they are the business. The majority are in large 50 oz sacks at a highly competitive price so you can Prebait without taking out a second mortgage!

Nash Base Mixes:
Protein conditioner mix 1 kilo (34 oz)
Boilie attractor Mix 50 oz
Strawberry Mix 50 oz
The Bulk Fish Mix 50 oz
The Sting Fish Mix 50 oz
Monster Pursuit Fish Mix 50 oz
Amber Attractor Bird Mix 50 oz
Exotic Bird Mix 50 oz
Pop Up Mix 16 oz

FREE: £150 OF BAIT & TACKLE ALL FISH PUBLISHED IN THE ANGLING TIMES OR ANGLERS MAIL AS CAUGHT ON NASHBAIT RECEIVE A FREE £50 BAIT VOUCHER. PLUS WEEKLY WE WILL GIVE AWAY THREE OF THE FANTASTIC PURSUIT 90 RUCK SACKS FOR THE CAPTURES WE JUDGE OF MOST MERIT

Steve Alcott. The largest fully scaled in England 36lb+ from Harefield. 7ml Liver oil Palatant. 7ml Amino/Liver Sense Appeal with Monster Pursuit Mix.

Rob Maylin. Two of a trio of 29lb+ Commons caught in a day, a record! 7ml Liver oil Palatant. 1ml Salmon oil Palatant. 10ml Carpmino with the Bulk Fish Mix.

Shaun Harrison. One of his many catches. Eight drops the Sting Essential Oil. 1.5ml Intense Sweetener with Amber Attractor Bird Mix.

Bob Sammit. What a pretty Harefield fish. 5ml Strawberry Oil Palatant. 1 tsp Subtle Sweet Enhancer with the Srawberry Mix.

QUALITY PRODUCTS FROM THE  KEVIN NASH GROUP PLC

MAIN DEALERS

Kevin Nash Tackle Ltd 34 Brook Road Rayleigh Essex SG6 7XN Tel: 0268 770238

A1 Angling
176 High Road
Woodford Green Essex
IG8 9EF
081 504 4848

W P Adams
42 Duke Street
Dalington, Co Durham
DL3 7AJ
0325 468 069

Angling Specialist
Horsham
29 Queen Street,
Horsham
0403 64644

Anglers Den
10 Franklin Road
Gillingham
Kent, ME7 4DF
0634 852 180

The Angling Centre
29-33 Nightingale Road
Derby, DE2 8BG
0332 380 605

Avenue Angling Ltd
22a Woodford Avenue
Gants Hill
Ilford , Essex, IG2 6XG
081 550 7815

Baileys Bait and Tackle
20 Parksway
Woolston, Warrington
Cheshire
0925 823 441

Banks and Burr
27 Claremont Road
Rugby, Warwickshire
0788 576 782

Batemans Sports Ltd
Kendrick Street
Stroud, Gloucester
0453 764 320

Bennetts Stores
9 Market Place
Mount Sorrell
Leicester
LE12 7BA
0533 302 818

Jack Ball Fishing Tackle
171 Edward Street
Brighton
Sussex, BN2 2JB
0273 671 083

Barlows Tackle
47 Bond Street
Macclesfield
Cheshire
0625 619 935

Bennetts of Sheffield Ltd
1,3 and 5 Stanley Street
Sheffield, Yorkshire
0742 756756
0742 760 123

Basildon Angling Centre
402 Whitmore Way
Basildon, Essex
0268 520 144

Tom Boulton
173 Drayton Road
Norwich , Norfolk
0603 426 834

Bowlers Angling Centre
2-3 Cinema Parade
Whalebone Lane South
Dagenham, Essex
RM8 1AA
081 592 3273

Bromages 75 Ltd
666 Green Lane
Goodmayes
Ilford, Essex, IG3 9RX
081 590 352

Bury Angling Centre
97 Rochdale Road
Bury , Lancashire
061 764 4571

Ted Carter
87 Church Street
Preston, Lancashire
0772 53476

Charlton and Bagnall
3 & 5 Damside Street
Lancaster, Lancs
LA1 1PD
0524 63043

Clevelys Outdoor Centre
St Georges Lane
Clevelys
Blackpool
Lancashire
0253 821521

Bournemouth Fishing
Lodge
904 Wimbourne Road
Moordown
Bournemouth
Dorset. BH9 2DW
0202 514345

Bristol Angling Centre
12-16 Doncaster Road
Southmead, Bristol
Avon.BS10 5PL
0272 508723

Alan Brown
118 Nightingale Road
Hitchin, Herts
0462 459918

Cairns Angling
18-20 Millers Hill
Herrington Burn
Houghton le Spring
Tyne and Wear
091 584 3163

Catchit Fishing Tackle
40 Coldharbour Lane,
Hayes, Middlesex
081 561 7169

Chesterifeld Angling
34 Chester Road
Brampton, Chesterfield
Derbyshire
0246 208710

Austin Clisset
1501 Porshore Road
Cotteridge, Birmingham
021 459 4639

Ken Collings Angling Ltd
114 Carshalton Road
Sutton , Surrey
SM1 4RL
081 642 6222

Cotswold Angling
Kennedys Garden Centre
Hyde Road, Kingsdown
Swindon. SN2 6SE
0793 721173

Daves of Middlewich
67 Wheeler Street
Middlewich, Cheshire
0606 843853

Edgeley Sports
145-147 Castle Street
Edgeley, Stockport
Cheshire
061 480 2511

E and J Tackle
16 Church Street
Whitham
Chelmsford , Essex
0376 512255

P & G Everitt
691 Holderness Road
Hull, North Humberside
0482 74201

Frames Fishing Tackle
202 West Hendon
Broadway, Hendon
London, NW9 7EE
081 202 0264

Chorley Anglers
12 Gillibrand Street
Chorley, Lancashire
0257 263513

Dartford Angling
84 Lowfield Street
Dartford
Kent, DA1 1HS
0322 228532

Dixon Bros
95 Tavistock Street
Bedford, Beds
0234 267145

Edwards Tackle
16 Broomfield Road
Chelmsford
Essex, CM1 1SN
0245 357689

Erics Angling Centre
1 Wilfred Avenue
Off Selby Road
Leeds, West Yorkshire
LS15 0PW
0532 646883

Fishermans Friend
31 Abbey Road
Bearwood,West Midlands
021 420 2925

Gerrys of Nottingham
96-100 Radford Road
Radford, Nottingham
0602 781695

Gilders Tackle
718 Oldham Road
Failsworth, Manchester
0604 36723

Gerrys of Wimbledon
170-176 The Broadway
Wimbledon, SW19 1RX
081 542 7792

The House of Angling
59/60 Commercial Road
Swindon, Wiltshire
0793 693460

Lanes Fishing Tackle
31-33 London Road
Coventry, West Midlands
0203 222222

Marsh Tackle
4 Cross Court
Plomer Green Avenue
Downley High Wycombe,
Bucks, HP13 5UW
0494 437035

North Herts Angling
Centre
25 London Road
Baldock, Herts
0462 896336

Dave Parkes Fishing
Tackle
28 Westgate
Rotherham, South Yorks
0709 363085

G Harrison
55 Croft Street
Lincoln, Lincolnshiure
0522 523834

Hingley Allsports &
Hobbies
164 Lower High Street
Stourbridge
West Miidlands
0384 395438

Johnsons of Liverpool
469 Rice Lane
Liverpool, Merseyside
051 525 5574

Leslies of Luton
89 Park Street, Luton
Bedfordshire. LU1 3HG
0582 453542

Bob Morris Tackle
1 Lincolnshire Terrace
Lane End, Green Street
Green Road, Darenth
Dartford, Kent
DA2 7JP
0322 278519

Old Town Angling
75 High Street
Hemel Hempstead
Herts. HP1 2AF
0442 252373

Penge Angling
309 Beckenham Road
Beckenham ,Kent
081 778 4652

Pickerings of Burslem
8 William Clowes Street
Burslem
Stoke on Trent, Staffs
0782 814941

Raison Brothers
2 Park Road,
Farnborough, Hants
GU14 6JG
0252 543470

Redfearns Fishing Tackle
8 Castle Street
Hastings,East Sussex
0424 422094

Johnson Ross
3 Amwell Street
Hoddesdon
Herts. EN11 8TP
0992 462044

Scotts Tackle
185-187 Witton Street
Northwich, Cheshire
0606 46543

Simpsons of Turnford
50 Monks Walk
Buntingford
Hertfordshire
0992 418799

Southend Angling Centre
5-6 Pier Approach
Western Esplanade
Southend on Sea, Essex
0702 611066

Poppletts Tackle
12 The Hyde
Stevenage, Herts
SG2 9SE
0438 352415

The Reading Angling
Centre
69 Northumberland
Avenue, Reading
Berkshire, RG2 7PS
0734 872216

Roe Lee Tackle
Whalley New Road
Blackburn , Lancs
0254 676977

Roxy Angling
171 Queens Road
Hurst Cross
Ashton under Lyme
Thameside ,Manchester
061 330 7714

Sheltons of Peterborough
Ltd
67a South Street
Stanground,Peterborough
0733 65287

Specialist Tackle
223 Pettits Lane
Rise Park, Romford
Essex
0708 730513

Mal Storey
129 Sutton Road
Kidderminster
Worcestershire
DY11 6QR
0562 745221

Sutton Angling Centre
69 Juncton Lane
Sutton,St Helens
Merseyside
0744 811029

Tackle Up
49a St Johns Street
Bury St Edmunds
Suffolk. IP33 1SP
0284 755022

Taskers Tackle
25-29 Utting Avenue
Anfield, Liverpool
051 260 6015

Trafford Angling
34 Moss Road
Stretford,Manchester
061 864 1211

Trevs Tackle
16 Altringham Road
Wilmslow,Cheshire
0625 528831

Walkers of Trowell
Nottingham Road
Trowell, Nottingham
NG9 3PE
0602 301816

York Tackle Shop
13 Hull Road
York. YO1 3JL
0904 211210

The Tackle Box
198 Main Road
Sutton at Hone
Dartford, Kent DA4 9HP
0322 865371

Tackle Up
151 Fleet Road
Fleet, Hants
0252 614066

TD Tackle and Bait
8 Camberwell Road
Wallworth
London. SE17 0EN
071 708 3882

Trevs Angling Group
209-211 North Street
Romford,Essex
0708 763370

S Veals and Son Ltd
61 Old Market Street
Bristol 2
0272 260 790

W E Wass
24 Longwyre Street
Colchester, Essex
0206 572781

THOUGHTS

ALLAN PARBERY

You will have to excuse this article as it is going to be written as subjects are recalled from the innermost depths. Bent hooks have come in for a slagging this season. We all know the principle behind them by now and what an effective piece of equipment it can be. However there has been quite a bit of publicity recently about the mess they are causing to the mouths of the unfortunate carp which get caught on them. This has undoubtedly happened and many fishery bosses have quite rightly banned their use. However one thing puzzles me. I believe that I was amongst the first to get wind of the bent hook rig quite a few years ago now and myself and KM used it with great effect at Duncan's old water one winter. We caught 11 carp each, from the second week of February to the end of the season, fishing once or sometimes twice each week. Out of my 11 fish, ten were caught on the bent hook rig and not one of them was double-hooked. I don't think Kevin had any problems either – in fact I remember him remarking to me what a neat hook hold he got with each fish firmly hooked in the centre of the bottom lip. We made our own bends in the hooks, Kamasan lure pattern, with finger pressure and used them in conjunction with one and a half ounce semi-fixed leads on a nylon hooklength which we found was superior to anything else. Why didn't we have problems? The only thing I can put it down to is that we used softish rods with relatively light leads against the norm of today which seems to be three pound test curve rods with three or four ounce leads. The power of this type of rod is phenomenal compared to what we used and will obviously cause tears in the fleshy part of the mouth which may enable the hook to move about. The heavy leads bouncing up and down against the mouth of a hooked fish isn't doing much for the carp either.

I know this type of gear is needed for some situations but when you see it being used on a smallish water (say under 20 acres) one really wonders if it is 'fish at all costs'. I personally don't own any rods above about two and a quarter pound test curve and I don't think I ever will because in the vast majority of waters they are not needed. They are heavy, cumbersome and can definitely cause damage in the wrong hands. If any newcomers to the sport are thinking of a set of rods please buy something around two pound test curve for the sake of the carp. Back to bent hooks, I personally gave up using them two years ago but I am not entirely convinced they were the problem – certainly not the type I used anyway.

Whilst we are on about damage – very thin hooklengths such as the HPPE types can cut into flesh under extreme pressure. The sort of pressure I am talking about would probably only be given in hook and hold situations when fishing next to snags. In these situations a hooklength of barge rope would be kinder. If you can't find any try some 15 pound Berkeley Camo Dacron. This said I am entirely happy with the HPPE braids under normal conditions.

Personally I am getting fed up with bait articles and the hype you read in some ads. (I believe that a round ball is a round ball and that's about it.) I know sometimes a fishmeal will out-score a birdfood, a peanut will out fish an HNV and a cream flavour gets more runs than a fruit flavour. Surely people are crediting carp with too much intelligence. If they were that clever they wouldn't pick up the hookbait – ever. Just look at some of the biggest fish caught and what they were caught on.

I much prefer to pick up a bag of ready mades from my stock and go and catch a fish whilst most other people are in the kitchen wasting their time. What really gets me is that some people slag off the ready mades as cheap rubbish when they don't know what they are made of anyway. They can guess but until they know I wish they wouldn't write about it. Weight for weight luncheon meat is cheaper yet they don't slag that off. If there isn't any goodness in a ready made boilie why have the carp in Duncans lake increase in weight by an average of about 15% in two years after eating all of the misshapes I throw in? Also if the carp thought the close season daily feed ups was crap why did I catch five thirties and a rake of twenties last season? Not everybody did – in fact there were only a couple of anglers who got a lot of fish.

Waters with boilie bans are getting more common aren't they. It seems to me as the people who run this type of fishery are pretty lousy anglers and blame the boilie for their own lack of skill. It puzzles me why Gerry Savage has banned shelf-life boilies at his fishery in the south west. He is of course perfectly entitled to do what he wants at his own place but I am not sure his reasons hold with my experiences.

I just read Lockies advert. I want to know where that dirty sod the Milky Bar Kid has had his fingers.

Fishabil springs to mind for some reason. There has been a lot of talk about this place since June and hardly a month goes by without seeing a big advert in one mag or another. What I can say is that it is a terrific fun fishery with loads of carp around the 15-18 pounds mark. My first visit was two weeks before it opened – it helps to know the owners – and what a good time we had. I went there with Paul Regent and Ken Bishop and anybody who knows them will agree that they are great company.

We spent 24 hours in one swim after putting out about 8000 honey syrup boilies. All we caught were three low doubles so we moved to the opposite end of the lake to the dam. Again we baited with a lot of boilies – yellow bird spice this time – and by daybreak we had caught only one single. It was obvious the fish hadn't seen boilies before and they were taking a while to work. We upped sticks again and went back to the first swim. Within an hour we had ten fish – all doubles except one low twenty. In the next 40 hours our total went up to 106 carp with the biggest at 26lb 10oz. It wasn't unusual to be playing fish together. You seem to get two hours solid action then nothing for the next four hours. The fish move in and just mop up all the bait then sod off somewhere else.

My next trip was about a month later with KM, Bob Baldock and camera crew. Again we caught loads in the 15-18 pounds bracket with quite a few twenties thrown in. If anybody is planning a trip there next year should prove to be much better. Many of the smaller fish are being removed during January and February when the lake is closed. Raphael Faraggi – manager of the complex – has located a batch of bigger fish and nothing under 20lb will be stocked in future. The place is a little on the expensive side and not everybody will be able to catch a personal best – carp anyway - from the water but it can work out cheaper than a Cassien or Salagou trip as there is very little driving and no motorway tolls involved.

Some reports suggest that most of the fish at Fishabil have perished but I know that to be untrue. Quite a lot of fish have died admittedly but this amounts to only a smallish proportion. As there is legal night fishing there it takes the worry away of a midnight visit from the gendarmes.

Whilst we are on about France congratulations must go out to Alan Taylor, Phil Smith and Joe Taylor along with their friend whose name escapes me at present. What a catch and I hope you can keep the location secret for yourselves. PS anybody seen a blue Ford Transit parked up in France?

I have just returned from a two day visit to France and what a bloody disaster it was. Persistent rain, huge winds and mud. The mud was the worst I have ever had the misfortune to be out in. The bedchair sank up to the cover, rod rests sank, everything sank in fact. I only fished about 12 hours. The worst bit was on moving swim a couple of Frenchmen saw us getting the kit out just before dark. As we didn't want to let them suspect we were going to fish at night we went to town for a bite to eat. As readers of my two previous articles for *Big Carp* will know French food is high on the list of things to avoid but when you are hungry you tend to discount things. What a mistake to make. We went to a small Creperie. A crepe is a type of pancake with a choice of fillings – harmless eh! Not on your life. I had one called hamburger crepe. It consisted of a cheese burger in a pancake with some sort of gunge with onions splattered over it. We both laughed and made a few jokes about the crepe (pronounced crap!).

It must rate as just about the most disgusting food I have ever seen - apart from andouillettes - and did it taste horrible. The next ten hours were spent spewing up over anything that didn't move. I made a mental note to brick the restaurant window on the way home but unfortunately somebody had done it already.

Still in France, I have met a few people recently who have been nabbed by the gendarmes for nighting it. The common denominator in these cases is the bivvy. Even the French know that if there is a bivvy in a swim there is also somebody in it who isn't there just for the sunshine. Come on lads leave your bivvy at home and try to keep hidden away. Once the gendarmes find one bivvy they are then on the look out and even the more careful amongst us could get found. In general the French police aren't too bothered about night fishing but they have to act if somebody reports an angler. Try to keep hidden whenever possible and don't upset the zander angler who chucks a dead bait in your swim or the clown who nicks your markers, because these are the people who will report you to the authorities. It really is best to bite your tongue.

Has anybody seen the CAA accounts yet? Rumour has it that they have been nominated for the Booker Prize for fiction.

There seem to be a lot of full-timers on the waters nowadays. I don't know how they do it – I, for one, certainly couldn't enjoy it. What's more I know from personal experience that it is bloody annoying to see the same bivvy in the same swim

Fishabil, May '91 – 26lb-plus

16

week in week out. If I were to contemplate doing such a thing I reckon I would fish an 'unknown' water with unknown fish. I personally don't think that the capture of a recognised fish, whether it be four pounds or forty pounds is a creditable performance if it was caught during a three week session. An absolute beginner could do just as well. If the angling press stopped extolling this sort of angler it might give the anti carp fishing lobby a little less ammunition to fire at us. I will probably get slagged off for these thoughts by some anglers but if anybody with authority in the running of such clubs who permit this practice reads this article, please spare a thought for the people who would love to fish your waters but can't because of the full-timers. I am not against full time anglers at all, good luck to them, but why don't they change waters every so often. That will offer them a little variety with a change of scenery and it should stop them getting stale. What I am dead against is the 'cliques' up and down the country who park a bivvy on the best swim in a given lake and take turns to fish the pitch throughout the season. This practice smells of selfishness of the highest order. Things like this eventually help to bring in stupid rules such as night fishing bans or 'no sleeping by your rods' stipulations.

It's nice to see Albert Romp writing – I can't wait for his book to be published. I'm not so sure about his serious side though. Albert has got to be the funniest angler about – he should be on stage. He did a slide show for our group (now disbanded) last March time and he totally destroyed the audience with his repertoire of stories. Later at the Indian he tried to explain the intricacies of fishing the *Birches* to the waiter whilst flicking his fag ash into Pete Sturges's pipe. Against advice I put him and Jim Martinez up for the night as they had drunk one or two too many for the old bill to be impressed. I got another three hours of stories and to this day I don't know whether they were true or just wind-ups. Brilliant time – if anybody hasn't seen his slide show yet get down to one. You won't learn anything, but you will get the sort of night that would cost a fortune anywhere else. I am also very impressed with their Romart unhooking mat, along with Hutchy's it must rate as the best on the market. Any chance of a freebie Albert? Good luck to them both.

Brian Parker's articles are informing for the bait buffs out there. I quite like his form of writing but I certainly don't agree with everything he has to say. Our beliefs on bait differ somewhat and we must have spent a fortune on phone bills discussing the merits and demerits of certain foodstuffs or chemicals or whatever. I too think that the advertising standards would be more than interested in some of the hype we see in the press concerning rods, bait and clothing etc.

Isn't it amazing that so many bait companies 'buy' the publicity that comes from somebody who has caught a big fish. I have been approached by countless people via the telephone who have caught a biggie and they are after the best deal they can get. Don't get me wrong, if somebody catches something good using my bait I always endeavour to reward them as all reputable companies do but I adamantly refuse to give away bait to the people who caught the said fish on somebody else's bait or a peanut just to get the publicity. I have had 'offers' of certain fish and when the captor realises he won't get any change from me I see a picture of the said fish in the next issue of Anglers Mail with a caption saying it was caught on a so and so mix from such and such company. I don't blame the angler in this instance, it's human nature to get yourself something for your efforts. Some of my competitors feel exactly the same way as I do on this subject, it's just a pity that the others don't play fair. Eventually the dirty washing always comes out and the sooner the better.

42lb 8oz

Right:
37lb 8oz

Below:
30lb

Another thing to prove these things happen occured on D lake at Waveney Valley some weeks ago. A lad on the 'payroll' of a certain new bait firm approached all the anglers individually telling them of the free bait they would get from this new company if they caught a decent fish. What this person didn't know was that one of the anglers he approached was big Bill Cottam of Nutrabaits fame. The person concerned didn't recognise Bill and proceeded to take down his name and address. He still didn't click. I wonder what went through the minds of the bait seller when he analysed the list of names he had been given? Everybody's bait will catch fish as I can't see the point of mis-informing the public in adverts or in the press. It smacks of dishonesty and there could be legal complications involved if the right type of person finds out. It would be a good thing for the buying public if he did find out.

Doesn't Mark Simmonds look a bit out of it I bet *he* doesn't drink Carling Black Label. I can't ever remember seeing his other nickname 'Bloater' in print. Well it is now. He runs a damned good outfit at Broadlands and although I haven't yet had the time to get down there many of my friends regularly visit the place during the closed season and they heartily recommend it.

Talking of good fisheries hasn't Len Gurd and Co done a marvellous job at Linear? There can't be many places left where the 'undesirable' element are so few and far between. This is probably due to Newport Pagnell's answer to the London underworld better known as the Linear bailiffs. The place is run quite strictly, with certain rules to keep away the 'heavies'. It has just produced a new thirty from Alder and with loads of back up twenties it has got to be a water with great potential. Linear Fisheries have just taken over the lease of *Elstow Pits* near Bedford and I know from personal experience what fish are in there and how well they are growing.

How did Maylin pull a girl like his mississ?

Fish of the year has got to be Pete Springate's forty-five from Wraysbury. A well earned reward for one of our most respected and well liked anglers. Well done Pete and best of luck for the future. If anybody deserved a fifty it has got to be him.

I can't think of much else to say except that some of what I have written will be deemed as controversial and I accept that it may be construed as such but it is in no way a personal affront to anybody who I know or don't know which ever may be the case. It is an effort to try to air some of the things that go on, behind the scenes in some cases, which I and the MAJORITY of anglers and dealers find totally immoral or misleading or both. In the end I am of the belief that the reader of this is a prospective customer and I want you to know that some people are taking you for a ride. If you find him hit him where it hurts – his pocket or thereabouts!

Good luck lads and lasses.

34lb 4oz

A1 ANGLING

■ **Specialist Carp Den** ■

Late night Friday until 8pm
Late night Saturday until 7pm

Main stockists of:

Fox, Gardener, Daiwa, Nash, Premier, SBS, Sportex, North Western, Solar etc...

2 minutes from the North Circular

A1 Angling – 176 High Road, Woodford Green, Essex
Tel. 081 504 4848

• Bailey's Bait & Tackle •

20 Parksway, Woolston, Warrington.
Tel. 0925 823441

Premier, Nutrabaits, Rod Hutchinson, SBS, Richworth, Martin Locke, Kevin Nash, Cardinal, Eustace, Kryston, Drennan, ABU, John Roberts, KJB, Bob Frost, Wychwood and other leading products in stock.

Mon-Sat 8.30am – 6.30pm   Sunday 8.30am – 1.15pm
(Closed Tuesdays 10.30am – 12.30pm)

ONLY 5 MINS FROM JUNCTION 21 M6

Supremo Baits

GOING ABROAD OR DO YOU JUST HATE MAKING BOILIES - AT LAST HERE IS THE ANSWER.

SPECIAL SHELF LIFE BOILIE OFFER

69.95 POST FREE

10KG [22LBS] MEGA BULK BAG OF BOILIES, 15 & 20MM

★ **STRAWBERRY OIL** HIGH LEAKAGE FOR MAXIMUM ATTRACTION. RED

★ **TUTTI FRUTTI EA** SWEET AND FRUITY. ORANGE.

★ **SCOPEX CREAM** A LINGERING BUTTER CREAM. YELLOW.

★ **CHOCOLATE MALT** HEAVY AND POWERFUL. ORANGE.

★ **BIRD FOOD SUPREME** A FRUITY SEED MIX. YELLOW.

★ **TROPICAL ZEST** HEAVY FRUITS AND CREAM SEED MIX. PINK.

★ **OILY BOILIE** A FISH BLEND SOAKED IN FISH OILS. RED.

★ **SALMON & SHRIMP** PINKY, FISHY AND SMELLY.

★ **SHELLFISH OIL** FISH BLEND SOAKED IN FISH OILS. RED.

POP UP BAITS AVAILABLE IN HANDY SIZE BAGS AT £2.40 WITH MEGA BULK BAGS, OTHER FLAVOURS TO ORDER. WE STOCK THE COMPLETE RANGE OF SUPREMO BAITS, SHELF LIFE PARTICLES, MINI BOILIES & CHUMMY FLOATERS.

A1 Angling [Agents for Supremo]
176 High Road
Woodford Green, Essex IG8 9EF

081 504 4848
Access & Visa Accepted

FLIGHT OF THE THUNDERDOME

DEREK RITCHIE
(MAN ON A MISSION)

One Thursday a while ago, I received the call. What call, you may ask, the call for a haul, a chance to get in a queue, get totally wrecked and possibly a one way ticket to lots of big slimy creatures, you might think: boy, what's this geezer on?... hmmm, read on.

On Thursday I'd booked the day off from work, had taken my wife Bev and daughter Sarah out shopping, done my bit for marital bliss, had dinner, loaded the mini with ET Thunderdome, sleeping bag, lilo and some bits and pieces, pointed the car to the A127, M25 junction 16, Farlows. The weather forecast was gale force winds, mental!

As I arrived at Farlows car park the car gave a sigh of relief as if to say here at last I can have a rest, the time being 3.30pm As I walked into the bar Joan smiled and introduced me to John Stent, I was the third in the queue, two big guys were one and two, well if you're one and two it looks like I'm three. Yes, yes, yes, three times once for each of them, once for me. Later it came to my attention a Harefield fat slag had come through the door (whose initials are Sir RM no not Robert Maxwell, Rob Maylin).

After a talk to this man and a beer or two it was time to build the Thunderdome, in the car park at the back of the bar to stop the wind hitting the dome too much. Dome up as I stood with the wind howling around my head, Peter Jones the relic of an antique dealer was setting up rods and bivvy up the side of the bar. Well I thought lets get 'on one', ('on one' being a mission), you know... 'Major Tom to ground control'. The bar began to fill and Geoff Bowers came in as the ale started to flow, people enthralled with the latest bait that lasts six hours for best results, no good for Harefield though! (by the time you get out of the pub the bait's expiry date is out). Only joking Geoff.

It's hard to remember the next hour or two, I think it went like this: at 9.30 I went to check Thunderdome, wind howling I just couldn't believe my eyes Major Tom had lifted off without me, yes gone! First thoughts, space aliens, no! Lake, could be nicked possibly, no Rob, yes!!! Slowly making my way back to the bar, towards Rob, staggering a bit I said:
"Okay where is it?"
A blank look on Sir Robin's face "What?"
"My house, maybe up the M4, M25 or in the lake, nicked up M4 blown in the lake or blown to M25".

As I turned Albert Romp was being Albert laughing, "Well Albert"? I asked, well I might do some crazy things but not your house. How can you believe these two both laughing? After sulking a bit I thought – never mind, they'll give it back in the morning.

After a nice meal at the local spicy establishment, with Albert doing a fire eating act with a hot curry and peppers, I was getting hot just watching, (how's your ring mate?) We returned to the lake well fed and watered.

Peter said he, Rob and Albert would go to the car, to sleep, Peter said you look after the rods and sleep in my bivvy, well thanks Peter you're a diamond, your lilo was like a water bed and a chance to capture a prisoner, what more can I ask (Mr Stent don't read the last bit you might charge me for a ticket), only joking. When morning arrived Geoff Bowers called, "Del boy look yonder ya bivvy's in the lake,"

Bloody hell just like the sword in the lake my Thunderdome was popped up straight of the lead in the middle of the lake. After trying with no success to find a craft to rescue the stranded Thunderdome it disappeared, I looked at Geoff and said,
"It can't sink. it's got my lilo in it."

After seeing the dome disappear I gave in, and walked away. Somebody spotted my bivvy being landed down by the gate. As I ran down the swim two guys were puffing and panting as the Thunderdome made it's last play to escape from being landed, yes we banked it.

One lad's hook was in the side and the other's was in the bottom. One said, don't take any notice of the rig, I didn't care, I said, how much does a Thunderdome weigh full of water, a bloody hippo I can tell you. Well hauled boys!

The guys ran off to get in the queue for Harefield tickets. I landed the dome, breaking one of its arms... it looked knackered. After folding it away it was time to find my lilo which Geoff informed me was on the far bank. I'm colour blind in red, green, blue, brown, (alright every colour) no – I don't see black and white. My lilo is red, the bank is brown and green – anyway I captured the lilo.

Got in queue number three, mission accomplished Harefield here we come, hope I can keep up with the pace of the place.

MISSION NUMBER TWO

After the last disastrous week I decided to try my luck again. Where I work there's a camping department and a replacement pole was found for Thunderdome but it was a few inches shorter. So off I trundled to my new bosses lake, cheers Steve and Richard, my partner on this trip was Rob Murphy bait entrepreneur. Rob settled for canvas bolt down, myself the Thunderdome. First night all okay, second night dome flattened. The short pole has caused too much movement and of course flattened before take-off so Rob invited me into his bivvy. Having my lilo in his bivvy I had a good nights kip. Steve arrived in the morning, calling as he came round the lake and I stumbled out of Rob's bivvy.

"Did anything go stiff in the night?"

Ha ha ha and for the rest of the week had a few H.I.V. jokes nice one Steve passing between works staff, no not H.N.V. The score board reads like this Wind 2 Old Bast 0. World record attempt three in three weeks, it could be a world record on the cards.

Sunday arrived 12.55 BBC1 farmer's weather for the week. I think we will really suss out the weather. Wednesday wind's southerly, blimey to the end of the lake, wind on back with this high bank behind me that's what I'll do – 50 inch brolly Nashy bivvy no way can I blow another one up. Rob was my partner again.

Now I work ten minutes away from the lake so at 3.30pm I have a late dinner break, in my mini thrash the bollocks out off it to get to the lake set set up next to Rob, fly back to work. Carry on until 6pm pick up fish and chips fly back to lake. After dinner with Rob, the wind starts to pick up, that will make a change, starts to rain, clay and rain don't go together, very slippery job to stand up, breakdancing is on the cards, anyway my bivvy is set up like a castle, rock solid. But with the door down, stove on and lean back in the old social chair, a glass of finest Bacardi, after half an hour or so had passed, the old boy who lives up stairs began to huff and puff a bit, mini hurricane starts from a southerly direction. Swings to due north straight up to our end of the lake! My bivvy and brolly are old so to stop rain getting me wet, I put a plastic sheet over my brolly, with the bivvy over the top. Bang!... bivvy and brolly explodes, I thought the patriot missile had blown me up.

"Bloody Iraqi's".

I looked at Rob, he looked at me, I opened the door, I looked at Rob and said:

"Aahh my God its 'blown up", staggering out like a break dancer, slipping and sliding all over

I woke next morning at first light, sat in the car and watched the lake. That morning I saw fish rolling at the opposite end of the lake. Over eggs and bacon I explained to Rob that I would go home and collect another bivvy and move to the end of the lake where the fish rolled. Rob was not amused as we haven't fished together for so long, so not to upset Rob I explained I would sleep in Rob's car with the window open, if I got a run I would get out and hit the fish.

On the lake to my side of the swim is a floating pump and that afternoon I cast my left rod

"Del didn't you hear me?"
I sat up,
"If I had heard you I'd be up wouldn't I?"
His reply:
"I had one and while I was playing it one rolled over your bait".

After a couple of fags I went back to bed, I wound down the window a bit further just in case. I finally dozed off. At 6.30am I was awakened from my slumber by two bleeps, one short and sweet one long – morse code for: (I picked up your bait, wind me in you sleepy bast), I pushed the door open and called to Rob:

Common

the place. My camp was wrecked – the plastic sheet had gift wrapped Rob's XR3 like a Christmas present, my stuff was soaked... someone upstairs is trying to tell me something. Rob helped me to get my chair and soggy sleeping bag into my mini and suggested I sleep in his car, so later I retired to his car, reclined the seat I went out like a light.

20 feet to the left of the pump, middle rod on the pump, right hand rod 15 feet to the right of the pump, firing ten baits (mission creamy passion) round each. Rob placed his baits two in front of a weed bed, one on a drop of.

That night I retired to the car about 12 o'clock. At 3.30am I woke to Rob knocking on the car door:

"Yours or mine?"
Rob's reply:
"Yours – middle".

My boots were on quicker than you can say Haulin' Hippos, I was break-dancing to my rods with Rob shouting slow down otherwise you'll end up in the drink. I got to the rod, the fish had run towards me, drop back, gotcha a lovely little mirror was in the net Haulin'

22

went up.

When we had put the prisoner in the sack that was it, we had got it right. I turned to Rob whilst waiting for daylight I feel better than James Brown I feel better now. At about 8.30am it was time for prisoners on parade. Rob's weighed 18lb, a mirror; mine a scaly 15lbs.

As we sat there at first light I was waiting for roll-call! I saw several fish rolling at the other end of the lake again. Rob had to leave at nine. I explained to him I would move to the other end for a couple of hours before going home. While we were taking pictures a guy arrived and walked down towards the area where I saw the fish roll I looked at Rob and said "Oh shit", but my luck was changing I'd paid my dues all summer, he stopped two swims short, put his gear down, stood looking at the lake for five minutes turned and started to arrange his gear. I saw a fish roll again two swims down, said goodbye to Rob, pulled my bank stick out, rods in hand 1955 stalking chair (pre Dick Walker chair) baits in pocket net broken down, and moved along the bank like a bat out of hell. I passed the gentleman setting up, and wishing good morning moved on to the swim. It was like Kings Cross station, the angler arriving at swim number ten is going to haul a hippo.

I felt good sitting on my chair I baited rod number one and cast out without standing up, right on top of where I had seen the fish 20 yards out and left the line slack. Number two rod same line 20 yards out, number three further down the bank, lines slack. Within two minutes the line tightened on rod number one, whack! I hit it. I hadn't set my net up, so I called to the guy down the bank,
"Geezer do us a favour come and net this fish for us"

After ten minutes and nice work a 13lb 12oz mirror was in the gentleman's net. You didn't hang about! I went back to the car got my camera and he did the honours for me, standing and chatting for about five minutes before starting to walk back to his rods. I then noticed the line tighten on rod number two before the buzzer could signal a take, whack I was in, my one three-quarter pound North Western haulin'.
"Here mate can you come and net this one?"
"Hell!" he said "another one", yep this fish felt better and weeded me up, after a bit of haulin' it came free. I thought the hook had pulled as there was more weed on my lead and hook than in the whole of the Sargasso sea but the guy said: "It's still on", as the net went under the fish and weed, (lend us your scales mate as mine were in the car)... a nice little 13lb 6oz common. These last two fish fell on single baits.

Well you could say I was pleased moving to the swim and within fifty minutes catching two fish. The cursed wind had gone. The old boy upstairs had taken pity and made the old bast happy.

The following week couldn't pass quickly enough. I was 'on one' again, Tuesday arrived I got all set in the swim I'd had the two fish previously, buzzing single baits in the same areas. I fished the first night, woke up in the morning, nothing. Mr gutted of Eastwood, at 8.30am a fish rolled down the bank to my left so in a flash I wound in, plop right on top of the fish. The excitement was too much a tortoise started to appear in my pants, must be the fag I lit up or the coffee. So before disaster occurred I scrambled to the top of the bank to a set of bushes one piece down, pulling hood between my legs not to deposit a torpedo in it, pulled trousers and suit back up, two bleeps was all I heard ran back to my rods the one I had cast out on the fish the tip was round but not out of the clip. I picked up the rod slammed over into the fish rod buckled over and then nothing, shit! Wound it in to find out I had been chomped off, the hook length was flattened.

Rob arrived that afternoon and he couldn't settle, he set up about 2pm and at 6pm said he was going home, he's in love you know (bad for ya). That afternoon a chap called Brian arrived and fished further down the lake. At about 7pm I saw a fish roll 45 yards out to the right of my swim, yet again before you could say 'haulin' hippos' my right hand rod was propelling my bait towards the area of activity, ten minutes passed and I put five (mission creamy passions) in. After an hour I fired another ten baits,

Rob, 18lb mirror

FIGHT FOR YOUR SPORT WITH THE ACA.

If you love angling, isn't it time you did something to stop the destruction of your sport?

The most positice step you can take is to join the Anglers' Co-operation Association.

The ACA is the **only** organisation which makes polluters pay up for the harm they do. Only the ACA uses the power of common law to help fishery owners and angling clubs clean up and re-stock their waters. Over the past seven years alone, the ACA has won more than £¼min damages.

No-one else is fighting this battle. But it can't be fought without funds. It costs just £5 a year to join the ACA. For your own sake — for the sake of angling — join today.

Join the ACA and we'll send you a sew-on badge. **FREE**

I want to join the fight against pollution — please enrol me in the ACA. I enclose £_____ (Yearly membership is £5) but donation are more than welcome).

NAME _____

ADDRESS _____

If you'd like more membership forms for your friends please tick here ☐

The Anglers' Co-operative Association
23 Castlegate, Grantham, Lincs

---

half an hour later another five baits, I didn't want to put all the baits out at once in case I spooked it.

Now when Rob left he said if you get a good 'un give us a ring and I'll take some pictures. After spending the evening drinking Brian's brandy from his hip flask and having a good chin wag I returned to the Thunderdome for lots of zzzzz's at 11.15. At 1.30am prisoner was about to shatter my slumber, two bleeps and then one tone, having my rods right next to the dome I leapt to my feet, hit the rod, all went solid as a fish started to move off slowly to my left covering more and more ground the fish sprinted sixty yards making a bee line to a sunken tree, by this time haulin' was resisted at least ten times to a sleeping Brian who must have been frightened out of his life. At 60 yards it had to be stopped – 12lb Berkley Big Game was hammered and the fish turned at this point, it started to come to me. It was time to put booties on. Boots on, sliding towards the lake the old girl was beaten, flop, flop, prisoner captured.

Brian was on his way round I opened the net in the bottom was a nugget a golden nugget one of the top prizes in the lakes raffle, Brian I said it's the big common, pxxx off was the reply "Honest", I said, Brian and sone of his friends have been trying to catch this girl for some time and here it was mine for the rest of the night.

At 2 o'clock I drove to the phone to phone Rob, well Kev who lives with Rob and is part of Mission Baits team was having his leg over answered the phone it went like this:
Del: "Had a nice fish 29lb 4oz"
Kev: "That's alright mate"
Del: "Yeh pukka, a common as well, tell Rob to get his arse down in the morning".

Rob was as happy as me on arrival and boy was I happy, that morning the camera was smoking.

The following week I captured another scaly fish, a 19lb 4oz mirror and alas the lake has frozen so I'll have to wait but I will definitely be back.

Once, twice, three times a blow up. But I loved it. The flight of the Thunderdome is over, we think!

Choose from 15 ranges of British Carp Hooks!

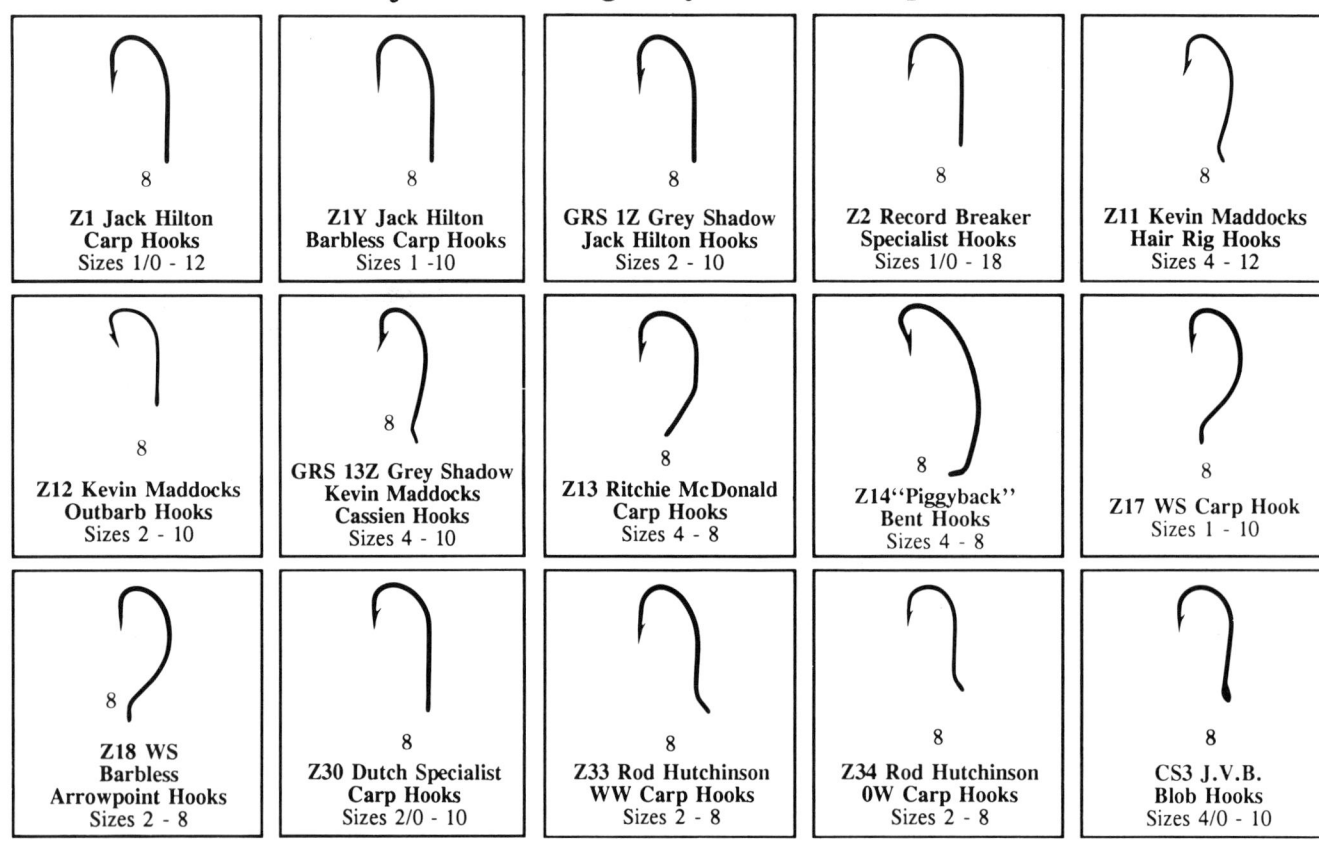

15 ranges of Carp Hooks from Partridge of Redditch!
If you take sizes into account - over 80 different Hooks!!

Write for your free copy of our Carp Hook leaflet and samples of some of the latest Hooks.

Partridge of Redditch,
Mount Pleasant, Redditch,
Worcestershire. B97 4JE
Tel: (0527) 541380
Fax: (0527) 546956

APPLICATION AND VARIATIONS

STEVE BRIGGS

These days it's possible to walk into a fishing tackle shop and buy everything you would ever need to catch a carp. You can buy all the ingredients possible to make an excellent bait, and even manuals to tell you how to make it. But the one thing you can't buy is experience, which has to be more valuable than any book you can read.

In reality there is very little differnce between what the top anglers do, and what the rest of us do, at the moment most of the rigs and baits are fairly similar, and at the end of the day it's often the application that makes all the difference, or to put it another way "It ain't what you've got, it's the way that you use it".

It was way back in the early seventies that this was first brought home to me. I used to make my way down to Brooklands every weekend armed with my tin of sweetcorn, and then watch in amazement as people like Dickie Caldwell caught several fish in a day while I was perhaps averaging one or two fish a month! It took me a while to realise that the few grains of corn that I was putting out wasn't going to hold them for five minutes, while the others were doing it right and reaping the rewards.

Thankfully I've learnt a bit more since those days. Although I'm still a long way from knowing everything, at least I catch a few more now.

Knowing how much bait to use in any given situation is one of the key factors. It's all very well having a bait that carp like but they won't always want to eat thousands of them, on the other hand if the bloke next door has got all the carp in front of him, just one bait's not going to attract them away. It's often just a matter of common sense, but also weather conditions, amount of pressure from other anglers and amount of bait they've used, all have to be taken into account. For instance if you've just moved in a swim where an angler's been all week, he may have put out ten thousand baits and not had a run. In that situation it's hardly worth putting any more bait out, a single fresh hookbait over the top would probably be far more effective, or if the lake's been packed and hardly anything's been caught, then the chances are the fish just aren't having it, and filling the swim in will probably do your chances more harm than good.

Of course there are times when putting a lot of bait out will double your chances. There are different reasons why it will work. One reason could be that the weather conditions are just right, and all the fish are in front of you just ready for a right old feed up. Another reason which has become more apparent over the last few years to me is the use of a new bait. Providing the carp like it and no one else is using it, it's often possible to put a large amount of bait out and attract carp from all over the lake. Darenth was a prime example of this.

A few years back when everyone was on high milk proteins and not getting to much action we went on there with Richworth's and the carp loved them. We were able to use three

One of four different fish taken in six hours after casting to a different area

or four hundred baits even on the coldest winter nights and still get runs where others wouldn't. And of course Terry Dempsey did even better with the fishmeals. But the trouble with finding a good bait and method is that people soon catch on, and eventually everyone ends up doing the same thing again. But that's the time to keep one step ahead and move on to something else. Not neccessarily a different bait, but just a different approach. The carp aren't that stupid, and they soon learn that where there's a large bed of bait there's also danger, and the results begin to dwindle away, again that's the time to try a single hook bait or a 'stringer'.

SIMPSONS
OF TURNFORD
EUROPE'S NO. 1 SPECIALIST TACKLE SHOP

FOR PROMPT EFFICIENT SERVICE TELEPHONE 0992 468799 USE YOUR ACCESS OR VISA CARD. JUST QUOTE YOUR CARD NUMBER STATING YOUR REQUIREMENTS

Whether you're a novice or experienced carp angler you'll find our Turnford Tackle Superstore is stocked with everything you'll need for modern carp and specialist angling. We've been established for 20 years and all members of our staff are capable carp anglers who can answer all your questions on choice of suitable tackle and bait making problems. Mr Jack Simpson, the proprietor, has been in the tackle trade over 30 years, so you can have every confidence when dealing with us.

RODS – over 300 specialist and carp rods on display in our Turnford Tackle Superstore. Sole suppliers and manufacturers of the exclusive Simpsons/Kevin Maddocks **Dual Taper** Carbon Carp Rods. Also, Rod Hutchinson IM6 Carbons, Century Composite 'Armalite' range, Daiwa's Kevin Nash Amorphous and the superb Simpson's Multiply Ceramic Carbons including the ultimate long range carp rod the Multiply 'Magnum' 12½', 3lb test curve – a legend in its own lifetime!

SPECIALIST TACKLE – we stock the full range of specialist tackle from Kevin Nash, Drennan, Gardner, Streamside, Terry Eustace, Solar Tackle plus the full range of top quality Wychwood rucksacks luggage and holdalls. Our self-service displays contain every conceivable gadget and accessory invented to improve your chances of catching carp.

REELS – we have the full range of Shimano reels in stock including the oustanding 'Aero' Baitrunner models. Also the Daiwa Bite'n'Run reels plus selected models from ABU, Ryobi, Mitchell and DAM, plus of course, full after sales service and spare spools on all models stocked.

HOOKS – we literally have millions of hooks in stock. The full range of handmade hooks from Partridge of Redditch, including the Kevin Maddocks selection, Rod Hutchinson, Ritchie McDonald and Gardner, also Kamasan, Drennan, Mustad and Terry Eustace. If you're having problems getting particular hooks give us a try, there's every chance we stock it.

LINE – we stock Tri-lene Big Game, Sten, Maxima, Drennan, Sylcast and Simpson own Carpcatcher brands. The clear high abrasion and the ever popular 'Sorrell', all on economy bulk spools. Also hook length braids, florescent dacrons from Krystons, Cortland, Black Spider and Masterline. We also have our own line spooling service where we fill your spools with the line of your choice – this service is free you only pay for the line.

BAIT – at least ⅓ of our tackle Superstore has been set out with bait ingredients, mixes, flavours, enhancers, oils, stimulators, soluble dyes and ready-made boilies from Streamselect, KM Maestro, SBS, Rod Hutchinson Developments, Martin Locke's Seed Mixes, Zenon Bojko's mixes, oils, flavours, plus the full range of mixed and ingredients from Nutrabaits, plus over 1000 flavours plus bait guns, rollers from Gardner, KJB and Streamside. We pride ourselves in offering the best range of quality bait products available – if you have a bait problem contact us.

DOUBLE THE SIZE – From April 1992 we will have doubled our shop size, offering one of the best personalised stocks and service in Europe. We accept payment by cheque, p.o, Eurocheques, Access, MasterCard, Visa credit cards, with split payment credit facilities up to £1000 (subject to status), send 50p for our rod brochure.

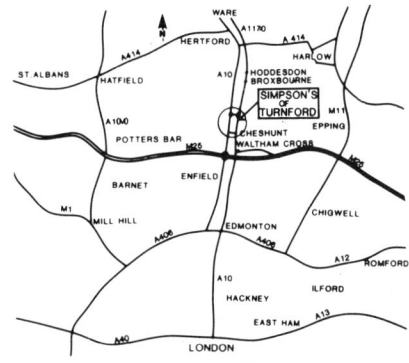

HOW TO FIND US – most major motorways now lead into the North Orbital London M25. Leave the M25 on the A10 northbound road indicating Cambridge. Travel north up the A10 for approximately 2¼ miles. You will see Tescos Brookfield Farm Superstore on your left. Leave the A10 on the next slip road indicating Broxbourne A1170 and come down to the new River Arms roundabout (Berni Inn). Go straight across on the Cheshunt B176 and we are 400 yards down the road on your left at the end of Nunsbury Road. Parking is unrestricted in our own forecourt in front of the shop.

SIMPSON S OF TURNFORD
(CRAFTSMEN RODMAKERS) DEPT. A.T.H.
NUNSBURY DRIVE, TURNFORD, BROXBOURNE, HERTFORDSHIRE · TEL: HODDESDON 468799
BUSINESS HOURS Mon to Sat 9am to 6pm Closed all day Thursday Late evening Fri 9am until 8pm
THE SPECIALIST TACKLE SHOP FOR THE SPECIALIST ANGLER

Of course it's not always that easy. You may not be able to fish a lake regularly and keep up with the developments, but there are still things you can do to improve your chances. Fig 1 shows what I quite often do when I'm not too sure of the right approach. By using one rod with just a single bait while the other one is over a bed of free offerings, it must give you more of a chance. If you fire a load of bait out for both rods as soon as you start fishing, as many people do, then you have to be confident that the carp are going to eat all of the bait. I think it's always best to go on the lighter side, you can put more bait out if needed, but if you've put too much out, you can't go and get it back.

But getting away from bait and more on to the location side of things, it's just as important to know where to put a bait as it is to know how much to use. A lot of people may look no further than the surface of a lake... casting to islands, jumping fish etc. without actually knowing what's on the bottom of the lake. This is where the marker float comes in. I've written about it before, but on most lakes I've fished its been invaluable for finding areas which otherwise I wouldn't know existed. Harefield lake for instance, where I've fished a bit this year is a mass of bars, gulleys, humps and plateaus. You can cast ten yards and be in twenty feet of water, or you could cast a hundred and forty yards and be in ten inches of water. Obviously a lot of hours could be wasted by putting baits where there's very little chance of a carp finding them.

But often the spots where carp will pick up a bait from can be very small. Sometimes it's essential to cast a bait precisely, within inches let alone feet to get a run. How many times does it happen, that you can have two rods cast out, ten feet apart, and get three or four runs on one rod and nothing on the other. Yet another day in the same place all the runs might come to the other rod. I wonder how many times we sit there getting nothing when all we have to do is cast one way or the other a couple of yards, to get a few runs? A lot of it of course, is to do with confidence as well. Quite often you know where you want to put a bait, but if it falls short it may be left there, but it always seems to niggle away in the back of your mind, and that always seems to be the bait that isn't taken. Whereas sometimes a cast seems to land 'spot on' and you 'know' that it's only a matter of time before you get one.

Again even if the areas are small, it's possible to increase your chances of action by the way you bait up. Fig 2 shows an area where the baits were placed, where the most likely places to get a run. But it was possible for fish to move along the middle of the channel and miss the baits. But by making a trail, joining the two areas together it was almost impossible for a fish to pass through without noticing the baits.

Probably the hardest water I've had to come to terms with was Johnson's Railway Lake. For a long time it seemed almost impossible to catch a carp off the bottom there, and I had to rely on the few chances there was to fish with floaters. There were so many things going against the angler. For one the presentation was always difficult because of the deep water and the weed. Secondly no area of the lake seemed to produce more action than any other so the choice of swim wasn't easy. And lastly the carp very rarely ate *any* anglers bait, most of it stayed on the bottom until it rotted. We knew this because we had friends who had dived in the lake and seen it for themselves. This was enough to actually make some people stop fishing the lake. But where there's problems there are also solutions, if you can find them. Pete Jones and I discussed the problems and came up with the following answers. By using baits popped-up six to seven inches off the bottom, they would be far more visible and should sit just above the silkweed which covered most areas. Secondly location was difficult, so I would fish one of the middle swims of the lake where I could cover a greater area plus there was more chance of intercepting fish that were moving through. And as far as bait went, it seemed that any amount of bait would lower the chances so I just used hookbaits with no free offerings. It all sounds quite simple but there were other things to take into account, rigs, flavours etc. But at the end of the day it worked, and I caught more carp in one week than I had caught in all my previous time there. I also felt a great sense of achievement in having succeeded at last on a lake which had been a stumbling block for me.

The preparation of the pop-ups was an important factor. While I was on Darenth, I used baits baked in the oven for a

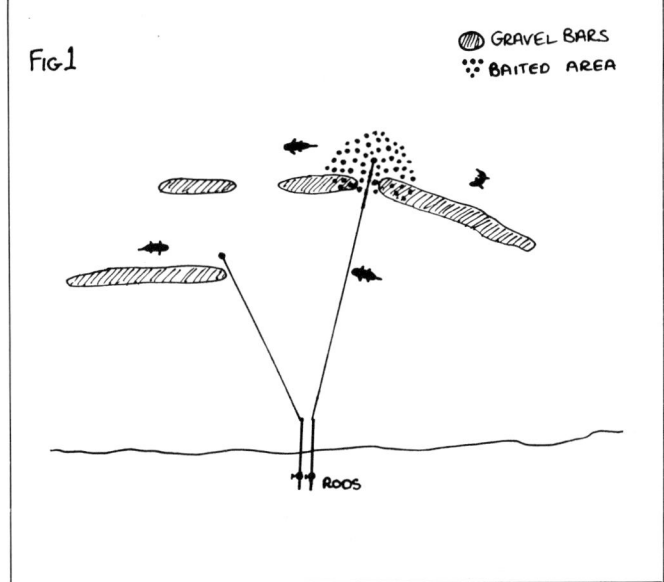

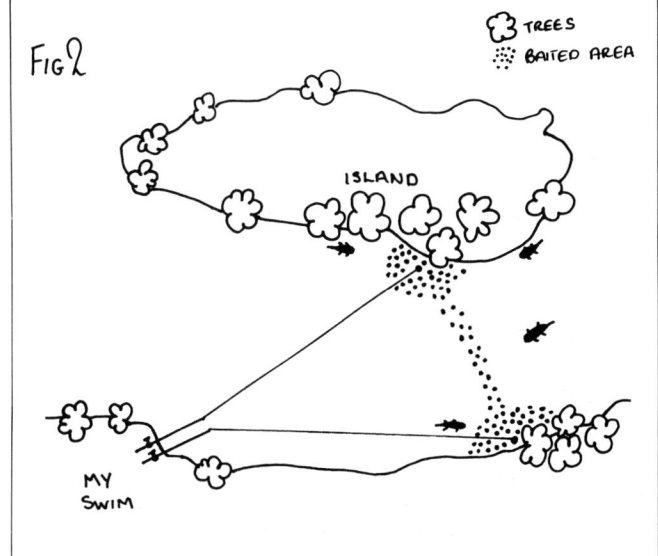

short time, making sure they weren't too hard. Then once they were on the rigs I would pierce the bait with a needle and squeeze the bait under water to release some of the air until they were critically balanced. This worked fine in the depths which were about five to seven feet. But in twenty feet of water this method proved to be useless. The extra pressure at that depth made them take on water far quicker, and within a few hours they would be laying flat on the bottom. I tried all sorts of variations to get over this and eventually the best way I found was to cook them in a microwave for as long as possible on full power, without actually burning the baits. This made the baits as hard as bullets, but far more water resistant. The other thing which helped was tying the baits on rather than making a hole through the middle where water could get in. By doing this I now had baits which would stay buoyant for over 50 hours.

Well that's a few things that have helped me catch the 'odd' fish down the years. Carp fishing doesn't seem to get any easier (just like writing these articles) but as I said, where there are problems there are also solutions if you can find them. Sometimes it seems almost impossible to catch anything. But why not try something different instead of just sitting there behind the rods, going through the motions, you never know you might end up catching fish you only dreamt of before.

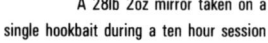

A 28lb 2oz mirror taken on a single hookbait during a ten hour session

BASILDON ANGLING CENTRE

402 Whitmore Way
Basildon Essex
Tel: 0268 520144

COUNTY ANGLING

19 Suttons Lane
Hornchurch Essex
Tel: 04024 77834

County Angling Manager Derek Ritchie with a 29-4-0 common on Mission Boilie

DAIWA

KEVIN NASH AMORPHOUS CARP RODS
12ft 2¼lb Test	£210.00
12ft 2½lb Test	£215.00
12ft 2¾lb Test	£215.00
13ft 3lb Test	£225.00
13ft 2¾lb Test	£220.00

KEVIN NASH WHISKER KEVLAR CARP
12ft 2lb Test	£140.00
12ft 2¼lb Test	£145.00
12ft 2½lb Test	£150.00
12ft 2¾lb Test	£155.00
13ft 2¼lb Test	£155.00
13ft 2½lb Test	£160.00

POWERMESH CARP RODS
11ft	from £76.99
12ft	from £85.99
13ft	from £94.99

BR FREE SPOOL CARP REELS
BR 2050X	£49.99
BR 2650X	£54.99
BR 2050	£69.99
BR 2650	£74.99
SS 3000	£175.00
PM 4000H	£85.99

FOX INTERNATIONAL

NEW Ultra Deluxe Bedchair	£219.90
Super Deluxe Bedchair	£189.90
Standard Deluxe Bedchair	£139.90
Standard Bedchair	£99.90
Super Adjusta Level Chair	£74.90
Standard Adjusta Level Chair	£49.90
Lite Weight Adjusta Level Chair	£34.90

SLEEPING BAGS
−30 degrees	£134.90
−20 degrees	£89.90
−10 degrees	£49.90
Supa Bivvy	£154.90
Supa Brolly	£131.90
Supa Brolly In-fill	£54.90
Jekk Shelter	£79.90

FULL RANGE OF FOX ACCESSORIES IN STOCK

KEVIN NASH

NEW Titan Carp Dome	£211.95
NEW Titan Carp Bivvy	£185.95
NEW Titan Carp Brolly	£141.95
NEW Titan Rucksack 120	£125.95
NEW Titan Rucksack 90	£98.99
NEW Titan Rucksack 60	£89.95
NEW Titan S Carp Bag	£119.95
NEW Titan Artic Suit	£203.95
NEW Titan Undersuit	£67.95
Hooker Holdall 12' Deluxe	£87.95
Hooker Holdall 13' Deluxe	£89.95

PLUS COMPLETE RANGE OF LUGGAGE AND ACCESSORIES

MAINLINE PRODUCTS
Zenon Bojko mixes, oils, flavours, boilie boosters

Complete range
NUTRABAITS
mixes, flavours, oils

Full range of
PREMIER BAITS
mixes, flavours, oils

EXCLUSIVE FOR '92
MISSION BAITS
FROZEN BOILIES, MIXES, FLAVOURS AND OILS

***NEW* JRC DELUXE BEDCHAIR**
Deluxe Padded Mattress, Fully Adjustable Legs, Strong Reinforced Frame £159.99

HANDBUILT RODS by VIC GIBSON
ARMALITE, NORTH WESTERN

COLEMAN
Unleaded Stove £41.95
PLUS SPARES

MAGNUM STAINLESS STEEL PRODUCTS

SOLAR TACKLE
Stainless Steel Banksticks, Buzz Bars, Needle Systems, Lite-Flo Indicators, MixMasters, Savay Seed Mixes plus all accessories

Full range of
GARDNER TACKLE
PRODUCTS
including *NEW* Baitmaster Giant Rolaball Boilie Roller £29.99

ARMALITE MAIN DEALER

BIG RANGE OF
TERRY EUSTACE GOLD LABEL TACKLE

KJB
Rod Pods – Electronic Swing Arm (2 rod)	£99.99
Rod Pods – Electronic Swing Arm (3 rod)	£119.99

KRYSTON ADVANCED HOOKLENGTHS

LARGE RANGE OF
WYCHWOOD LUGGAGE
PLUS *NEW* REDDICAT BOILIEPULT

ROD HUTCHINSON
BAITS AND PRODUCTS

RODS
IMX 12' 2lb Test	£197.75
IMX 12' 2¼lb Test	£197.75
IMX 12' 2½lb Test	£203.00
IMX 13' 2½lb Test	£208.00
IMX 13' 3½lb Test	£225.00

***NEW* GREY SHADOW RODS**
12ft 2¼lb Test	£134.95
12ft 2½lb Test	£134.95
13ft 3½lb Test	£145.95

HIGH PROTECTION HOLDALL
12ft	£85.95
13ft	£87.95
The Ultimate Bivvy	£159.95
NEW One Man Bivvy	£139.95

(when available)

PLUS COMPLETE RANGE OF MIXES AND FLAVOURS

SHIMANO

Aero GT 3500	£89.90
Aero GT 4000	£96.90
Aero GT 4500	£99.90
Aero 3000	£59.90
Aero 3500	£64.90
Aero 4000	£69.90
Aero 4500	£74.90
Aerlex 8000 FB	£64.90

TWIN POWER CARP RODS
12ft 1¾lb Test	£107.00
12ft 2lb Test	£112.00
12ft 2¼lb Test	£117.00
12ft 2½ Test	£123.00

DIAFLASH CARP RODS
12ft 2lb Test	£163.00
12ft 2¼lb Test	£174.00
12ft 2½lb Test	£179.00
12ft 3lb Test	£183.00

LESLIE'S OF LUTON

Mail Order by return post, or visit our 11,000 sq.ft. shop, only 3 minutes from the M1 motorway, Junction 10.

THE WORLDS NO 1 SPECIALIST
89/93 Park Street, Luton, Beds. LU1 3HG
Tel:0582 453542 20 Lines Fax:0582 357405

All prices correct at time going to press. Item subject to availabili

TOMORROW'S TACKLE TODAY

THE ROBIN MAYLIN RANGE OF SPECIALIST RODS

During the 1988 close season Leslies's Specialist Tackle Centre approached me regarding the introduction of a new range of carp rods. Not the same old blanks with a different name range of rods, which seem to be so commonplace these days, but a totally exclusive set of blanks; a set of blanks manufactured by the country's top rod manufacturer, built to my own specifications by Ian Crawley, leslies own rod builder, whose work as you will see is second to none. So it was that during the 1988-89 season a total of twenty six different blanks were field tested by myself. The one and only method to get what I wanted from a rod was by trial and error, by field testing one design and then altering the taper, the test curve, the wall thickness or the action until a perfect fishing tool was created. After almost fifteen hundred hours of field work by myself the result is the new Rob Maylin "Pursuit" range of rods.

The range consists of 3 basic models, all manufactured from high modulus carbon Kevlar fibres combined with two fibres which are now ready to revolutionise the carp fishing spectrum; the very latest in carp fishing technology. There is no single rod which can enhance every situation in fishing but these three will undoubtedly cover them all.

PRECISE PURSUIT - 12ft 2lbs TEST CURVE - £159.95

Close - medium range, optimum casting weight 1 3/4ozs, range margin to 80yards.
Line weight 6-12lbs

This rod is beauiful both in action and in feel. Once you hold it you instinctively tell that it's right. The balance and the curve of a perfectionist's rod, someone who wants to stalk his quarry, or accurately present a bait under close in snags, under bushes or up against island margins. Alternatively sit over a large bed of particles, or present a tiny floater with finesse and accuracy. Even for boilies up to 80 yards range this rod is the one for you.

INTERMEDIATE PURSUIT - 12ft 6ins 2lbs 6ozs TEST CURVE - £165.95

Medium - long range, optimum casting weight 2 1/4ozs, range close - 100+ yards.
Line weight 6 - 15lbs (6 with shock leader).

The middle rod is the best way describe this rod. A rod which can be used close but also has the backbone to present a bait accurately past the 100 yards mark. For the angler who does a variety of fishing from pouch range particles to throwing stick range boilies, a brilliant multi-distance rod.

EXTREME PURSUIT - 13ft 2lbs 9ozs TEST CURVE - £175.95

Long - extreme range, optimum casting weight 3ozs, range medium - 140 yards.
Line weight 6 - 15lbs (6-8 with shock leader).

My rod, the rod you will see me using this season on almost all the venues I intend to fish this year. I feel confident enough to use it at almost any range. It has superb casting abilities which even allow for the silly mistakes I make when playing. All in all the rod which will, in my opinion, revolutionise carp fishing.

THE K.C. CONTOUR RANGE OF SPECIALIST RODS

This range of rods has been our best seller in the past two years. Using the same materials as the range above but staying with the most popular lengths and test curves. Also finished by our resident rod builder.

12ft EXTREME DISTANCE 2 3/4LBS T.C. OPIMUM CASTING WEIGHT 2 1/2OZS - £159.95

This rod has been designed specifically for long range fishing. During extensive field testing this rod proved its potential to out-cast other specialist rods on the market, and proved it also had the power to set a hook at the extreme distances fished on some of the large pits today. This rod has become increasingly popular over the last season, as more people resort to long range fishing.

This rod has the power to cast a stringer further than you could catapult a bait thus making it a very useful weapon for the big pit angler. If you want a long range rod that still has a good fighting curve, see this rod before you buy anything esle that may not do the right job.

12ft MULTI-DISTANCE 2lbs T.C. OPTIMUM CASTING WEIGHT 2ozs - £149.95

This is the versatile rod in the range and has been designed for the angler who wants one rod to do several jobs. It is capable of putting 1 3/4oz lead plus bait over 90 yards, yet can still be used under the rod tip with a reasonable amount of care, without fear of the hook pulling out when you apply a bit of pressure. This is now the only rod we use on our local waters. An ideal rod for small lakes and pits.

11ft 6' 1 1/2lbs T.C. OPTIMUM CASTING WEIGHT 1 1/4ozs - £139.95

This rod is unbelievable. It is the most forgiving rod we have produced for margin fishing. In extensive testing it has landed fish to 35lbs and made us realise the enjoyment and excitement of this style of fishing we sometimes forget with long range angling.

THE G.B. CONTOUR ULTRACAST SPECIALIST ROD

13ft 6' G.B. CONTOUR ULTRACAST 3 3/4 lbs. T.C. OPTIMUM CASTING WEIGHT 4ozs - £180

During the 1987-88 season I had been fishing Harefield Lake for nearly a seaon, when I, along with numerous other angler's noticed the fish were showing at distances in excess of 150 yards. A distance that no rod or angler could cast, even with single baits. Something had to be done.

After some thought I contacted Kevin at Leslie's, where I work during the close season.I searched through all the blanks on the market but still couldn't find the one to suit my purpose. Both Kevin and I soon realised that what was needed would have to be built from scratch.

After a visit to his blank makers and three month wait, Kevin came back to me with the 13'6" 3 3/4lb blank which had incorporated in the new fibres which are included in the Rob Maylin and K.C. Contour Rods, as well as the Carbon and Aramid fibres.

Following a season's field testing we have found this Rod to outcast any other on the market, casting stringers in excess of 110 yards and hookbaits well over 160 yards.

Any of our own ranges can be built to your own specifcations, in our shop rods we have specific ring spacings and handle lengths to suit each particular blank. We put Fuji FPS fittings and abbreviated Duplon handles and Fuji rings on our rods as standard but any variations can be cated for.

We also stock a large range of other rods including the full range Daiwa, Shakespeare. (Silicon Carbide Rings. £25 extra.)

LESLIE'S EXCLUSIVE PRODUCTS

TWIN REST STAINLESS STEEL BUZZER BAR (PATENT No 8506849)

This unique buzzer bar enables the use of two banksticks, one at either end, thus creating an extreme stable set up. When using the buzzer bar in this fashion any turning or dipping of the rods can be eliminated, thus cutting out any unwanted noise from the buzzers. Also this system creates a stable se when fishing with tight lines, when with a conventional buzzer bar a certain amount of movement of rods may be encountered. These bars are now being used by many of the leading anglers in the coun today, i.e. Rob Maylin, Kevin Nash.

2 ROD BAR £17.95   3 ROD BAR £18.95   4 ROD BAR £22.95

SUPER STAINLESS STEEL MONKEY CLIMBER SYSTE

This is the strongest and most stable monkey climber system on the market today. The groundpins made of 7.5mm solid stainless steel as is the main bar. The needle holders are manufactured with a thumbscrew into the top of the holders. The groundpins and needle holders have a small hole drilled side so that a tommy bar, which is supplied, can be used to get a really firm hold on the main bar.

The system is supplied woth 20in stainless steel needles. The way this system works eliminates t to use spanners or pliers to get the needles to stay upright. All initial stocks of this system sold out quickly despite the higher prices. You really do get what you pay for.

2 ROD SYSTEM £26.95   3 ROD SYSTEM £30.95

PTFE SUPER ADJUSTABLE BOBBINS

These bobbins allow you to use several different weights of indicator without having to carry severa different bobbins. Each part of the bobbin has a thread on it so a good hold can be obtained between different sections of the bobbin. Also so the weight of the bobbin can be changed while it is still on line. These have been made from top quality PTFE so that you get minimal resistance which is cau other materials against the needles. It also helps to get a good indication when fishing dropbacks a range in drag or windy conditions, because the indicator does not stick to the needle. These bobbin available in two different sizes but extensions are available if more weight is required.

BOBBINS £6.95   EXTENSION £2.75, P&P 80p

BLACK TULIP BEADS

as used by many of the country's top anglers including Rod Maylin

The most efficient method of fishing both fixed lead or running lead without having to retackle. Su for all standard or in line leads. Fits Berkley and Diamond Eye swivels. Use on their own or for an tangle rig add valve rubber or our new rigid sinking tube.

LOOSE TULIP BEADS (per 10).................
BOLT CLIP PACK (beads and clips).................
NON TANGLE BOOMS Pack (per 5).................
ANTI TANGLE PACK (10 beads, clips, links and 5 yard tubing).................
RIGID SINKING TUBE (large bore).................
SEMI STIFF SINKING RIG TUBE.................

ROBIN MAYLIN SPECIALIST LINE

This line has performed well beyond expectations during last season, especially as far as abrasion resistance is concerned. There have been reports of many twenties, several thirties and one forty cau the line last season. The colour of the line has proved a great advantage. Being almost clear it is as being invisible as you can get in the water, and does not cause as much of a shadow or silhouette, proved a winner for floater fishing.

ALL SPOOLS - 1000 YARDS.

8lb	£14.95	9lb	£1
10lb	£16.25	12lb	£1
15 1/2lb	£17.75	p + p on line	

LARGEST FISH CAUGHT TO DATE - JOHN ALLEN 55lb

STAINLESS STEEL BANKSTICKS

These have been designed with both lightness and strength in mind. We have used highest grade stainless steel in specific lengths and diameters to produce a slimmer bankstick which is still strong enough to use in the hardest ground without fear of These banksticks are extendable and have a large knurled thumbscrew, easier to t than those on most banksticks.

14in. BANKSTICK £11.95, 22!n. BANKSTICK £13.95 - P&P £1.75 ea
EXTRA HEAVY DUTY 12 in. BANKSTICK £12.95, 16in. BANKSTICK 22in. BANKSTICK £14.95

LESLIE'S *NEW* MULTISTRAND HAIR RIG LINE

Our new Hair Rig Line is supersoft for excellent bait presentation. The bait acts so na it's hard to believe, while on test last year it produced devastating results.

White, 30 metre spools £4.95

SLIDING RIG STOPS £1.30   COLOURED ISOTOPES
Availabe in green, blue, orange ar

LESLIE'S EXCLUSIVE LEADS

LESLIE'S NEW TADPOLEBOMBS
Patent No. 91137430

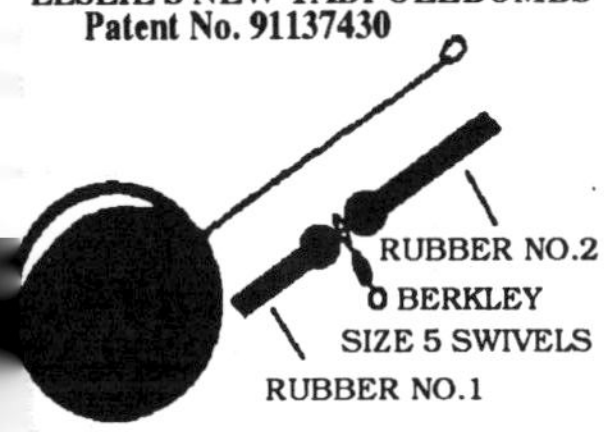

ew design in bombs to be used the copter rig to stop breakages on main s. A spherically designed bomb with a to withstand the pressure of the ked fish. All the pressure of the swivel g spread along the bomb shank ead of one point on the main line and . Designed with conservation in mind, ish can also part with the lead if kages occur further along the main

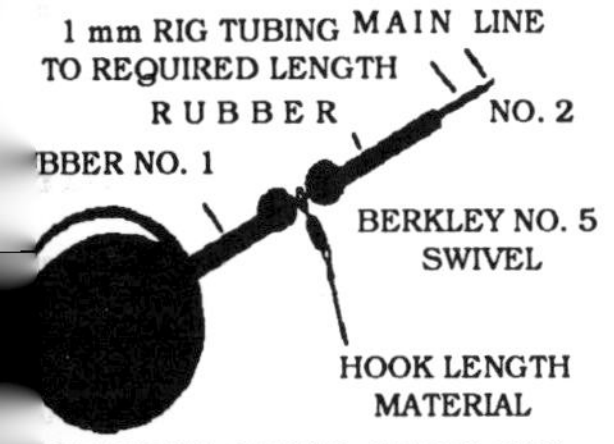

W A SMALL GAP SO SWIVEL CAN ATE AROUND BOMB SHANK

uctions on use: Take bomb and er No.1 onto shank which can be cut t required distance from lead. Next a No.5 Berkley Swivel on shank with ength material attached. Then slide er No.2 onto shank so it covers nder of shank and eye. 1mm Rig g can be pushed into Rubber No.2 if ed. Both rubbers are made from a l material to allow for shock bancy within the rig itself.

OLE BOMBS -
0p, 2 1/2oz 85p, 3oz 90p, 4oz 95p
pplied with 2 rubbers
Rubbers per pack of 10 £2.25
y No. 5 Swivels per pack 10 75p

LEADS

BLACK CARP BOMBS
z 47p, 1 1/2oz 52p, 1 3/4oz 57p, p, 2 1/4oz 62p, 2 1/2oz 67p, p, 4/5oz 75p

BLACK RISER BOMBS
z 42p, 1 1/2oz 48p, 2oz 52p

ZIPP LEADS
z 57p, 1 3/4oz 62p, 2 1/4oz 67p, z 75p

NTI TANGLE ZIPP LEADS
z 72p, 2oz 77p, 2 1/2oz 82p, z 92p

RY EUSTACE BUZZ BOMBS
With fins for added stability
70, 2 1/2oz £1.85, 3 1/2oz £2.15

ON LEADS 11p PER OUNCE

LINES

SYLCAST SORRELL
6/7/8/9/11/13lb............£4.25
7lb....................................£10.95
/13/15lb...........................£11.95
Specimen, 100m.
9/11lb...............................£11.95

MAXIMA

	o/shot	600m	1000m
75	£6.99	£11.45	£18.00
95	£7.39	£11.90	£18.50
99	£7.65	£12.25	£19.30
.14	£7.90	£12.75	£19.90
25	£7.99	£14.45	£21.45

ARDNER LINE BROWN
.26 7lb....£9.67 8lb....£10.48
1.25 11lb...£11.25 15lb...£11.82

NAN DOUBLE STRENGTH
0m. Brown.
.90 7lb....£6.90 10lb....£7.73
7.73 15lb...£8.75 17lb....£8.75
10.18 22lb...£10.18

BRENT
mono high grade. 1000m.
45 9lb...£10.18 11lb...£10.80
1.80

LESLIE'S NEW PEARPOLE BOMB
Patent No. 91137430

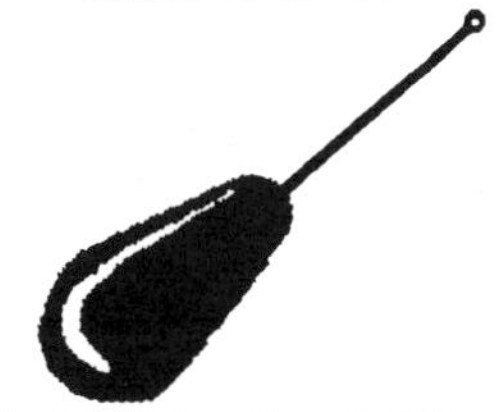

To be used where steep sided gravel bars are a feature in larger gravel pits. A more areodynicly designed bomb with tapered sides to slide up the sides of the bars without locking up. **See Tadpole bomb instructions.**

PEARPOLE BOMBS -
2oz 80p, 2 1/2oz 85p, 3oz 90p, 4oz 95p
Supplied with 2 Rubbers.
Spare rubbers per pack of 10 £2.25
Berkley No. 5 Swivels per pack 10 75p

LESLIE'S NEW PATPOLE BOMB
Patent No. 91137430

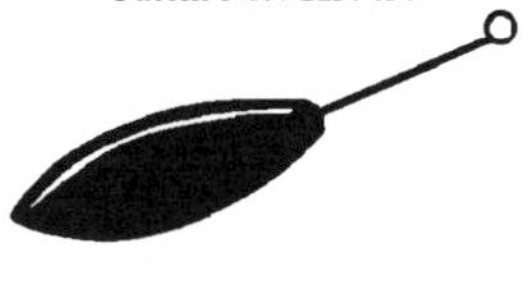

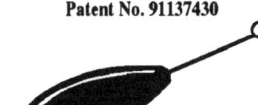

A combination of our patriot and pole bombs the new patpole bomb has been developed to increase casting distance by some 10 - 15%. While also retaining the advantages the range of pole bombs offer. **See Tadpole bomb instructions.**

PATPOLE BOMBS -
2oz 85p, 2 1/2oz 90p, 3oz 95p, 4oz £1.00
Supplied with 2 rubbers.
Spare rubbers per pack of 10 £2.25
Berkley No. 5 Swivels per pack 10 75p

THE FOLLOWING LINES ARE RECOMMENDED FOR SHOCK, SNAG AND ABRASIVE RESISTANT USE

AMNESIA
Black. 200ft. 20lb...............................£2.40
Green. 200ft. 20lb.....£2.40 30lb.....£3.65

BIG GAME
Trilene/Big Game. White.or Green
10lb/1500yds; 12lb/1175yds; 15lb/900yds; 20lb/650yds; 25lb/595yds; 30lb/440yds; 40lb/370yds; 50lb/275yds................£15.99

GOLDEN MARLIN
New formula in Sorrell 2oz spools.
8lb/875yds; 10lb/750yds; 12lb/630yds; 15lb/520yds; 18lb/393yds..................£4.95

DACRON & MULTISTRAND HOOK LENGTH MATERIAL

KRYSTON SILKWORM
Brown & white. All 40m spools.
4/6/8/10/12/15lb.....£11.39 25lb....£11.77
Ultrasoft 40m. 12lb...........................£11.39

KRYSTON MULTISTRAND
White. 40m. 15lb................................£11.39
Black or white. 40m 70lb..................£12.25

KRYSTON SUPERSILK
White. 40m. 14lb................................£11.39

KRYSTON MERLIN
Green/white. Ultrasoft, camouflaged. 40m.
8/10/12/15lb..................................£10.66

KRYSTON QUICKSILVER
High abrasion resistantance. shock leader material. Gravel brown. 25m spools.
25lb....£10.99 35lb....£10.99 45lb....£10.99

KRYSTON R.D.O.N. NO TANGLE GEL
for Multistrands.................................£3.49

KRYSTON SUPER STIFF GEL
for men with real problems..................£3.49

KRYSTON HAWSER
New Permanent Stiffener in a tube .£3.75

CORTLAND MICRON WHITES
The most reliable braided line we have ever used, strongly recommened. All 100yds spools.
15lb.........£7.95 20lb.........£8.95
25lb.........£9.50 30lb.........£9.95

CORTLAND CAM-O-FLAGE
Braided nylon line alternates between brown,green,grey and sand, every 9". 100yds spools.
10lb....£6.00 12lb.....£6.30 15lb.....£6.80

GARDNER DACRON
Black. All 100 metres, (except 1lb 50 metres).
1lb....£4.68 6lb....£6.38 8lb......£6.82
10lb.......£6.92 12lb.......£7.29

DRENNAN CARP DACRON
Olive/Brown 20m hair/8/10/12/15lb.£2.16

LESLIE'S NEW PATRIOT BOMBS

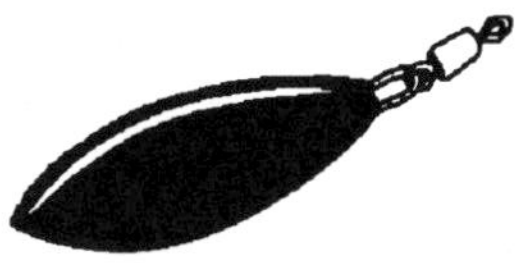

Developed with aerodynamic effiency in mind, this new concept in bombs has been designed to increase casting distance by 10-15% with greater accuracy.
As used by the country's leading carp anglers, including Rob Maylin.
PATRIOT BOMBS - 2oz 62p, 3oz 77p
4oz 82p, 5oz 92p, 6oz 98p

LESLIE'S NEW CLUSTER BOMBS

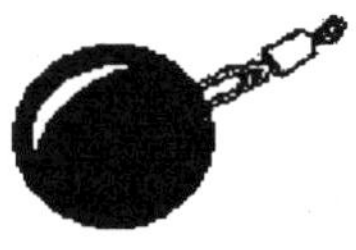

As opposed to other bolt bombs, the spherical design of this totally new dumpy lead means greater efficiency when used in conjunction with bolt rigs.
CLUSTER BOMBS - 2oz 62p, 3oz 67p,
4oz 72p, 5oz 77p

KEVIN NASH FINESSE TG
4/10/12/15/25lb..x20m...................£6.62

KEVIN NASH FINESSE HAIR BRAID
Hair braid...x20m..............................£1.90

KEVIN NASH FINESSE ENTICER
4/10/12/15/25lb..x20m...................£6.62

KEVIN NASH FINESSE DENTAL FLOSS
DENTAL FLOSS.................................£1.50

DRENNAN HI TENACITY BRAID
Green/brown. 20m.
8lb................£6.09 12lb................£6.60
15lb..............£6.90 25lb................£7.11

HOOKS

LESLIE'S SEARCH HOOKS
A powerful hook-short shank and forged, designed originally for catching King Salmon up to 100lb in the U.S.A., but found to be the Carp hook that everybody had been waiting for. Used with devasting results in 1990.
Sizes 2/4/6/8...£1.25 per 10

LESLIE'S BENT HOOKS
Sizes 2/4/6/8...£1.25 per 10

KEVIN NASH HOOKS
Outpoint sizes 4/6/8/10 per 10..........................£1.15
Specialist sizes 2/4/6/8/10/12 per 10....................£1.15
Snag sizes 2/4/6/8 per 10....................................£1.15
Spec Boilie 4/6/8 per 10.......................................£1.15

DRENNAN HOOKS
Super spec sizes 2/4/6/8/10/12..................£2.87 per 50
Boilie Hooks sizes 1/2/4/6/8/10/12/14...........93 per 10
Starpoint sizes 4/6/8/10/12.........................£1.55 per 10
Starpoint Barbless sizes 4/6/8/10/12..........£1.55 per 10

PARTRIDGE HOOKS
Z1 Jack Hilton sizes 2/4/6/8/10/12............£2.97 per 25
Z1Y Jack Hilton Barbless sizes 2/4/6/8/10..£3.33 per 25
Z2 TE Record Breaker sizes 2/4/6/8/10/12..£2.97 per 25
Z11 K/Maddocks Hair Rig Hook sizes 4/6/8..£3.79 per 25
Z12 K/Maddocks Outbarb sizes 2/4/6/8.......£3.79 per 25
Z18 S/H Arrowpoint Barbless sizes 2/4/6/8.£2.16 per 10
Z17 W.S Specimen Hunter sizes 2/4/6/8......£1.85 per 10

ROD HUTCHINSON
Z33 Weedywater 4/6/8...............................£4.50 per 25
Z34 Open Water 4/6/8................................£3.70 per 25

GREY SHADOW HOOKS
GRS1Z Jack Hilton sizes 2/4/6/8/10............£3.79 per 25
GRS13Z K/Maddocks Cassien
sizes 2/4/6/8/10.......................................£4.61 per 25

RITCHIE MCDONALD
Z13 Sizes 4/6/8...£4.50 per 25
Z14 Piggyback sizes 4/6/8............................£1.85 per 10

MUSTAD HOOKS
34021 sizes 2/4/6/8.....................................£2.82 per 50
3406 sizes 4/6/8...£2.82 per 50
34007 sizes 4/6/8...£3.89 per 50

SCALES & S/ACCESSORIES

KEVIN NASH
Hooker 56/112lb...............................£50.39
Hooker Scale Pouch..............................£7.79
Waymaster Flyweight Scales 30lb......£22.50
Reuben Heaton Spec Scales 60lb.......£87.50

E.T.
Avon Scales Pouch..............................£9.99
Dial Scales Pouch.............................£12.99

NEEDLE BAR SLEEVES

KEVIN NASH
Needle Bar Sleeve 65cm.......................£8.95
Needle Bar SLeeve 90cm......................£9.95

SACK, WEIGH SLINGS & S/WS ACCESSORIES

KEVIN NASH
Sack 3'x4'...£8.83
Sack XL 3'x5'..£9.99
Sack XL + Extension Cord.................£12.55
Big Sack 4'x5'.....................................£11.18
Zip Sack 50"x30"................................£10.12
Zip Sack + Extension Cord...............£13.70
Sack Clip...£2.07
Sack Extension Cord...........................£3.20
Standard Sling.......................................£7.45
Big Sling..£8.60
Specialist Sling......................................£8.60
River Sling...£4.45
Monster Carp Sling..............................£15.45
Hooker Sling Sack Combo...................£12.95
Wet Sling Sack Bag...............................£3.90

E.T.
Supersoft Zip Sack £11.20
Savay Standard Sack.............................£8.25
Savay Jumbo Sack..................................£9.16
Deluxe Weigh Bag Small........................£8.16
Medium £10.20
Large..........................£12.10

ROD HUTCHINSON
Weigh Sling and Sack Combined......£12.50

QUIVERS & SLINGS

KEVIN NASH
Stalker Sling..£18.35
Deluxe Stalker Sling.............................£22.11

WYCHWOOD
Specialist Quiver..................................£24.50
Carp Quiver..£27.50

TERRY EUSTACE
Brolly Stormside Sling..........................£25.51

UNHOOKING MATS

MARTIN CLARKE
No flaps or anything fancy. This is for the fish you catch and not to catch the fishermen. A 36" x 24" mat with 1 1/2" covered foam with two retaining rings. Large enough to place your knees on when unhooking. No work manual needed with this one. A value for the money product.
Price..£17.95

KEVIN NASH
Carp Unhooking Mat............................£12.10
Monster Carp Unhooking Mat...........£16.07

E.T.
Ritchie McDonald Unhooking Mat.....£10.80
Carp Mat...£20.00
Jumbo Carp/Pike Mat.........................£24.00

ROMART
Blow up unhooking mat, absolutely brilliant. £32.00

ROD HUTCHINSON
Carryall Unhooking Mat......................£65.95

ANDY LITTLE
Blow up unhooking mat which can be floated on the water, as seen in the Andy Little 'La Carping' Video, supplied with pump...£15.35

ROD POD & R/P ACCESSORIES

KJB
2 Rod..£61.30
3 Rod (ex wide)......................................£71.50
4 Rod Stand...£85.76
Extending main bar..............................£20.44
Stalker Pod...£47.77
12" extension legs..................................£8.14
15" extension legs..................................£9.16
Indicator Needles
2...........................£3.04 3.........................£4.05

GARDNER ROD PODS
30"................£16.80 44".................£19.99
Mega Pop telescopic............................£28.18
ProPod completely folding into one unit to fit hodall..£37.52
Mini tripod for canals and hard banks extending..£6.73
Pod Aeriel System..................................£5.92

FOX ROD POD
30" non adjustable...............................£24.90
48" adjustable.......................................£32.50
Needle bar system..................................£8.60
Needles to suit
2.........................£5.75 3...........................£7.75
Rod Locks...£6.40

SLEEPING BAGS & STOVES

COLEMAN
Unleaded Stove 2 burner.....................£61.65
Deluxe Unleaded Stove 2 burner........£74.65
Deluxe Unleaded Stove 3 burner........£85.85
1 Litre Coleman Fuel.............................£3.00
Peak One Unleaded..............................£42.00
Multifuel 8000 BTU...............................£60.95
Filter Funnel..£2.72
Coleman 4 seasons bag -15c...........£103.15
Coleman 5 seasons bag - 30c..........£118.00

ROD HUTCHINSON
Cyclone Sleeping Bag........................£149.95
Cyclone Coverall...................................£82.95

LESLIE'S INSIGHT COLUMNS

At Leslies we decided to donate this part of our advert to certain companies and products we believe are of outstanding quality and value, or are going to be very beneficial to the carp and the carp angler. Products will be rated by star quality - 5 stars being the maximum for quality and value.

THE SOLAR SOD POD

The Sod Pod has taken us a year and a half to design, and finally we have come up with what we believe is the finest pod available. It has a unique one-piece deisgn, with no "kit" type parts to assemble and yet weighs less than 3lbs.
Designed to be strong and sturdy with a low centre of gravity for maximum stability, fully adjustable in all directions with the legs and banksticks hinged from our unique Centre Boss Locking System, the whole set-up is complete in seconds.
The adjustable, pointed legs give maximum grip, whatever the ground, and banksticks are fitted with coin-slotted screws for tightening at the required height.
The SOD extends up to 40" long and closes down to 22", drops into a protective tube for packing into your tackle bag.
Price £89.99

THE SOD POD NEEDLE BARS

The SOD has a needle bar fitting incorporated on it and any of the three versions screw onto it and can be locked into position along the pods length. The two and three rod bars have a milled flat along their length with the needle's simply screw down and locked in any position along the flat.
There is also an adjustable bar which is of the same design as our adjustable bars, extending up to 16" wide for three rod use and closes down to 9" for two rods, and packing away.
If you have a satalite system there is no need for any extra needle bar as the cross bar screws straight onto the pod.
Price ..2 Rod £13.99, 3 Rod £18.99, Adjust £29.99

LESLIE'S SAY

When Martin told us that he was doing a 100% stainless pod our first thought was that it would weigh a ton, and when he was telling us how simple it was to set up, how stable the design was, and how compact it packed away, we thought well we had better have a look at one of these. They can't be as good as Lockie say's because he is biased and were not, in fact were are very critical, but when we saw this system, we were in a word "gobsmacked". It did everything Martin had told us and was manufactured to SOLAR's usual high machining standards, we couldn't fault it, no matter how hard we tried.
STAR QUALITY *****
STAR VALUE *****

SOLAR STAINLESS LOCKEY BACK REST

Stainless "Lockey" back rest. U shaped butt rest formed in stainless steel with a layer of foam to cushion and grip the rod. They can also be adjusted to clamp the rod in position when fishing snaggy swims complete with a stainless locking ring and rubber 'O' ring for alignment onto the buzzer bar. The smartest back rest ever produced.
Price £4.95

LESLIE'S SAY

A very well made product which is simple to use which holds the rod tightly without damage, at £4.95 extremely good value.
STAR QUALITY *****
STAR VALUE *****

BOW - LOC LANDING NET

It seems that until now no-one has looked at the Landing Net design, and they are just an awkward piece of equipment and nearly everybody has lost fish because of this.
The problems are that they are too heavy, especially if you are on your own, the mesh needs to be "swished" about in order to sink it. Once the fish is netted gathering the mesh and trying to turn round with the pole waggling around and catching up on everything from the nearby bushes to poking someone's eye out! Whilst trying to manovere it with fish to the awaiting mat. If this brings back memories how about this :
The Bow-Loc is made from reinforced carbon fibre, and is unquestionably the lightest net on the market. The 6'3" carbon pole is thin in diameter at the spreader block end, allowing for easy movement through the water. There is a stainless clip whipped onto the pole so you can clip the bottom of the mesh into it which completly gets around the problem of sinking the mesh as well as stopping it catching in brambles etc. With these problems out of the way, once the fish is netted the handle can be detached as there is an overfit spigot near the spreader block (which is just like taking a rod apart). Then, rather than gather the mesh, the unique alloy Bow-Loc spreader is simply disengaged and the arms folded together, for carrying and supporting the fish to the mat. The whole procedure of detatching the handle and closing the arms takes less than 2 seconds!
We believe that the Bow-Loc has taken care of ALL the problems of netting fish and cannot be bettered. This is the ultimate net.
Price £125.00

LESLIE'S SAY

What more can we say about the Bow-Lock that hasn't already been said, a class above any other net that has been marketed. Solar have thought of everything and although a pricey item, when all things considered they have cut no corners and used the best quality materials available. as they say you get what you pay for. What price the carp that was lost because you couldn't quite lift the net under it? The Bow-Loc might just make the difference. Fantastic step forward, brilliant design throughout, the Bow-Loc's indeed!
STAR QUALITY *****
STAR VALUE *****

THE SENSORISER INDICATOR ARM

This is the alternative to the traditional monkey type bobbin. A stainless armature which incorporates two hinges along its length that will pick up on even the slightest movement of the line, as they register from both the hinge points. The indicator rises and falls parallel to the bankstick giving full view anywhere on its axis. There are six versions in the range, four in the light flo material in red, yellow, blue and green, a white PTFE and a super stainless head all fitted with our unique line clip. To tension the clip it is simply screwed deeper into the indicator body, this tensions the point at which the clip meets the line where it is tucked under for use with baitrunners etc., just at that point where the clip meets is an area where the line can be trapped like a run clip, so as the arm can be fished slack and as it picks up it reaches a point where it 'snaps' out, creating a bolt rig effect which has proved effective to such a point that fixed leads can be disregarded as the clip creates the same effect.
Along the length of the SENSORISER arm is an adjustable weight which can be mived up to the buzzer bar, leaving only a few grams of the indicator for sensitive pick-ups. It can be set at any position along the length right upto sit underneath the bobbin when using tighline tactics.
The SENSORISER can be positioned underneath the buzzer or on a satellite needle system.   **AVAILABLE MAY**
Price....Lite-flo heads Red, Green, Blue, Yellow..£19.99
Price....White PTFE..£19.99
Price....Super Stainless Head..............................£23.50

LESLIE'S SAY

Is this the ultimate indicator system ?. We believe that it's the nearest we've ever seen to it. The hinged arm and unique clip set-up makes this indicator the for runner on today's market.
STAR QUALITY *****
STAR VALUE *****

THE DELUXE OPTI - POLO

The polo that everyone has been asking for is now available. The "see your face in it" finish sets of ar stainless set-up and incorporates a shoulder each side for rock solid positioning of Optonics, as well a full hole. For security purposes the bolt must be fully removed before the buzzer can be lifted from polo. Supplied with an 'O' ring for 'squaring' onto buzzer.
Price £2

COIN SLOT OPTI-BOLT & N

This is a stainless steel bolt which has a suregrip knurled head for tightening onto the POLO, also has a slot for tightening with a coin which is sup
Price ....£

FLOURESENT CARP EAR

Bright, flouresent yellow ears that definately loo business, as well as stopping the rod being pulle blown off the buzzer. Also abailable in black sup with nuts and bolts as required.
Price..Per Pair ....£

TWITCHER WHEELS

Twelve vane twitcher wheel converts rod knocks bleeps and bleeps into wackers! Roughly 1 bleep 1/8 of an inch of line movement.
Price ....Per Pack ......£

SPEAKER COVERS

These speak for themsleves. They stop the rain a mud getting into the buzzer, whilst not cutting d the sound level.
Price ....Each ....£

LESLIE'S SAY

Everything for the OPTONIC that you could ever is in this range. The Deluxe Polo is superb and s with a stainless coin slotted bolt ensures that everything is as solid as a rock.
The Flouresent Ears had us ammused, will defi get noticed and are a refreshing change from an other ear! Sunglasses may be useful when walk past anglers with them on his gear.
STAR QUALITY *****
STAR VALUE *****

STAINLESS BOILIE AN STOP NEEDLE

A totally unique little tool designed by us with hooked needle which is kind to all types of hair hooklink braided materials, as well as being ex for stringers unlike the barbed and crochet nee types which damage braids and PVA, (as well a being rather nasty to stab yourself with when s The clever part about this needle is in the back where the boilie stops stick out like a pig tail. put the bait on the needle, turn it round and th put the stop in. No hunting around for stops o ground at night or squashed in the mud.
The stops are stored inside the needle and onc strip is used just unsrew the cap and push an strip through.
Supplied with numerous stops, with refils ava
Price ....Available May..............Needle...
Price ....Refil Stops..

LESLIE'S SAY

Fantastic little gadget that EVERY carp angler want. Praticle, no fuss item, saves messing ab looking for stops as you have always got them hand. With the spares being stored inside, yo run out and have to resort to using twigs or matchsticks as we have all done in the past. to the usual "Solar" standard we predict that be the top selling item of tackle this year.
STAR QUALITY *****
STAR VALUE *****

LESLIE'S INSIGHT COLUMNS

...eslie's we decided to donate this part of our advert to certain companies and products we believe are of outstanding quality and value, ...or are going to be very beneficial to carp and the carp angler. Products will be rated by star quality - 5 stars being the maximum for quality and value.

...t last Kevin Nash has launched "THE RANGE" of baits. ...e have been hearing about these baits for the last two ...ars, and some of our customers have been lucky enough ...be in on the field testing. The word is they have ...en taking waters apart, so we had better have an ...sight look.

Proven baits that my mates and I always use. Fish well and I guarantee you will have a result.
Kevin Nash

HIGH QUALITY BASE MIXES

Extremely high quality base mixes which are nutritionally balanced with added vitamins, minerals, and powdered palatants. They come at bulk prices so that you can afford to bait up and also buy those new rods!

...ein Conditioner Mix 34oz £9.77
...e Attractor Mix 50oz £4.24
...vberry Mix 50oz £5.66
...Bulk Fish Mix 50oz £5.66
...Sting Fish Mix 50oz £9.14
...er Pursuit Fish Mix 50oz £7.40
...er Attractor Bird Mix 50oz £8.44
...ic Bird Mix 50oz £7.08
...Jp Mix 16oz £4.34

RISER PELLETS

These pellets are for the waters where the fish have been hammered off the surface. On certain occassions when we have used these pellets we've had fish boiling on the surface when other types of floaters haven't induced them to feed. A fine pellet sprayed ...eding inducer really does get surface fish feeding.

Pellets 1Kg £2.74

CONCENTRATED SWEETENERS

Three different sweeteners which are highly concentrated. Don't forget sweeteners blow just like flavours. These sweeteners do taste sweet, and are not the usual bland taste.

...se Sweetener 50ml £2.09
... Sweet 100g £3.66
... Sweet £3.13

LIE'S INSIGHT RECIPE
AMBER ATTRACTOR BIRD MIX

... special bird food mix. This mix ...ns a high level of quality Milk ...ns which make it stand out from the ... has a light base which produces one ...most versatile baits we have seen. ...ly a winner on the gravel pits, but ...eal for fishing over silt or weed. A ...Y SCORER FOR THE NASHBAIT ...ESLIES FIELD TESTERS.

RECOMMENDED RECIPE

... STRAWBERRY OIL PALATANT
... BIG STRAWBERRY FLAVOUR
... NTENSE SWEETENER
... TWO EGGS
... D TO AMBER ATTRACTOR BIRD
... O REQUIRED CONSISTANCY

NASHBAIT FLAVOURS

Of all the hundreds of flavours available, it seems to be the same few that always catch consistantly. Here they are to the original recipes. **All flavours are 1000:1 concentration.** Some superb results were taken during field testing.

Sweet Cream 50ml £2.50
Maple Essence 50ml £2.72
Seafood Concentrate 50ml £3.50
Big Strawberry 50ml £4.25
Strawberry 50ml £3.80
Chocolate Malt 50ml £3.43
Maple Cream 50ml £3.67
Mega Tutti Frutti 50ml £3.79
Scopex Number 1 50ml £3.76
Lobster Thermadore 50ml £3.90
Megaspice 50ml £3.85
Sweet Maple 50ml £2.72

SENSE APPEAL STIMULANTS

Brilliant fish catchers that not only attract and induce feeding, but also improve the food source. Look at the new Oily Sense Appeals for loose textured fish meals & bird food mixes. The strawberry concentrate is highly recommended by ourselves.

Amino Liver Concentrate 100ml £5.81
Oily Amino Liver 100ml £5.81
Shellfish Concentrate 100ml £8.92
Oily Shellfish 100ml £8.92
Strawberry Concentrate 100ml £5.81
Sweet Spice Concentrate 100ml £5.81
Natural Sweet Concentrate 100ml £5.81
Carpmino Concentrate 250ml £8.12

GENUINE "STARBRIGHT" BAIT DYES

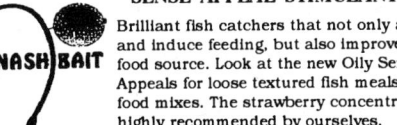

Well what can you say about bait dyes! Kevin has kept to the four main colours not making it too complicated. They did stay in the bait longer for us than the majority of the dyes.

White 20g Tub £2.02
Yellow 20g Tub £2.33
Orange 20g Tub £2.26
Red 20g Tub £2.34

LESLIE'S INSIGHT RECIPE
THE BIG CARP MIX

This is only for the boy's who want to catch the "BIG CARP".

RECOMMENDED RECIPE

7.5ML PEACH OIL
1/2 TEASPOON FRUIT POWDERED PALATANT
1/2 TEASPOON SICKLY SWEET
10ML CARPMINO
4 SIZE TWO EGGS
& ADD TO AMBER ATTRACTOR BIRD MIX
TO REQUIRED CONSISTANCY

SUPASENSE OIL PALATANTS

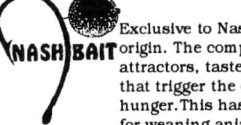

Exclusive to Nashbait and of American origin. The complex composition of attractors, taste enhancers, and palatants that trigger the chemical receptors of hunger. This has been primarily developed for weaning animals, or inducing sick animals to feed.

Salmon 100ml £5.89
Mature Lobster 100ml £7.74
Grouper 100ml £7.74
Arouser Bird Mix 100ml £5.73
Sweet Cumin 100ml £7.74
White Chocolate 100ml £7.74
Peach 100ml £7.74
Strawberry 100ml £7.74
Red Liver 100ml £7.74

SUPASENSE POWDERED PALATANTS

This is the powdered version of the above stated oil, with again complex composition of attractors, taste enhancers, and the palatants that trigger the chemical receptors of hunger.

Fruit 15 mix tub £2.69
Sweet 15 mix tub £2.74
Spice & Savoury 15 mix tub £2.78
Liver 15 mix tub £2.78

ESSENTIAL OILS

Out of all of the hundreds of oils tested, only these four blends consistantly caught fish. We know of some amazing catches made by anglers using these oils. Kevin has not tried to confuse anglers by introducing to many flavours.

Jamaican Special 20ml £6.99
The Sting 20ml £6.99
Almond & Spice 20ml £6.99
The Secret 20ml £6.99

LESLIE'S INSIGHT RECIPE
SUPASENSE STRAWBERRY OIL PALATANT

We are convinced this will be the top selling attractor of the 1990's. Anyone who is anyone, has been trying to get hold of some, and it has already produced over fifty 30lb plus fish to the field testers. Kevin Nash informs us it is an instant fish catcher and works in any type of base mix. Guaranteed next season to be catching in a swim near you.

RECOMMENDED RECIPE

7.5ML STRAWBERRY OIL PALATANT
3ML BIG STRAWBERRY FLAVOUR
2ML INTENSE SWEETENER
4 SIZE TWO EGGS
& ADD TO AMBER ATTRACTOR BIRD MIX TO REQUIRED CONSISTANCY

BIVVIES & B/ACCESSORIES

KEVIN NASH BROLLY OVERWRAPS
Lightweight Overwrap 45"................£52.54
Lightweight Overwrap 50"................£59.37
Zig Wrap 45" Nylon................£78.43
Zig Wrap 50" Nylon................£88.65
Zig Wrap Oval................£97.36
Zig Wrap Canvas 45"................£122.94
Zig Wrap Canvas 50"................£128.84

ROD HUTCHINSON
Bivvy Tent................£159.95

FOX INTERNATIONAL
Supa Bivvy................£147.95

E.T.
Bivvy Dome................£99.76

KEVIN NASH
Ground Sheet 45"................£21.05
Lightweight Ground Sheet 45"................£9.74
Ground Sheet 50"................£22.30
Lightweight Ground Sheet 50"................£11.69
Oval Ground Sheet................£26.86
Lightweight Oval Ground Sheet................£13.63
Ground Sheet Bag................£3.90
Storm Rods & Caps................£8.35
Swival Storm Caps................£9.66
Bivvy Stick 26"................£9.45
Bivvy Stick 36"................£9.91
Thumbscrew x2................£1.55
Bivvy Pegs................£5.65
Peg Extractor................£2.33
Velcro Pack................£11.20
Nylaproof................£8.96
Canvaproof................£8.96
Seam Sealant................£4.08

K J B
Storm Rods 50"................£22.50
Super Storm Rods 50"................£25.99

KINGFISHER
Storm Bolts................£5.37
Kingfisher T. Pegs: 2.....£2.68 8.....£8.18

FOX STORM ATTACHMENTS
For Fox Products................£6.03
For non-Fox Products................£6.03

BAIT MAKING PRODUCTS
Rollaball Baitmakers Long Base 12/14/16/18/20/22/24mm................£7.86
Rolling Table 12/16mm, 14/18mm, 20/22mm.......£2.63
Rollaball with Table 8mm................£5.45
Sidewinder Boilie Machine................£53.49
Sausage Gun (8 nozzles)................£9.25
KJB Professional Baitmate Sausage Gun................£31.90
Boilie Foam.
Black ..£2.25, Orange, yellow, green......£1.35
KJB Large Poly Pop-ups................98p
Ivel Boilie Pops for 20ml+ above boilies...£1.10
3 Pippettes................£1.03
The last word in Rollaball Bait Makers: Extra Large size rolling over 80 baits at a time 16 or 18mm................£59.95

OPTONICS/ALARMS BOBBINS & SWINGERS

LESLIE'S BLEEPER DICS
An ultra sensistive dics to replace 2 or 4 vane wheels in Optonics. Ideal for twitch bites. Absolutely brilliant .
3 per pack................£2.25
OPTONIC New Super XL................£77.00
Super Special Compact................£66.00
Special Compact Hi or Lo................£55.00
Compact Hi and Lo................£39.95
Magnetonic Hi and Lo................£49.95
Basic Hi and Lo................£32.95
Optonic Extension Leads
5m Special................£7.95
7.5m Special................£8.95
Sounder Box 2T................£27.95
Sounder Box 4 channel................£69.95
BITECH VIPER................£49.95
Sounder Box................£35.26
Leads................£5.07
DAIWA SENSITRON ALARM................£76.99

KEVIN NASH
Opti Polo................£2.95
Opto Fork................£2.25
Opti Bolt and Nut................£2.15
Bite Alarm Bolt and Nut................£1.99
Twitcher Wheel................£2.15
Opto Pouch................£2.98
Caps Ears................£2.10
Optonic Vee Betalights................£2.01

FOX INTERNATIONAL
Swingers................£11.30
Spare Heads green, red, yellow................£3.85

K J B
Swingers with Isotope................£10.82

SOLAR
Lite Flo Bobbins, red,blue,yellow, green Small 15mm Dia 7gr, Medium 20mm Dia 15gr, Large 25mm Dia 26gr. All at £5.95

FOX INTERNATIONAL
3 in 1 Light Reactive Luminous Indictors. Adjustable Weights to Allow Four Different Sizes From 10g to 25g.
Clear, yellow, red, orange................£7.50

HAIR PRESENTATION BITS

GARDNER
Mini Hair Needle................82p
Needle Guard................£1.14
Braided Hair needle................£1.19
Stringer Needle................£1.26
'V' Hair Stops. Green, yellow, orange........50p

KEVIN NASH
Boilie Baiting Needle................£1.28
X-Long Stringer Needle................£1.52
Boilie Hair Bead and Needle................£2.02
Replacement Hair Beads for above................98p
Boilie Hair Stops, black, orange, yellow....65p
Nut Drill................£1.75
Marvic Boilie Punch................£2.36
Marvic Boilie Pop Foam................82p

CONTROLLERS & FEATURE FINDERS

GARDNER
Controllers Clear, 5gm....82p 10gm......92p
15gm................£1.15 20gm................£1.45
30gm................£1.88 40gm................£2.21

TERRY EUSTACE
Floater Floats
Small................£2.82 Large................£3.05

E.T.
Feature Finder for finding different depths.........£1.14

IVEL
Swim Marker................£1.39

PVA PRODUCTS

LESLIE'S
MARTIN CLARKE NON RESIDUE CORD
A cord which dissolves while staying in string form rather than shrinking into a blob first before dissolving. A non-taste, non-residue P.V.A. which increased catch rates when used in preference to other makes of P.V.A. 20 or 40 seconds dissolve available. Supplied on 20 metre spools................£4.95

K J B
200 20 sec Dissolve Time................£3.17
400 40 sec Dissolve Time................£3.70
Cord 60 sec Dissolve Time................£4.20

TERRY EUSTACE
P.V.A Thread 240"......£1.70 1000"......£4.05

KEVIN NASH
P.V.A. String Quick Melt................£3.00
P.V.A. String Slow Melt................£3.50

RIG BITS, TUBING, BEADS ETC

LESLIE'S
Supersoft Valve Rubber, available in clear or black, 5 yards, 0.5/1/1.5/2/2.5/3m...£3.00
Semi-stiff Tubing, black................£2.85
Black Sliding Rig Stops................£1.30
Shrink to Fit Tubing................£1.25
A very special plastic rig tubing which has the ability to shrink to half its original size when exposed to direct heat.
We see the main advantage of this product to secure flosses and dacron hairs firmly to hooks. The thinking angler will be able to find many applications for joining/bonding parts of rigs semi-permanently.

KEVIN NASH
Large Bore Rig Beads................66p
Anti-tangle Bead and Tube................£1.10
Bolt Beads................£1.31
Swivel Beads................£1.37
Micro Swivel Beads................£1.37
Casting Booms................90p
Feeder Booms................85p
3/5/8mm Beads................86p
Knot Beads................66p
Rig Foam, black, orange, yellow................£1.35
Polypops................£1.12
Rig Rings................£1.00
Micro Rig Rings................£1.00

TERRY EUSTACE
The Rig................£1.95
Carp Beads 4m Olive................£1.45
Carp Beads 5m Black................£1.55
Carp Beads 6m Brown................£1.65
Sliding Knot Beads................99p
Rig Glue................£2.16
Rig Putty................£2.45

GARDNER
Pop-up Putty................£1.52

E.T.
Tungsten Rubber, green, brown, black..£2.21
Helicopter rig beads................£1.40

KEVIN NASH
Stiff Boom Tube................91p
Fine Stiff Boom Tube................91p
Boom Tube, black 1.5/2/3mm................91p
Boom Tube, clear 1.5/2/3mm................91p
Rig Tube, 0.5/1mm................91p

SPOOL, LEAD & ROD BANDS

KEVIN NASH
Spool Bands................£1.07
Spool Bands Aero................£1.07
Rod and Lead Bands................£3.81
Velcro Rod Straps................£2.60

TERRY EUSTACE
Rod and Leads Straps................£3.45

E.T.
Velcro Rod Bands................£2.73
Lead Band Rod Protectors................£3.03

BAITING ACCESSORIES & BOILIE BAGS

WYCHWOOD
New Reddicat Boilie Pult £6.95

COBRA
Throwing Sticks.
20mm Standard 14mm Boilies 90yds.........£11.95
23mm Super 18mm Boilies 100yds.........£13.95
23mm King 18mm Boilies 110yds.........£16.95
29mm Jumbo 20mm Boilies 120yds.........£18.95
Groundbait Thrower great for particles......£13.25

GARDNER
Mixer Fixer................£2.33
Bait Rocket................£3.50

DRENNAN
Boiliepult Catties, Small, Large, and Multi Pouch................£5.78

BARNETT
Black Widow................£9.05
Diablo................£15.14
Spare Bands................£2.95

E.T.
5" Leather Catapult Pouch................£3.33
5" Nylon Catapult Pouch................£2.62

KEVIN NASH
Standard Boilie Bag................£5.99
Jumbo Boilie Bag................£7.99
Special Boilie Bag................£16.99

UMBRELLAS & S/SIDES

FOX INTERNATIONAL
Supa Brolly................£124.90
Supa Brolly Fill-in................£54.90

KEVIN NASH
Oval Umbrella................£97.28
Brolly + Brollywrap Oval................£188.73
Mini Side 50"................£27.66
Mini Side Oval................£29.67
Brolleywrap 50"................£41.46
Twin Zip Door 50"................£13.54
Hooker Special 50"................£67.37
Hooker Special Oval................£76.13

STEADES WAVELOCK BROLLIES
45" Nubrolli MK2................£47.99
50" Nubrolli MK2................£52.99
50" Camouflage Nubrolli MK2................£62.99

GARDNER
Brolly Poles 29"................£8.25
Brolly poles 36"................£9.41
Guy Rope Set................£2.75

LANDING NETS & HANDLES

KEVIN NASH
Standard Landing Net 42" complete....£48.45
Standard Landing Net 52" complete....£55.50
Hooker Landing Net 42" complete........£56.95
Hooker Landing Net 52" complete........£59.82
Arms 42"................£15.11
Arms 52"................£15.50
Standard Pole................£19.28
Hooker Pole................£24.72
Nylon Spreader Block................£3.52
Standard Mesh Net 42"only................£16.55
Standard Mesh Net 52" only................£19.43
Hooker Mesh Net 42" only................£17.91
Hooker Mesh Net 52" only................£20.54
Landing Net Bag................£4.13

GARDNER
Landing Net 42" complete................£49.30
Landing Net 36" complete................£45.93
Specimen Nets, black fibreglass arms, brass spreader block 28"........£13.02 32"................£16.50
Dual Mesh Nets 42" Hex/Micro Base...£16.35
42" 3/4 Micro Base................£16.35

LESLIE'S
Extra Strong 6' Landing Net Pole, Parallel Glass, *Absolutely Brilliant*................£22.95

LESLIE'S SLEEPING BAG
3 Seasons Sleeping Bag....Very Good....£40.83
All Seasons Sleeping Bag....Brilliant....£87.83

A very good value sleeping bag of high quality at a very reasonable price.(All Seasons Bag used to -10, we must have been fools).

VIDEOS & BOOKS

VIDEO'S
Carp Fever by Kevin Maddocks
No1 The Revolution................
No2 Rigs................
No3 Baits................
Cat Fever *very enjoyable*................
Carp Action at Lake Salagou................
Carp by Tim Paisley and John Lilley
Part 1 & Part 2................each...
Carp Bait - The Video................£
La Carping by Andy Little
Brilliant, very enjoyable................
Canary Carping by Kevin Nash................
Russian Fishing Adventure by Kevin Maddocks & Bob Baldock................
Big Cats of the Volga Delta by Kevin Maddocks & Bob Baldock................
Gravel Pit Carping by Andy Little................
Carping on Particles by Andy Little................
Euro Carp Quest by Kevin Maddocks................
Carp From The Start Part 1 by Kevin Maddocks................
Carp From The Start Part 2 by Kevin Maddocks................
Startin Carpin Part 1 by Kevin Nash................
Startin Carpin Part 2 by Kevin Nash................
Canary Carpin by Kevin Nash................

BOOKS
Beekay Guide to 1000 Carp waters................
Big Water Carp by J.Gibbson................
Carp Now & Then by R.Hutchinson................
Fox Pool by Robin Maylin................
Tiger Bay by Robin Maylin................
The Quest for the Queen by Bailey & Page..
Ritchie on Carp by R.McDonald................
Redmire Pool by Clifford & Arbery................
In Pursuit of Carp & Catfish by K.Maddock
Carp by Robin Maylin................
Big Carp by Tim Paisley................
Carp in Focus................
For the Love of Carp................
Carp Season by Tim Paisley................
Carp Fishing by Tim Paisley................
Big Fish from Famous Waters................
Kevin Nash Rig Book................
Kevin Nash Advanced Rig Book................
Kevin Nash Annual 1992................
Carpworld Yearbook................

BEDCHAIRS, CHAI & B/C ACCESSORIE

FOX INTERNATIONA
Super Deluxe................
Standard Deluxe................
Super Adjustable Level Chair................
Standard Adjustable Level Chair...
Spare feet - 2 sizes................
ALL SPARES AVAILABLE F
FOX BEDCHAIRS AND CHAIR
ORDER ONLY

KEVIN NASH
Fox Bag Cover & Mattress................
Deluxe Fox Bag Cover................
Deluxe Breathable Fox Bag Cover.
Fox Deluxe Wellie Wipe................
Sleeping Bag Kit Bag................
Standard Bedchair Cover................
Fox Bedchair Cover................
Fox Mattress................
Bedchair Kit Harness. ....
Bedchair Bag................

RUCKSACKS & BA

KEVIN NASH
Hooker Rucksack................
Specialist Rucksack................
Carp Carryall................
Carp Carryall Specialist................
Stalker Bag................
Monster Specialist Carryall................
Pursuit Rucksack 60................
Pursuit Rucksack 90................
Pursuit Rucksack 120................

ROD HUTCHINSON
Pukka Rucksack................

WYCHWOOD
K2 Rucksack................
Ruckman Rucksack................
Ruckman Lightweight................
Packer................
K2 Stalker Bag................
Lugger................
Stalker Bag................
Carry All................
John Wilson Carry All................
John Wilson Shoulder Bag................

TROLLEY & T/ACCESSORIES

FOX INTERNATION
Load Shift Trolley................
Load Shift Strap System................

DZUS
Warrior MK3 Trolley................

LESLIE'S INSIGHT COLUMNS

At Leslie's we decided to donate this part of our advert to certain products we believe are of outstanding quality and value, or are going to be very beneficial to carp and the carp angler. Products will be rated by star quality - 5 stars being the maximum for quality and value.

KRYSTON 'MAGMA' LIQUID TUNGSTEN WEIGHT

first ever liquid tungsten weight in a
, Non toxic, easy to apply, adds that
a heavy weight to wherever its
ired. Its super adhesive qualities
e it the ideal tool for balancing
ded rigs, braided hooklengths &
i-strands, adds vital weight to mono
ackleading situations for carp
ng. Totally universal, 1001 uses.
e.....................£3.75 per tube.
'LIE'S SAY
one is for the carp boys, it is
lastly in it's self, absolutely brilliant
ritical balanced baits.
R QUALITY *****
R VALUE *****

KRYSTON KLIN-IK CARP CARE ANTISEPTIC

fically formulated for todays caring
r, one shot treatment following
removal will help speed up the
ng process. Can be used directly on
s body to aid protection against
se. Where torn fins, missing scales,
nfection from lice exist. Klin-ik will
to be invaluable on todays
ured waters, suitable for all
es. This product will help todays
r treat fish in a totaly safe manner
posed to using substances which
tully toxic.
......................£3.25 per Bottle
IE'S SAY
hould not be just for the careing
but for all anglers.
R QUALITY *****
R VALUE *****

KEVIN NASH HOOKER DELUXE HOLDALL

Further update for 1992. Now manufactured entirely from Creek total performance laminate. Massive umbrella pocket and bankstick pocket zipped and buckled for easy and quick access, luxury padded shoulder and carrying handles. Fully lined inside with additional cushioned padding plus rod seperators for total protection. Accomodates six rods, three tackled up and three without reels, 12' and 13' models available.
Price 12'.......£87.93 13'........£89.47

KEVIN NASH PURSUIT SLING

Designed for the mobile specialist Carp angler. To cover any permutation of carrying requirement, with total rod protection. Roomy main compartment for brolly with sides if required. Two external pockets with quick release buckles and zipped for easy access. Luxury padded shoulder and carrying handles, rear pocket for rods, foam lined for tip/butt protection. Quick release rod straps with foam lined protectors. Nylon base for life time durability.
Price............................£30.68

LESLIE'S SAY
Now is the time of year when our customers start to think about there new rod requirements for the coming season. We are proud of the craftsmanship built into our rods each one is treated like an individual work of art by us. We like to think you'll give them the care they deserve. You will not find better systems for rod protection than Kevin's Hooker Holdall or Pursuit Quiver Sling. They are simply the best.
STAR QUALITY *****
STAR VALUE *****

KRYSTON 'HEAVY METAL'

Using space-age technology for its formulation this revolutionary non-toxic enviroment friendly compound exhibits the highest specific gravity and adhesion of any lead putty substitute product on the market. The extreme high density of 'Heavy Metal' ensures the product weighs in at more than twice the given weight as other alternatives. Containing the highest quality tungsten powder available plus rare materials this compound is not only heavier than steel and cast iron but is also the most dense material of its type available and must be comparable size for size with lead.
A purpose designed feature of 'Heavy Metal' is its incorporated hardening agent. After moulding onto line thermal shock and micro-crystallisation will automatically cure and 'set hard' the adhesion when immersed in water. For further use this hardening process is reversable with manipulation, at the end of the session the angler simply removes the used piece from his line or rig to be stored back with the original slug where it can be used over and over again.
The unique formulation of 'Heavy Metal' has been engineered specifically for the critical balancing of pop ups and for close proximity back leading.
Price...........................£4.35 per Tub
LESLIE'S SAY
Heaviest putty on the market, low profile presentation, reusable long lasting, easy application, self-curing, totally versatile, non toxic and environmentally friendly. Absolutley brilliant.
STAR QUALITY *****
STAR VALUE *****

LESLIE'S CELEBRITY SHOWS

March 21st.....Rod Hutchinson
March 28th.....K.J.B Products
April 4th.......Tim Paisley & Julian Cundiff From Carpworld
April 11th......Dave Chiltern From Kryston
April 18th......Zenon Bojko From Mainline Bait
April 25th......Rob Maylin
May 2nd........Andy Little & Dave Keeves
May 9th........Martin Clarke
May 16th.......Des Taylor
May 23rd.......Kevin Nash
May 30th.......Martin Locke Solar Tackle
June 6th.......Mathew Hayes (Barbel)

After last year's great success, we are doing CELEBRITY SHOWS again during the close season. At Leslie's you can meet them, and also ask the questions that have been on the tip of your tongue. The shows will run on each Saturday form March 21st to June 6th, there be at least two Celebrities, on Match fishing and one or more on Specimen fishing.
Most of the CELEBRITIES will be launching brand New products.

HOLDALLS & HODS

IN NASH HOOKER HOLDALLS
ITH REEL POCKETS
ard 12'........£49.97
  13'..........£52.10
  12'..........£87.93
  '............£89.47
ITH SPOOL POCKETS
ard 12'........£44.79
  13'..........£47.86
  12'..........£72.41
  3'...........£73.99

SAVAY ROD HOD
  Hod..........£78.88
  Hod..........£82.96
  Sleeve.......£21.10
  Sleeve.......£21.90

ROD HUTCHINSON
otection Holdall 12'...£85.95
                 13'...£87.95

WYCHWOOD
Select 12/13'..........£65.50
hes 12/13'............£18.50
ght System Select
th....................£25.52
12/13ft..............£69.50
elixe. Fully Padded for protection
.....................£84.50
.....................£84.50

ERAL ACCESSORIES
KEVIN NASH
fe....................£1.90
t.....................£1.64
monopod - plastic.....£1.13
ief...................£4.72
.....................£4.72
m 18/30mm.............62p
Tubing natural/black..£2.33

GARDNER
Camera monopod - brass.........£1.39
Adjustable line clips..........£1.29
Rig bin........................£4.76
Back leads.....................£1.94
Heavy back leads...............£1.94
Suspender......................£2.33
Magic markers clear, yellow, orange..£1.55
Power Gum 7lb..£1.63 11lb..£1.79 22lb..£1.98
Run rings......................77p

E.T.
TERRY EUSTACE
Spool cases....................£5.07

IVEL CAMO
Bomb coating powder.
A selected blend of low melt special plastic powders which produce a camouflage effect to lead bombs and protects from damage/sharp edges that may cause abrasion to line if left untreated.
Colour:
Sand/Brown Mix..................£2.20
Green/Brown Mix.................£2.20
All Brown Mix...................£2.20
Black/Sand Mix..................£2.20

EZEE LAP
Diamond Hook sharpeners.........£8.25
Tube Threaders..................£1.70
Braided Threader................72p
Middy Hair Rigs - Sizes: 4,6,8
2 in a pack + tubing............£1.24

DRENNAN CARP SYSTEM
Drennan brass rings - mini & small...82p
Sub - surface controller........£1.39
Surface controllers -
5g...£1.60 10g...£1.65 15g...£1.70
Bait drill......................£1.70
Bait needle.....................97p
Stiff Anti-tangle tube..........98p
Shock beads, 5mm, 8mm...........72p
Shock swivel beads..............98p
Link beads......................67p

Hair stops - Small, large.......87p
Bolt Beads......................87p
Anti-tangle beads...............77p
Free-run beads..................77p
Floater loops...................77p
Boilie bayonets.................67p

SOLAR TACKLE
Buzzer Bars
2 Rod 6"/8"/10"................£8.95
3 Rod 12"/15"..................£10.95
3 Rod Adjustable Front.........£21.50
3 Rod Adjustable Back..........£21.50
Extending Banksticks
12".............................£12.25
16".............................£13.25
20".............................£14.25
Needle Systems
2 Rod...........................£19.95
3 Rod...........................£23.95
The Satellite
3 Rod...........................£40.95
3/4" Bobbin/18" Needle..........£4.75
1" Bobbin/18" Needle............£4.75
Indicator Bodies (solar Bore)
3/4" Acetol.....................£2.50
1" Acetol.......................£2.50
PTFE Flip Top (small)...........£3.95
PTFE Flip Top (medium)..........£4.25
PTFE Flip Top (large)...........£4.50
All above available in Gardner bore
Guy Ropes.......................£4.95
Bivvy Pegs......................£10.95
Stabilizer......................£5.50
Adjustable Stabilizer...........£6.95
Stainless Coin Optonic Bolt.....£2.95
Stainless Lockey Back Rest......£4.95
Carp Sack Pegs x 2..............£4.95

Savay Seed Mix   1kg   3kg
Red Mix   £7.45   £18.95
Yellow Mix   £6.95   £17.95
Spiced Seed Mix   £6.95   £17.95
Quench Mix   £6.95   £17.95
Neptune Mix   £6.45   £15.95

Savay Mix Masters   100ml
Squid/Octopus Koi Rearer   £8.90
White Chocolate   £6.50
Golden Plum   £4.50
Esterblend 12   £4.90
Stimulin Amino Comp   £4.90
Stimulin Amino with Garlic £4.90
Liquid Candy Sweetener   £8.90

ONE PIECE SUITS
LESLIE'S
Leslie's Alaskan under suit....£49.95
BOB CHURCH
Waxed, Proofed 8oz
Small/Medium/Large.............£81.71
Ex. Large......................£84.36
Ex. Ex. Large..................£88.84
ROD HUTCHINSON
Cyclone suit. S/M/L/XL/XXL.....£208.75
MAINSTREAM
One piece Suit with hood, without lining
S/M/L/XL/XXL....£67.39 K1, K2...£81.71
Summer Lining
S/M/L/XL/XXL....£20.40 K1, K2...£24.49
Winter Linning
S/M/L/XL/XXL....£36.74 K1, K2...£44.92
KEVIN NASH
Pursuit Actic Suit S/M/L.......£194.77
Pursuit Actic Suit XL/XXL......£203.09

DAIWA SS3000 TOURNAMENT CARP REEL
The ultimate in quality carp reels
This reel has best of everything. A 35mm long stroke mechanism allied to a large capacity coned spool which has a 3 degree taper to give perfect even line lay, incorpating 5 ball bearings.
Reel............................£175.00
Spare spools....................£35.00
Phone for availability

ELEPHONE
0582 453542
swering Machine after 6pm

POSTAGE AND PACKAGING
UP TO 10 SMALL ITEMS : eg pkts of hooks, floats, line etc............£1.00
UP TO 20 SMALL ITEMS : £1.75
UP TO 50 SMALL ITEMS : £2.75
LEADS   : Please allow 11 pence per ounce
OVERSEAS & BFPO   : Please contact us for Postal Charges

FAX
0582 35740

24 Hour Working Day Delivery On orders above the value of £50.00 = £10.00 eg Rods, Poles, Bedchairs, Holdalls, or Multiple small items weighing up to 30 kilos. UK ONLY
48 Hour Working Day Delivery On orders above the value of £50.00 = £5.42 eg Rods, Poles, Bedchairs, Holldalls, or Multiple small items weighing up to 30 kils. UK ONLY

THE BIRDHIDE AND THE BOG OF CORRUPTION

ANDY SPREADBURY

My wife Chris maintains that I always fish in the area of the lake that is:
a) Furthest from the car park, and thus the longest walk with the gear.
b) The muddiest, most rat-infested, bug-ridden, litter-bound and smelliest pitch on any of the club's lakes, and
c) Generally the area least likely to appeal to all but the most significant of fish. (Very droll Chris...)

Whilst the *bird hide* may satisfy at least some of these criteria, I take exception to the view that it does all... it's not muddy – just completely under water! For the *bird hide* is one of a number of constructions built by the owners for the use of the duck shooting syndicate. These are dotted about the lake, located in strategic areas and consist of raised wooden platforms approximately ten feet long by four feet wide, with a raised wooden panel three feet high (situated to prevent the occupier from falling off into the water).

My reasons for choosing to fish off this particular platform was that since I wished to start the season on this water and it was certain to be extremely busy, I needed to choose a pitch that would be both available the night before the season started, and would stand a good chance of having some fish in it. (It does help).

This particular hide was a bitch to get to. Not quite the furthest pitch from the car park, it was certainly not high on everyone's list of 'swims I would most like to fish.' To get to it, *the bog* had to be negotiated; this entailed stripping down to the undies and wading with the gear held aloft through some of the foulest, most insect infested muddy corruption imaginable. The lake in question being a badly silted clay pit, the bottom of which consisted of three feet of mucky ooze overlaying two to three feet of water, it was usual to sink down to the thighs in the silt with the water level somewhere up near the chin! This swim automatically ruled out some of the more diminutive members, unable to negotiate the terrain without the aid of snorkels, stilts, divine assistance, or an ability to hold the breath for a very, very long time...

Since a three-day stint was envisaged, some consideration was given to creature comforts; because of the restricted space available, it was impossible to bivvy on the platform – in fact there was just sufficient space to position the bedchair with the rods at the foot of the bed. The best protection that could be achieved was to stick a long pole of the right diameter into the silt off the right side of the platform and position an umbrella directly over the head end of the bed, covering rucksack, stove, bait etc from the elements; the bottom half would have to take care of itself and make do with a ground sheet.

The *hide* (hide was a joke, it opened right out onto the lake where the occupant could be seen by every carp in the vicinity!), was perfectly positioned to intercept carp moving out of their night time dwelling areas away to the right. At dawn, fish would move up the lake, across the front of the pitch to their usual dawn feeding area which was some way to the left. Their usual route was to follow a narrow sand bar which ran across the pitch, ten to fifteen yards out, the 'hotspot' being the shallowest spot on the bar near to where marginal bulrushes formed the start of a serious snag – where any carp that was hooked would make for, for sure!

The sand bar was baited with chick peas, some being distributed along it, and some thrown out in trails leading from the marginal bulrushes as it was previously observed that some of the fish would hug these margins, swimming across the gap in front of the pitch. The diagram makes it all clear I hope... (as mud).

Work commitments prevented me being at the lake any earlier than opening night, another reason for choosing this pitch). When I arrived it was as well that I had made preparations to fish it as every recognised swim on the lake was occupied, (and apparently had been so since the evening before!) Having suffered the walk round, stripped down to my St Michael's and braved the 'wade of corruption', I was on the hide washing off the yuk that had affixed itself like a limpet to parts I never knew I had......!

The evening was glorious; a cold, wet, windy and depressingly dreary spring had, suddenly at the eleventh hour given way to bright sun and a light, warm breeze which in the evening was now dropping. Copper gold caressed every leaf and limb, and as swifts whizzed and swooped over the surface of the lake, I noticed at once that there was suddenly the most tremendous hatch of caenis – what trout anglers call the anglers curse! Tiny broadwing flies by the million upon million! Everything was covered in them – including me! I looked like a homepride flour grader! I was spitting flies from my mouth, and snorting them from my nose, they were in my ears, in my hair (and had found their way to a good few other places besides!) The little insects, about a quarter of an inch long or so, crawled up reed stems and other emergent vegetation, and underwent their miraculous transformation into winged adults by splitting their skins and emerging from the spent shucks. It was one of the heaviest hatches I had ever seen, and carried on for some time.

Away over on the right-hand side of the lake, it seemed that a barbeque was in progress; judging from the noise the lads were having a real stonker of a time – wine flowed, sausages, burgers and bacon crackled and popped in the evening air – the smell was agonisingly mouth-watering! Saliva ran like a river around my tongue...

Needless to say, tea that evening was baked beans...

With the two rods set up, and simple running rigs attached I awaited the onset of the new season. Bats wheeled and flitted in and out of the trees, and overhead a heron called, making it's way back to it's nest far in the distance. Coots clucked, and frogs croaked, and as the evening wore on and flow of wine slowed, voices became quieter; people whispered excitedly and fussed with their tackle.

It has always been my practice to wait until the stroke of midnight before starting to fish – believing that to start sooner is guaranteed to put the mockers on things for the rest of the season; so whilst everyone else had cast out (it seemed), I patiently waited for the 'starters whistle'.

Out in the blackness of the dark, all was now utterly quiet. Nothing interrupted the cloaked silence of the lake, except for the occasional flutter of fowl. On the stroke of twelve I cast out and snuggled down under the covers beneath the umbrella, pulling the ground sheet

CUSTOM MADE BOILIES
187 Beacon Road
Chatham
Kent ME5 7BS

CUSTOM MADE BOILIES

MEDWAY'S NO. 1 BAIT STOCKIST

FED UP!! OR NOT ENOUGH TIME TO MAKE YOUR OWN BAITS

BORED! WITH SHOP BOUGHT READY MADES

NEED A LARGE QUANTITY AT SHORT NOTICE, FOR THAT LAST MINUTE SESSION, HOLIDAY OR PRE BAITING CAMPAIGN.

IF SO LET US SOLVE YOUR PROBLEMS AT VERY COMPETITIVE RATES

Just simply choose your bait mix from the list below

SOLAR   PREMIER   MAINLINE

or from our own range of mixes (Spice - Seedmix - Fishmeal)

Choose your own size: 14mm   16mm   18mm   20mm   22mm
or even chopped boilie - THE BOILIE PARTICLE EQUIVALENT

ANY COLOUR!   ANY FLAVOUR!   ANY QUANTITY!
(all mixes are Shelf Life)
All above mixes also available in unrolled form.
Special North Kent area delivery service.

Immediate return mail order service available.
(Postal rates vary to size of order).

IT'S JUST A PHONE CALL AWAY. IT'S THAT EASY

OR JUST POP IN AND SEE US

Telephone: 0634 403108

up under my chin. After all the weeks of waiting for the new season to start, all I now wanted to do was sleep – hopefully to be awakened by the sound of the Optonic's urgent call.

Excitement and fatigue overcame devotion and sometime after 2am I dropped off.

I awoke in the half light of dawn, (somewhere around half past three or four at this time of year), to the sound of bite alarms screaming, – only thing was – they weren't mine! Away to my right, members of the 'Barbecue Gang' were crashing into one another and getting in each others way as one of their number attempted to convert a chance. Amid great oaths, and crashing and slashing of rods and reeds, an encouraging cry of "I'm in" rent the dawn.. Unfortunately, he wasn't – certainly not a carp anyway as a few minutes later, a three pound foul hooked tench was dragged unceremoniously to the bank. Later, it was followed by another – this time fairly hooked in the mouth – and then another – and before long Optonics were in top gear as the entire tench population decided to spawn in the Gang's baited area giving continual line bites to every rod! Half asleep, (or hungover), the recipients of this unwelcome attention attempted great feats of contortion as they tried to out perform each other in the striking and playing of fish, crashing into each other and tripping over each other's rods, standing on bait boxes, and casting into each other's swims!

At six o'clock I decided to recast both baits and in the now clear light could position them with much greater accuracy near the 'hot-spot' just over the bar. On the edge of the marginal rushes, a dark shape glided along at speed – obviously intent on making its way down to the dawn feeding area to my left. I had long since learnt that it was futile to try and catch these rapidly moving fish, having many times before tried to intercept them on their peregrinations. I left him alone, hoping that my baited area over the bar would cause at least something to stop in it's tracks and go down and feed.

Both baits landed inch perfect and I topped up the area with several pouchfuls of chicks. Minutes later along the bar, mud clouds could be seen rising from the bottom and the tips of tails breaking the surface! Things were definitely looking up and I expected action at any moment.

At five minute intervals, the line to the right hand rod would pull tight and the Optonic would give a two bleep signal – the fish were obviously inspecting the bait but were being extremely wary. I pulled everything tight and put the line in the clip hoping to prick a fish bolt fashion. I didn't have long to wait...

At some time after six thirty, the right hand rod exploded into action – the Optonic was screaming, the rod was flapping up and down and shaking on the rests and a great boil over the sand bar signalled where the fish had picked up the bait – had hooked itself, and was desperately trying to put as much distance between us as it could!

There was no question of striking to make contact with the fish – it was more a matter of giving line fast enough so that I didn't become 'pointed!' The fish powered away like a steam train and I was just able to back wind sufficiently to prevent a disaster; away to the right he went, in the direction of the marginal rushes and in seconds he was five, six, seven yards into the danger area! Standing right on the left hand edge of the platform, I leant the rod right over, trying to make the angle of contact as parallel to the bank as possible; the rod creaked and groaned, and the eleven pound line strained to the limit – I could vaguely hear splashing in the margins to the right and bulrushes rocked and swayed as the fish desperately tried to get in them...

Bending the rod round and straining everything as hard as I dare I pulled for dear life, and gradually, inch by straining inch he came, thrashing and protesting back along the margins. However, the bulrushes to my right were at their thinnest, and it was here that he temporarily found his haven, – but not for long, more heaving and humping soon had him swirling at my feet and just when I thought that it was all over, he dived under the other line and shot into the bulrushes to my left! What a cock-up ensued! The Optonics to this rod began screaming as line was ripped from the reel, so I hopped along the platform to the right to reduce the angle again, over balanced, and knocked the other rod off the rest and into the water! Panic station! Groping after it with my left hand I lost balance again and fell against the bedchair tipping it up like a see-saw! Blankets, bedding and bait flew into the air and landed in the bog behind me! – Meanwhile, the fish discovered its sense of humour and decided to swim out of the bulrushes and under the platform! Frantically I wound down to try and make contact – I was in contact all right – with about ten tons of vegetation, the line was a veritable 'cat's cradle' around it!

At this point, my guardian angel must have assumed responsibility for the subsequent events, because quite anticlimatically, the fish lay quietly off the end of the platform while I managed to get the meshes of the net up around him and hoist him up onto the boards. The scene of devastation on the platform however, was without equal...

Line from the other rod was massed in a great birds nest of a ball caught up around one arm of the landing net and wrapped around half a bed of bulrushes; the bedchair was upside down with one end in the water and various items of bedding and bait lay in the 'Bog of Corruption' behind me; the other rod was somewhere in the lake, presumably at the other end of the line...

The fish by the way was a long, lean and mean 10lb 6oz common, whose performance I think you will agree, was out of all proportion to it's size!...

It goes without saying that it took most of the rest of the day to retrieve lost gear, apprehend and dry out bedding from the bog, and respool with line; the birds nest unquestionably being a lost cause. Meanwhile, the 'Barbecue Gang' continued to fall over each other as they kept the tench (and the rest of us) entertained well into teatime when unfortunately the activities of the tench began to subside and normal services were resumed. By the evening, some semblance of normality had returned and we all turned our attention to the catching of a reasonable fish of which the lake held quite a few.

It had been a glorious day of light winds and relentless sun, and now in the evening as the lake calmed, anglers prepared themselves for the night's activities. Rods were rebaited, warm clothing was donned (all carp anglers know how chilly summer nights can be), and bait was catapulted about the lake. Once more, voices were hushed and expectant. The joining of battle was in the air...

To the seasoned and habitual carp fisher, it doesn't take long to fall back into the habits acquired during years spent at the waterside. The primeval instincts that lay dormant within all hunters – normally eroded and submerged beneath the façades of modern day living, gradually re-emerge, and in the quiet, reflective moments, when the owls hoot and the bats swoop; when voles scurry and foxes stalk, men may see through the darkness and sense the unseen...

It was one of those nights when I knew something was going to happen...

I was asleep dreaming. I was in the High Street with my rods set up pointing down the road... people were rushing past and kept pointing and laughing, and then someone I knew asked me whether I'd caught anything. I replied very seriously that I'd had no action but that a group of six carp were about to commence feeding in my 'swim'... I couldn't understand why people kept looking and laughing at me?... Suddenly I became anxious... there was obviously some crisis... Panic! They're here! They're here!... Leave me alone!... Go away!...

I woke up with the sweat pouring down my face; cloud had come rolling in and the night had suddenly become hot and oppressive. I looked at my watch – twelve fifteen. All was utterly quiet. Nothing stirred the calm and the stillness. For some reason that I cannot fathom, I carefully and ceremoniously cast the covers aside and knelt down beside the rods... I guess I just knew...

As I crouched there in the dark, it was the right hand rod that was suddenly and without warning away! – The fish was going and going, the clutch was screaming in staccatto rasps and the rod bucked and lurched! It headed straight for the middle of the lake and there wasn't a thing I could do to stop it! – I just hung on, praying that it wouldn't go to the right, that it would stay out in the open water and for the few moments that it took to recover my senses it did, boring and jabbing, making a bed of weed out in the middle. Suddenly, it gave this up and made off to the right, straight into the danger area! – I couldn't allow it to get into the snags so I gave it as much as I

Not a monster but meritorious enough

DRAGON BAITS

Run by carp anglers ... for carp anglers

Here at Dragon Baits our aim is simply this — to supply the carp angler with top quality, food value base mixes at the lowest possible prices ... prices that will allow you to pre-bait and offer 'freebies' in quantity. Confident, pre-occupied feeding reaction is becoming the most crucial factor for success on many of our lakes; give your carp a bait they recognise as a valuable food source in abundant 'nature-occurring' amounts and this can be achieved.

Our base mixes contain the finest natural ingredients plus added vitamins and minerals, providing carp with an all round dietary requirement.

MÊLÉE — A blend of four bird foods, plus natural attractors, appetite stimulators and a dairy-based taste enhancer ... 50oz bag **£5.20**

SPICY DRAGON — A rich blend of energy and vitamin and mineral sources, including robin red, dried yeast powder and a combination of several spices known to attract carp.
... 50oz **£5.60**

SEA DRAGON — A mix that combines both fishmeal and bird foods, creating a bait that contains the best that both forms of base mix have to offer ... 50oz bag **£5.00**

Further base mixes, plus a range of essential oils, flavours and additives are being field-tested for release in the near future.

Make out cheque including postage payable to 'Dragon Baits' and post to the address below. No credit cards.

Postage and packing rates
1 Bag – £3.15   2 Bags – £3.70   3-5 Bags – £4.25
6-15 Bags £5.50   Over 15 Bags – Post Free

6 The Drift, Culford, Bury St Edmunds, Suffolk, IP28 6DR
(0284) 728829

Trade enquiries welcome

---

thought the tackle would stand, straining the gear to the absolute limit!

Suddenly the fish came to the top in a great flurry and boil – it was way round to the right and there seemed no way I was ever going to get it back into the gap. Perhaps I could go in after it? Take the net and net it out there in the lake; – no that was daft – by the time I'd got out there, the fish would be well through the bulrushes and out the other side...

In the dark, I could just make out the profile of the stems waving in the air, it felt as if the fish was trying to force it's way through. If I could only just get it to move...

It was solid. No jab of life or semblance of contact came down the line at all – it must have got stuck fast around the rushes. What to do? Think man – think quickly! Do something! Don't just stand here in the dark like a lemon while the fish buries itself deeper and deeper in... DO SOMETHING!

My old mate Brian Mills had often advocated slackening off on a weeded fish or one that was making for weed, the idea being to try and kid the fish into thinking that it had escaped, hoping it may do an about turn and swim out again... I let the line go slack and waited for a few moments – how long to wait? When would it realise that all was well and make a run for it? Would it make a run for it at all? I waited.

Ten seconds went past – then twenty; should I wait longer? Should I tighten up now? Thirty seconds – something has got to have happened by now – if it hasn't come free by now it never will – forty seconds went by... I could stand it no longer, winding down as fast as I could I gave a great heave on the rod and something on the end responded! He wasn't out by any means but at least I was in contact. I was right on the end of the platform with the rod absolutely parallel with the water, straining for all I was worth – and suddenly – I managed to gain a few feet of line – not much – but a little! He was moving!... I wound down and heaved again, pulling the rod this way and that, trying to get a slightly different angle of pull on the fish – I gained more line! The commotion out on the edge of the rushes was moving more and more to the left... that was it! The bulrush stems were so thickly packed in that area that he was having trouble forcing his way between the stems! I knew I was going to win!

After about three minutes of heaving and hauling I'd got him right to the edge of the rushes and it was then that the fireworks really started! The rush stems there were much more loosely packed and as I moved him within sight of clear water, he really started to scrap. Knowing that freedom was there for the taking he made a determined lunge for sanctuary. I could see the bulrush stems bending in the dark, bobbing and dancing as the line lay them flat. White water churned from out of the blackness and the rod was hit by a series of violent lunges as the fish desperately tried to force his way in. I was having none of it though – I wasn't going to get him in this far and give up now, I bent the rod as never before, swinging it first one way, then the other. Then all of a sudden I knew he was beaten; with sanctuary denied, he kited right across and to the left, attempting to get under the platform! But it was no good, once in the open water of the gap it was just a question of controlling his ever diminishing runs and after ten minutes or so of boring under the rod tip – he was mine!

No disasters with the other rod this time – I'd taken the precaution of dunking the rod tip and was able to net him, clean as a whistle.

First job was to get on reasonably firm ground; there was a hump of grass about four feet square in the middle of the bog, and this was wadeable to with the aid of thigh waders from the platform – though it was deeper further on. With the fish and net in one hand and weighing sling and scales in the other, I squelched and groped my way in the dark to the grass hump where the usual formalities were carried out – 23lb 12oz of Italian leather in absolutely mint condition. All that remained was to negotiate my way back to the platform, sack it, and maybe catch another before Chris turned up in the morning when she'd be able to do the honours with camera...

At 23lb 12oz it wasn't a monster by today's standards, although a meritorious enough fish given the circumstances of it's capture; but one thing does puzzle me though, if I had all that trouble getting out onto the *bird hide*, how the blazes did the duck shooter manage it...

OPENING WEEK ON HAREFIELD

ISLE OF WIGHT PAUL

It was in 1984 when I first saw Harefield, I was amazed at the sheer expanse of water in front of me, like a landlocked sea, a windswept expanse of water. I had no idea how I was going to be drawn more and more to this water over the next seven years, but I like a challenge in my fishing just like the next man, and Harefield looked the 'place'. My friend and I applied for our tickets in the close season of '84, during which time we heard so much about the place; the cutoffs, mountainous bars, certain wind directions and their effects etc. At first it sounded more like a nightmare than a challenge! At that time the lake did not hold half the stock it now has. Due to good management Harefield is now a fine venue to fish. Although it has been enlarged a lot since I first fished it, the lake was still being worked in the '80's and about 40 yards of bank on the road side dug out which made the first bar about 100 yards out. Enough of the history...

The start of the 1991-92 season was fast approaching, and with it the date for the draw. I still had a lot to do – rods to whip, bait to make... I had spent the back end of last season testing a bait I planned to use at Harefield with great results, so I had confidence in it before the start. The date of the draw arrived, and late, as always I just had time for a quick walk round the lake. I narrowed it down to just three swims I fancied. Noting the peg numbers I made my way to the car park in the hope of getting a draw. I was lucky and got the one I fancied most. Knowing the swim well, I was fairly confident as I had fished there at the start of the season and done well. Time flew to the 15th of June and I got to the lake at about 1.30pm, leaving time to set-up, bit-up, and map out the swim (and a quick pint) before 'the off'.

Returning to the lake after a pre-season drink with friends, fish were showing close in and there was a lot of activity in the first half of the lake, but not much in the bottom half below the island and stick bar. Where I was fishing looked devoid of fish. Still it was only the first night... 'give them a chance', I thought, casting one rod on the face of the stick bar and the second behind the first bar. As I settled in for the night the wind was a light south-westerley which had been blowing for a week before the season started. I began to wonder whether I was fishing the right end of the lake, as anybody who fishes there will know the carp move on a wind. Opening night passed without any action from my end of the lake but fish were coming out above me, in fact everywhere. Above the island five fish, including a 30lb common, came out on opening night. I decided to give my swim another chance of producing a fish. Both Gary and I, drawn side by side, fished through Sunday without seeing a fish our end of the lake. Although only 17 hours into the season I felt a move was on the cards already. The news came round the lake that *Nelson* had been out at a new weight of 38lb 4oz to Rob on the *Causeway* – a new lake record and the new season only hours old. With the wind still blowing up the other end of the lake I walked up the bank to see if a swim was available above the island. Gary told me he was off in the morning and his swim would be available, he'd had a good mirror the previous evening of 28lb. Close in looking at his swim it looked fishy – nice wind coming into the bank and the water nice and coloured. Back at my swim I gathered the gear together ready for a move early morning, I felt very confident of some action having seen fish in the bay where Gary was fishing. Tuesday morning still no sign of fish on the stick bar. By now it was obvious most of the fish were above me. By mid-day I was settled in my new swim. After a few alterations to the rigs and a plumb round with the marker float I had a rough idea of the bottom features I placed the first rod on the left hand corner of *The Pads* and the other rod on the edge of another set of pads to the right. Rods in place, Baitrunner set, it was kettle on and a well-earned cup of tea, it's hard work humping gear from one end of Harefield to the other. Looking out I saw a

Early Days
A brace of Harefield twenties caught in one night in 1985. Both carp fell to pop-up tiger nuts before the nut ban

Right:
Sunset over Harefield, often a very productive time

Below:
Getting the season off on a high note at 33lb 8oz, it's high enough for me

fish show twice behind *the Pads*, sitting on my bedchair my confidence on a high, it was not long before I was into my first fish of the season. At first it felt small as the carp ran towards me, but as soon as it saw the net it was away taking line off the clutch with ease, I now knew it was a good fish, for a minute I thought it had run over my other line, but no, it was a run on the right hand rod – I was in trouble I now had two fish on.

I gave the other rod to another angler to play out while I got on with my fish, it was very busy in the swim, luckily he was close by to help our. Thanks a lot. Gary netted my fish first attempt while the other fish, a common, followed shortly. Looking in the bottom of the net was a lovely looking low thirty mirror. As least we agreed on that figure as my needle went to the limit on my scales. Rob came to the rescue with his Nashy scales (I must remember to get a set), the needle settled on 33lb 6oz, what a result and only one and a half hours after moving swims. On the unhooking mat I recognised the fish as *Black Spot*, a fish I had seen on the bank before, but not had the privilege of catching. Pictures were taken and a few video shots for future reference, I slipped her back.

I rebaited with trembling hands and placed the baits out again. The common went 10lb. Lucky I had the runs in the order they came in, I would have been well sick with a 10lb common! Thanks lads for all your help. I sat back in the chair to take it all in, there was still a nice wind into the bay, conditions were perfect. I was just thinking of cooking a meal when I had a screaming take on the same rod, leaning into the fish I managed to clear the roots of the pads. The carp headed up the bay then went solid in a weedbed. I put the rod back int he rest and gave line, the rod tip pulled round and the carp freed itself. After a lot of give and take on the clutch I slid the carp over the net, it looked another good fish, I was well pleased when the needle on the scales settled on 27lb 6oz, a mirror and an old friend called *Bite Mark*. After Rob video'd the fish and pictures were taken I made a second attempt at cooking some food.

After baiting up and placing the baits again this time I dropped them short of the pads and baited up fairly tightly with about 50 baits round each rod forming a link up of baits in between each hookbait hoping to draw fish out of the safety of the pads. By now it was obvious the carp were holed up in the bay and had been there for some time. I had just finished eating when the Optonic sprang to life again on the right hand rod. I knew I was on a good mix but not that good, the fish headed straight for the weedbed but now I knew where it was, I was able to keep the fish clear. Rob came over for the third time in six hours with his video to hand. I soon had the carp under the rod tip and with a bit of pressure got it over the net, it looked another monster. We gently laid the carp on the mat while the scales were zeroed, gently I lifted the fish clear of the ground, the needle hovering between 31lb 14oz and 31lb 15oz. Two 30lb-plus carp in one afternoon! After Rob had done his video bit, and pictures taken we all agreed it was time for refreshments and headed for the pub.

News travels fast on Harefield, I wasn't even through the pub door before I was congratulated by the lads and met with an expensive bar bill.

Returning to the lake, the wind had dropped and it looked quiet, so I placed the baits back out and liberally baited up for the night. Laying on the bedchair I now had time to take it all in before drifting off to sleep. The night passed quietly until 5.30am Wednesday morning when I was woken by a screaming Optonic. Falling out of the sleeping bag I just managed to stop the fish going into the sanctuary of the pads, it felt like another good 'un the way it was going. Gary came to my assistance with the net and landed it first attempt, he's good at netting carp! Looking in the bottom of the net we both saw it could possibly go to thirty. I zeroed the scales and slowly lifted the fish clear of the mat, the needle hovering between 29lb 15oz and 30lb dead, it was that close. For a second opinion Rob re-weighed the fish on his set, 30lb exactly. Still dazed and half asleep I put the kettle on and had a smoke.

It was not until lunchtime in the bar that I realised I had caught three 30lb-plus carp in the space of 15 hours, an achievement I shall never forget – nor the bar bill. Here's to the rest of the season.

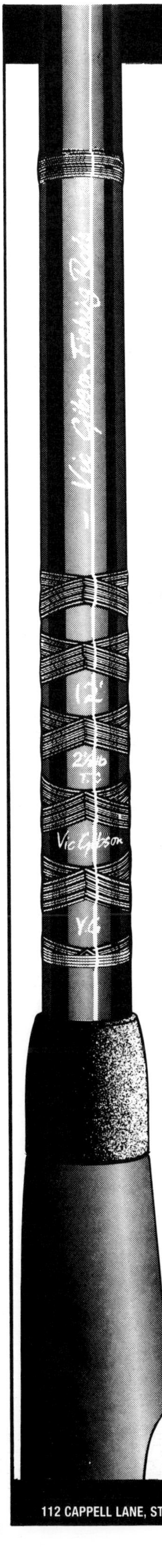

Vic Gibson Fishing Rods

"WHEN ONLY THE BEST WILL DO"

For over 15 years Vic Gibson Fishing Rods have specialised in building quality fishing rods for many of the biggest companies in the UK and Europe. Specialist skills of hand-building, combined with modern materials and techniques, have gained us a reputation beyond comparison. The care and attention that is given to every rod we build guarantees satisfaction.

Rods are not supplied from stock, but built to your own exact specifications. This attention to detail and commitment to perfection takes time and costs money. No discounts, no cheap quotes, quite simply rods which other anglers will admire. Rods that will do justice to the time and dedication which you give to your fishing.

Spoil yourself — you know you deserve it!

Century ARMALITE

	BLANK	STD BSVLG/BLVLG	SIC SVSG/LVSG
12' 2lb	£94.97	£139.00	£174.00
12' 2¼lb	£96.14	£141.00	£176.00
12' 2½lb	£99.75	£144.00	£179.00
12' 2¾lb	£101.34	£146.00	£181.00
12' 3lb	£105.66	£150.00	£185.00
12' 3½lb "TOP GUN"	£108.39	£153.00	£188.00
12' 4lb "TOP GUN"	£112.71	£157.00	£192.00
13' 2lb	£98.17	£143.00	£178.00
13' 2¼lb	£100.19	£145.00	£180.00
13' 2½lb	£103.28	£148.00	£183.00
13' 2¾lb	£105.57	£150.00	£185.00
13' 3lb	£112.09	£157.00	£192.00
13' 3½lb "TOP GUN"	£115.88	£160.00	£195.00
13' 4lb "TOP GUN"	£117.91	£162.00	£197.00

Century BLACKMAX

12' 3lb	£149.10	£194.00	£229.00
12' 3½lb	£150.25	£195.00	£230.00
13' 3lb	£154.92	£199.00	£234.00
13' 3½lb	£156.33	£201.00	£236.00

'PARAGON'
ULTRA SLIM SPECIALIST CARP RODS

These superb 12' rods are built on our own British made, spiral finish, carbon blanks of overfit joint construction. Progressively increased wall thickness in the butt section gives almost total 'lock-up' under compression, providing the power needed to cast good distances with accuracy — whilst retaining the ultra slim diameters only possible with the overfit joint. They are, in fact, two six foot blanks of different tapers, married together via the overfit, to give the perfect partnership of forgiving tip (for playing big fish) and powerful butt to give the casting abilities of much stiffer casting rods that leave so much to be desired when playing big fish under the tip where so many fish are lost.

If you have handled some of the other distance rods on the market and been discouraged by what are basically beach-casting blanks then be pleasantly surprised by — 'Paragon' — and get back to a fishing rod, a pleasure to use, a joy to own.

The 'Paragon' range are built to our normal exacting standards, using genuine Fuji rings and fittings — abbreviated Duplon/NPS handles finished in black as standard with superb hard epoxy resin or built to your own specifications.

			FUJI STD BSVLG/BLVLG	FUJI SIC SVSG/LVSG
'PARAGON 200'	12'	2lb TC	£125.00	£160.00
'PARAGON 225'	12'	2¼lb TC	£130.00	£165.00
'PARAGON 275'	12'	2¾lb TC	£135.00	£170.00
'PARAGON 300'	12'	3lb TC	£140.00	£175.00
'PARAGON E/R'	13'	3lb TC	£150.00	£185.00

Rods are available in either "distance ringing" (5 rings plus tip - 30mm butt ring) or "multi-range ringing" (7 rings plus tip - 25mm butt ring). We suggest distance ringing on rods of 2¾lb TC and above and multi-range ringing on 2¼lb TC and below. Alternatively, we can supply any ring pattern and spacing required.

As standard, the rods listed here have the new Fuji NPS-D18B reel fitting, with 1" domed Duplon either side and cigar butt grip with BNB butt cap. However, handles of any kind, full length or abbreviated, can be fitted to your rods.

Whippings to the colour of your choice (if not stated Rods will be supplied whipped in black). Your own name can be written on the rods. Spigots will be numbered 1/1 — 2/2 — 3/3 etc.

Also — **repairs and re-whips** undertaken — please 'phone.

Butt Whips — The illustration shows the classic Vic Gibson Chevron Butt Whip. This distinctive chevron design, achieved with individual windings of top quality threads, can be incorporated in your rods if so desired. We would love to say at no extra cost, but as each chevron will take a skilled whipper up to 2 hours, we cannot. A nominal charge of £10 per rod is made for chevrons.

Please 'phone Vic on **(0920) 870775** during working hours to discuss your requirements. We would be pleased to advise on any aspect of rod building.

The rods listed here are a guide to our range and prices.
Cheque with order please.
Carriage and insurance is charged at **£9.00** per consignment.
TRADE ENQUIRIES FOR ROD BUILDING WELCOMED

VIC GIBSON FISHING RODS
112 CAPPELL LANE, STANSTEAD ABBOTTS, HERTS SG12 8BY   TEL: 0920-870775

ALL THE BEST CARP GEAR FROM CHESHIRE'S TOP TACKLE STORE

Dave's of Middlewich
'ANGLING CENTRE of CHESHIRE'

The Carp Dept

MAIN AGENTS FOR:

- ☆ SHIMANO
- ☆ KEVIN NASH
- ☆ ROD HUTCHINSON
- ☆ ZENON BOJKO
- ☆ GARDNER
- ☆ KRYSTON
- ☆ FOX INTERNATIONAL
- ☆ DRENNAN
- ☆ TRI-CAST
- ☆ DAIWA
- ☆ OPTONIC
- ☆ ARMALITE
- ☆ K.J.B.
- ☆ TERRY EUSTACE
- ☆ SOLAR
- ☆ BITECH VIPER
- ☆ OBELISK
- ☆ STEADEFAST
- ☆ MARVIC
- ☆ COLMAN
- ☆ SBS
- ☆ RICHWORTH

etc etc

All this and of course the full range of NUTRABAITS PRODUCTS

The Angling Centre with the big reputation for fair play and honest dealing

Phone us first for all your carp goods

We will give you an immediate quote and dispatch goods to you without delay

Simply phone us with your Mastercard or Visa number and we'll take care of the rest leaving you free to go fishing

FOR TELEPHONE ORDERS USE THESE HOTLINE NUMBERS
TEL: 0606 833853
(24 HR ANSAPHONE)
FAX: 0606 737469

For personal visitors we are just five minutes from junction 18 on the M6. You'll be amazed at our vast stocks of tackle all on open display and at the best possible prices

STOP PRESS
We've increased the size of the shop yet again. To enable us to offer you an even bigger range of gear for the new season.

67 WHEELOCK STREET, MIDDLEWICH, CHESHIRE CW10 9AB   TEL: 0606 833853

A PERFECT DAY'S BLANKING

ROB HILL

The season was well underway and Harefield had seen its busiest yet. However, by this time of year weekends were the only busy time, as most anglers by now had already used up their holidays, also most guests had been and gone. I had taken a few days off work, not for fishing unfortunately or that's at least what I thought. I was due to do those things that interfere with fishing such as decorating, keeping the wife happy and killing the next door neighbour's dog for using my garden as a cesspit, you know – those sorts of things. Anyway on my first morning off I eventually dug my way out of bed expecting to start on the decorating when my wife Orla said to me "you can go fishing for a couple of days if you like". Am I hearing things I thought? I didn't ask any questions, when you get an offer like that you don't ask questions. I didn't have time to because before Orla even finished that sentence I had made 200 baits, packed the car and was pulling into Harefield's car park. I wasn't surprised to find that there were only two cars in the car park which goes to show that even the anglers who live here go to work come Monday morning. All except Tony Cheadle of course. Midweek fishing is so peaceful compared with the weekends. I wrapped all my fishing gear around me and charged up the causeway. By the time I had reached the halfway mark I was sweating and totally out of breath, I had to slow down, then a little thought popped into my mind. What the hell is the panic! There's hardly anybody here, I've got plenty of time and I don't even know where I want to fish. Well, that seemed like a good enough reason for racing up the bank like a lunatic with his hair on fire. So once I had got my breath back I was off, just as fast, I couldn't help it, I had to get to where I was going without knowing it, if you know what I mean.

I passed Tony Cheadle who was fishing on the causeway so quickly that I didn't even stop to ask him why he appeared to be using a seagull as an indicator. He was probably asleep anyway. I also wanted to remind him that if he doesn't reshuffle his bivvy within the next six weeks it would take root and end up a permanent fixture. I carried myself up to the top end of Harefield, into the bays, swims commonly known as *Sluggs* and *Goose* I was particularly interested in. As I have found in the past that when the weather is hot and it had been for some time and the pressure on the lake had died down, some good fish can often be spotted cruising around in these areas. I first stopped in the *Sluggs* swim and had a good look around, hoping to see some fish but I never saw a damn thing, which isn't unusual for me because a carp would have to jump clean out of the water, with a red light flashing on its head, waving its fins at me shouting: "I'm over here you dummy", before I would notice it.

I walked around to the point which is right next door to *Sluggs*. You can see a lot of water from here. I was almost tempted to drop in here, but thought that I had better have a quick look at *Goose Island* as I've gone this far. When I got to the white post which sticks up on *Goose Island*, I dropped my gear and walked along the gravel bar which was out of the water due to low levels, it also comes in kind of handy when you're snooping around looking for fish. Even if there were fish around, I wouldn't notice them. I like the look of it, maybe it's the peaceful, quiet surroundings, which is all part of fishing for me. It certainly wasn't the overwhelming fish activity that's for sure, unless I'm getting even worse at noticing fish, surely not, there just aren't any here. I had virtually made up my mind to give *The Goose* a try, when, you won't believe it, a huge mass of Canadian geese came heading towards me. And when there are a hundred of these things together, the noise they make is ridiculous, they took no notice of me standing there and proceeded to land all around me. After all it is *Goose Island* and this place lives up to its name. Who said anything about it being peaceful and quiet, it's like Piccadilly Circus now. I did fancy *The Goose* but not literally, sod this lot I'm off.

Before I collected up my gear I scanned the top bank. Yes – there was the answer. So off I went once again, climbing through six foot high stinging nettles and bramble bushes even higher, you would hope to get there without breaking your neck. But, oh no it's not that easy, because there's a booby trap! Just as you get up to the top bank there's a nice lump of unmovable metal, sticking up about four inches from the ground and it gets you every time, (including this time). I tripped over it but managed to stay on both feet. When I got to my chosen spot I collapsed in a heap.

Taking my time to set up it wasn't much before mid-day before I cast out. I decided to fish a small area alongside a gravel bar at about 60 yards. Both rods were fixed up the same way which I rarely alter, eight pound mainline straight through, I didn't need to use shockleaders which is a good idea in many of Harefield's swims, this particular area is tame compared with some of the line-ripping, lumps, bumps, boulders, craters, cars, trollies, prams, bikes and bodies – God only knows what lurks beneath the surface of Harefield! Fixed to this was a three ounce bolt rig, ten inches of 15lb Silkworm hooklength, tied up to a number six Drennan boilie hook, using a short hair rig and armed with Premier fishmeal, I was ready for some action, or even some blanking, whatever it's to be I'm ready.

Once I had cast out, I sat on the bedchair and watched the large amount of birdlife swimming around in this part of the lake. Certain boilie-eating birds like tufties, coots and seagulls were all patrolling around the area in which I was fishing, it was as if they were waiting for me to start baiting up. It's got to be more than a coincidence that with a lake this size, most of the birds, including all the seagulls were sitting in my swim. It's an achievement to get a hookbait past them so forget a free bait. Baiting up would have been a waste of time. It was a hot, sunny day, the water flat calm, perfect conditions for blanking. I proceeded along those lines and happily blanked for my first day (although this was preferable to being at home decorating). Just as the sun was beginning to set, I wound in both rods, put on fresh hookbaits, ready for my return after visiting the Harefield chip shop. On the causeway I saw Tony, he was awake and baiting up, so he came with me. Soon we were back at the lake and I left him in his swim as I couldn't wait to get back to my rods. There's something about this time of day, just before dark, when I always feel maximum confidence, I don't know why, because nothing ever happens, but when it does its always out of the blue, never when I'm expecting it.

I cast my rods out as accurately as I could, which reminded me that I still needed to put some bait out, but up until now I didn't want to please the seagulls and their friends. I intended to bait up in the dark. Soon enough I considered it too dark for the seagulls to see my baits. After a couple of baiting attempts it was obvious that it was also too dark for me to see the baits, let alone the seagulls. So, there I was fishing a swim with accurately placed hookbaits and very inaccurate free baits, well that should keep the carp guessing if nothing else.

After sitting by my rods until almost midnight, I decided to curl up on my bedchair and get some sleep. The night passed uneventfully. Early the next morning when I first peered through the bivvy door, I could see that once again it was going to be a beautiful day, bright sunshine, no cloud, no wind and no fish! Looked like a perfect day for blanking again, so first things first, bait up, feed the seagulls then off to the cafe. I dug Tony up who had also spent yet another undisturbed night. At that time the only other angler of the water was Isle of Wight Paul, who was fishing *The Stick Bar* and no prizes for why we call him Isle of Wight Paul - you've guessed it, his name's Paul. Anyway after our usual performance up at the cafe, we were soon walking back along the causeway. At this point I felt that we were lacking a few things, at the top of the list would have been enthusiasm, in fact the only thing that I was confident of was the bait. When we got to where Tony was fishing, I stayed with him just to watch him cast out, not to see where he was casting, because anybody who is fishing the causeway seems to cast out as far as possible, not any particular area, that seems to be par for the course along here. Anyway when Tony is aiming for the horizon he can be very entertaining as I have seen him have a multitude of mishaps including breaking a rod in half. Unfortunately he wasn't entertaining me this morning, and managed to cast out in his words 'perfect', in my words 'blind'. I left him to it and strolled on up to where I was fishing.

When I got to my swim I had a look around, it was a half-hearted attempt really. I went through the motions of putting on fresh hookbaits and casting out to the small gravel bar, perfectly and not blind I hoped just in case there was a fish out there swimming around with his eyes closed and his mouth wide open because in these conditions that's the only way I'm going to catch anything. Once both rods were clipped up I was set, I lay back in the bedchair enjoying the mid-morning sunshine and eventually dozed off.

Isn't it just amazing that even in the most perfect blanking time of a session you may still get an unbelievable surprise. This was more than a surprise, my left hand rod was on a screamer, I jumped up expecting it to be a supersonic duck, especially when I first glanced at the water, just as I was pulling into the fish and saw just how much duck life was still floating about in my swim, what's the attraction out there I wanted to know, but it would have to wait as I didn't have time to worry about it. The rod arched right over, I soon needed to click the reel into backwind motion, I much prefer to play a fish backwinding as opposed to using the clutch, although when a fish is on its first initial run, the clutch when set correctly can be a good idea. I soon realised that I must have upset the clutch setting on my reel and forgotten to check it as it was set too high, that's why I went onto backwind so soon which is taking a bit of a chance on a fish that is tearing off line at the speed that this one was. Have you ever tried backwinding for 80 yards at 200 miles per hour under pressure and then smile about it? After what seemed ages but was probably only a few seconds the fish slowed down, then came up into the upper layers of the water and proceeded to kite to my right, at this stage breaking surface, but it was still miles from me. The fish seemed to mess about on the surface for a while, which is fine by me, less chance of things like the line getting damaged, the fish snagging up or getting weeded up. If the fish wants to do battle close to the surface it might swim over my other line without catching onto it, which would make a nice change. When the fish got in front of me at about 50 yards it plunged into a semi-circle and steamed off once again in the opposite direction. The water was very calm and as the fish steamed off it was possible to see the bow-waves following along the fish's dorsal fin, which shows how close it was to the surface. The fish managed about 30 yards or so on that run before I managed to turn him. As the carp turned around, so the line pinged slightly, which for only a split second gives you a heart attack because you think that you have lost it, but

Harefield, 28lb 14oz mirror.
September 1989

I'm sure this is when a fish is turning, the line trips across his back catching his dorsal fin on the way (or something along those lines). Anyway after my brief heart attack I realised the fish was still on, and the carp then decided to see how fast I could wind in, he had already seen (on two occasions) how fast I can wind *out*. And to be quite honest I can do without this sort of punishment. The fish did a standing quarter of a mile in five second flat – straight towards me. Well, to talk about gain line on a fish rapidly would be an understatement. I was winding in so fast that had the fish suddenly stopped the rod would have broken! The carp was now about ten yards or so in front of me and went down deep, the depth here being about 12 feet in the margins, totally snag-free so I had nothing to worry about, apart from when the fish wanted to pass under the other rod more than once (not an easy manoeuvre at the best of times). The carp continued to swim up and down in front of me for a couple of minutes although it seemed like hours – you know the feeling. By now I was getting the better of him as he started to get closer towards the surface, until eventually it broke surface and I got a good look at him. A lovely looking mirror in the upper twenties I thought, as I got ready with the net trying not to panic (I have found in the past that this is a good time to panic!). The carp rolled on the surface and I slid the net under him, the fish was mine.

A great sigh of relief came over me as I lifted the fish onto my sleeping bag, which always ends up on the ground following a screaming run. After unhooking the fish I placed him back in the landing net, because at the time there was a carp sack ban. I whistled over to Paul who had me worried at first because I was on the third whistle before he looked up, I indicated to him that I needed his assistance and he was promptly on the scene. Thank goodness he was fishing *The Stick Bar*, he could have been fishing a lot of other swims out of earshot, then what would I have done? Break the rules and use a carp sack I hear you say – no – I didn't even carry one.

We weighed the fish – a mirror of 28lb 14oz. Paul took some great photos and then returned the carp to his home. I checked the time – 12.25pm. We had a chat for a while then Paul went back to his swim.

I sat back on the bedchair to recover, I was so pleased. I had a bit of a clear up as tackle was everywhere following all the excitement. I wound in the other rod and put fresh hookbaits on both rods. I cast the rods near enough to where I wanted them, I didn't really care to be honest as I was happy enough with my result. I lay back on my bedchair with a big, fat smile on my face and with the warm sunny day I was soon dozing off.

This time what can I say to describe my suprise when the right hand rod was on a flyer. I jumped off the bedchair so fast that I don't remember doing it, picked up the rod and leant into a fast-moving fish. This time the clutch was correctly set, as off went the fish until I was able to turn him. Trying to retrieve line on this fish was very slow. I was beginning to get the feeling that the fish was in some sort of large weedbed. The carp thumped around a few times before going off on another strong run, taking about 20 yards of line. By now however things didn't seem to be quite right, although

BRENTWOOD ANGLING CENTRE
118 Warley Hill · Brentwood · Essex · Tel: 0277 200985

Kevin Nash		Solar Tackle		Nutrabaits		Mainline	
Oval Brolly	£97.28	12" Banksticks	£12.25	Hi Nu Val	£15.95	Marine and Liver Mix	£7.50
Zig Wrap Oval	£97.36	16" Banksticks	£13.25	Enervite Gold	£8.72	Fish Base Mix	£5.75
Zig Wrap 45"	£78.43	2 Rod 8" Buzz Bar	£8.95	Enervite	£8.72	Marine Base Mix	£6.50
Zig Wrap 50"	£88.65	2 Rod 10" Buzz Bar	£8.95	Nutramix	£5.30	Yellow Seed Mix	£5.95
Zig Wrap Canvas	£128.44	3 Rod 12" Buzz Bar	£10.95	Big Fish Mix	£10.60	Supreme Bird Blend	£6.50
Oval Ground Sheet	£26.86	3 Rod adj Buzz Bar	£21.50	The Biollix	£12.86	High Leakage Mix	£4.95
45" Ground Sheet	£21.05	Quench Mix 1kg	£6.95	Fish Food Mix	£9.87	NRG Winter Blend	£6.95
50" Ground Sheet	£22.30	Red Mix 1kg	£7.45	*Full range of addits, oils,*		*Full range of flavours and Oils*	
Hooker Rucksack	£84.99	Yellow Mix 1kg	£6.95	*Nutrafruits and Nutraspices*		*and Booster dips*	
Spec Rucksack	£59.47	Squid/Koi Rearer 100ml	£8.90				
Hooker Deluxe 12'	£87.93	Golden Plum 100ml	£4.50	**Century**		**North Western**	
Stalker Sling	£18.34	Ester Blend 12 100ml	£4.90	12' Armalite 2¼lb	£159.10	12' Kevlite Mr 2¼lb	£132.50
Stalker Bag	£25.85	White Choc, Enha 4oz	£4.00	12' Armalite 2½lb	£162.50	12' Kevlite MR 2½lb	£135.00
Carp Carryall	£35.49	*Full range of mixes, flavours and*		12' Top Gun 3lb	£170.35	12' Kevlite LR 2¾lb	£137.50
Carp Carryall	£44.93	*stainless available*		12' Top Gun 3½lb	£173.10	12' Kevlite LR 3lb	£139.99
				Black Max's in stock		*Dyncema 92 available to order*	
Wychwood		**Optonics**					
K2 Rucksack	£123.00	Super XL	£77.00	**CUSTOM BUILT RODS BY VIC GIBSON AVAILABLE TO ORDER**			
K2 Stalker Bag	£28.09	Super Compact	£66.00				
Ruckman	£76.10	Special Hi Lo	£55.00	**Daiwa Reels**		**KJB Products**	
Packer	£91.43	Compact Hi Lo	£39.95	BR2050	£69.99	2 Rod Pod	£62.95
Carp Quiver	£25.48	Magnetonic	£49.95	BR2650	£74.99	3 Rod Pod	£66.95
Insider Deluxe 12'	£81.21	Bitech Viper	£49.95	BR2050x	£49.99	3 Rod Pod Spec.	£69.95
				BR2650x	£54.99	Bivvy T Pegs x 8	£8.95
Fox International		**Shimano Reels**		SS3000	£175.00	Coloured Isotopes	£4.75
Sup. Deluxe B/chair	£189.90	BTR Aero GT3500	£89.90				
Std Deluxe Bedchair	£139.90	BTR Aero GT4000	£96.90	**Daiwa Rods**		**Shimano Rods**	
Supa Bivvy	£154.90	BTR Aero GT4500	£99.99	Powermesh 12' 2¼lb	£89.99	Twin Power 12' 2¼lb	£117.00
Supa Brolly	£131.90	Biomaster GT7000	£96.90	Powermesh 12' 2½lb	£89.99	Twin Power 12' 2½lb	£123.00
Swingers	£11.90	BTR Aero 3500	£64.90	Whis. Kev. 12' 2¼lb	£145.00	Diaflash 12' 2¼lb	£173.69
30" Rod Pod	£26.50	BTR Aero 4000	£69.90	Whis. Kev. 12' 2½lb	£150.00	Diaflash 12' 2½lb	£178.77
48" Adj. Rod Pod	£34.50	BTR Aero 4500	£74.90	**THE NEW BEDCHAIR**	£159.95	*Powerloops available*	

Also main stockist for: Gardner · ET Products
ABU · Ryobi · Leeda · Silstar · Shakespeare
Beekay Products · SBS · Middy · Premier
Kryston · Drennan · Richworth · Sundridge
Coleman · Gold Label

★ **Interest Free Credit Available** ★
Orders up to £100 three or six monthly payments.
Orders over £100 three, six or nine monthly payments.
Mail order available on credit terms. Please telephone for details. Telephone: 0277 200985.

Large range of particles available including Moth Beans and Partiblend both cooked and uncooked. Maples, French Maize, Tiger Nuts, Hemp and Tares always in stock. Bulk orders taken for all baits and particles.

Three exclusive carp syndicate waters controlled by ourselves in Essex and Herts. Day ticket waters available. For details please contact us at the above address or tel: 0277 200985

the fish was moving around the line was entering the water in exactly the same place. Then a big shock came, the fish rolled on the surface about 70 yards out to my right, yet the line was entering the water in front of me at about 40 yards, I knew this was definitely the fish that I had hooked, although my line was going to the fish via a weedbed. I put the pressure on hoping to clear the problem. I managed a few yards of line but progress was still slow, then suddenly my lead and rig tube pinged out of the water just where my line was entering it, my line immediately went directly to the fish. Well, it seems that I'd cleared a problem and gained a problem. When the fish swam through the weed my lead and rig tube caught up in the weed but my line still travelled through it, keeping me in contact with the fish. The problem I had then was that the fish was about 40 yards from the lead, now that's what you call a long hooklength! As I managed to gain more line on the carp so my rig got nearer to the top of my rod – a small piece of weed was stopping it from sliding back down the line. I was beginning to think that with such a long hooklength things might get very difficult. If you are using shockleaders it is bad enough when the knot keeps travelling through the eyes of your rod whilst doing battle, but can you imagine trying to wind a three ounce bomb through the eyes of your rod? I had no choice but to hope that when the rig did hit the top of my rod that it would slide back down the line – and it did just that. Unfortunately, because I was watching my rig swinging around in the air, I wasn't watching where the carp was going and so he ended up once again in the same patch of weed. As he knew his way around in there by then better than I do I put pressure on, a bit of thumping, pumping, boiling and farting went on and eventually he came free from the weed. The fish stayed deep and was much slower than the first fish (thank God!). At this stage however he was showing signs of tiredness and I gradually managed to encourage him towards me.

The carp swam up and down in front of me a few times before breaking surface, and when it did I could see it was another big mirror. Normally this is where I panic, but this time I was reasonably calm. I lowered the net into the water and brought the carp over it at the first attempt. I dropped the rod and lifted the fish out and onto my sleeping bag (which was once again on the ground), looking at the fish I though to myself, the first fish was over 28lb – this must be a thirty. That was enough to bring me out in a sweat. I placed the fish back into the landing net and lowered him into the water. I checked the time – 2.20pm, less than two hours after the first fish.

Once again I called out to Paul who immediately came to my assistance. We weighed the carp at 31lb 6oz. Paul then watched over the fish while I ran all the way round to Tony to tell him that fish do swim around with their eyes closed and mouths wide open!

When I got to where Tony was fishing, I was so out of breath that I couldn't speak. Just for a change he was asleep anyway. I shook him a few times but nothing happened. I was just lighting up some explosives to throw into his bivvy – that normally wakes him – when there was a movement, yes he was still alive! I called him a couple of times, he woke up and said: "If it's not a thirty – don't bother", some people are hard to please.

Once I had told him that it *was* he dragged himself away. Off we went to show him the carp. On our way round I told him about the 28lb 14oz mirror that I had also caught. I'm sure that at first he didn't believe me. Whilst showing Tony the carp, Paul took some more excellent photos.

The carp was then returned to his home. Not a bad afternoon's fishing for a so-called 'perfect day for blanking'. In all this excitement I kept on forgetting to ask Tony about the seagull that he had fixed up on his line, his reply – well I'll leave that to your imagination.

By the way, my 31lb mirror carp is known by the members as *Black Spot* – but I'll be buggered if I know why!

Harefield, 31lb 6oz mirror. Steptember 1989

FATE

JAN WENCZKA

Fate plays some funny tricks on you when you're not looking. I was meandering down the lane that led to Longfield on that late Sunday evening, not for any pescatorial reason, quite the opposite in fact because I actually knew that immediate commitments meant that the one day a week I usually took off for fishing had to be shelved for that week, but I was passing and a bit of easy conversation would do me a world of good. Imagine my surprise when I found the carp park almost deserted. This water though only small was fished nine months solidly by a bevy of carpers. Confused but not deterred I made my way across the bridge that lead to the *Yodelling Corner* and from that vantage point I found the swims that were visible to be empty, so I decided to walk along the stream bank to the pier to view the lake from there.

Though still confused I nevertheless kept on looking into the margins for signs of fish, so when a voice said "What happened Jan?" I was somewhat startled. It was one of the twins, I've read somewhere that it is psychologically damaging to twins to refer to them as such, it somehow reduces their sense of identity and that people refer to them as twins because they can't tell them apart, well actually I *can* tell them apart, but carp fishing being what it is formal introductions are redundant – instead we just sort of get to know the other anglers and the twins were always referred to as such, and if they are psychologically scarred then they mask it very well because the seem perfectly normal to me. I didn't realise that the question was in fact rhetorical because on saying that I had no idea, he went on to explain what had happened. The bailiffs had a raid on the Saturday night and quite a few of the regulars were caught being naughty – for which they were banned for a period of time. He vocalized my thoughts when he said that he though the place would be empty for the week, he had a bait bucket in his hands so when I asked if he was going to fish during the week, that was also a rhetorical question. I was in a real dilemma, a perfect opportunity had arisen. I had always wanted to stalk the water unhindered from angling pressure, believing that this would give me more chances. But I had money to earn and promises to keep, so I drove back home still despondent.

I phoned my old fishing oppo' Chris Ball to tell him the bad news about the lads being banned and I swear that for nearly ten seconds he was genuinely sorry, and when I told him that I didn't think I would be able to go fishing that week, he had to be sorry all over again, but even with the previous rehearsal he didn't sound very convincing. Even by the time I had gone to bed a deserted Longfield was still playing on my mind. So Monday morning I was up with the lark, by 7am I was toiling over a hot easel and this hive of industry went on well into the night, which meant I could have Tuesday morning for fishing. I don't carry a watch, nor do I set alarms so the night was spent restless and before day-break I was up and loading the car, my arrival at the lake was far too early. On previous experiences the fish weren't in stalking positions till gone 10am. Still I was here but who else was there, the couple of cars in the car park were parked in such a way as to suggest that the occupants were fishing the other lakes. I quickly gathered my stalking gear, bags of bait and went off to investigate and put bait in what John Allen charmingly calls 'my little spots' which always sound like a disease, still it adequately describes my favoured areas. I started at the pier and did a complete circuit, baiting my 'spots' and ended up on the ruin. I sat down and looked out at Longfield completely devoid of human life.

I suppose quite a few of you might be wondering why I had bothered to start fishing Longfield if time was in such short supply? Firstly I was convinced that the group of large fish that inhabited the lake (known as the *A team*) are vulnerable to the stalking approach, so convinced was I that when I wrote a letter to Yatesy thanking him for coming to my side in an hour of need I told him to get a ticket as the right couple of hours could see a real monster in the net. Secondly, I just enjoy fishing for big fish irrespective of the difficulty involved. It's always been difficult to explain as the right words have never been forthcoming, but I recently read a piece by the poet Philip Larkin and in it he describes writing poetry as being as difficult as sainthood, yet at the same time as easy as breathing and that's exactly how I feel about fishing for big fish. I don't make a conscious decision one way or the other but just like breathing I do it instinctively. Anyway to get back to the ruin. The adrenalin rush hadn't subsided, I tried to have a coffee and relax but I couldn't, instead I hurriedly quaffed down the coffee, burning my mouth in the process, and made my second trip around my 'spots'. Nothing. On the third circuit I didn't even bother to bring my gear. After that my enthusiasm waned and I was just walking around the place looking for signs of fish. It was now past the watershed hour of ten and getting of for mid-day... it looked like all that angst was for nothing.

They say that artists see everything in patterns and I suppose this must be true because if I'm ever stalking with Bally and we put boilies in am area he always counts them, and on returning will recount them to see if any are missing. I don't, I just see the pattern of the baits on the bottom and just know when baits are moved or missing and I got that feeling when I looked at the baits under a bush close to the *goose pool*, I lay right across the bush and looked good and hard into the depths. After a short while I could just make out a dark shape moving very slowly along the furthest visible shelf. I hadn't rigged up the rod yet as I needed a vital piece of information so another ten minutes was spent looking at the fish to see how it was feeding. The margin feeders feed in two distinctly different ways, what I called 'clampers' and 'testers'. The 'clampers' would approach baits from directly above and clamp down on the gravel then suck up the baits, of course any tethered bait wasn't able to be sucked up and was left, it didn't even spook them and they would carry on eating every bait except one. The others were 'testers', they would travel parallel to the bottom and suck in the baits, but before the bait entered the mouth they would partially close their mouth and test the bait. Both 'testers' or 'clampers', once they had started on a bed of baits, would stay directly above them and carry on feeding unless anything frightened them, in which case they would leave not to return. Eventually I could see that the fish was feeding parallel to the bottom so it was a tester. The way I set about catching these fish was to use a pop-up one inch off the bottom, the bait then had to be positioned in such a way that the fish could only approach the bait so that when it scrutinised it, it was in my full view and not masked by part of the fish's body ie along a sunken branch or along one of the shelves. This was because the 'testers' would test the hookbait anything up to half a dozen times before they would sometimes test the bait in their mouths, on feeling the rig it would immediately spit the bait out again, but that split second that the hook was in the mouth was a window of opportunity to set the hook, not much of one I know, but an opportunity nevertheless. So I started to rig up the rod, a flattened Arlesley bomb (for easier positioning and stability) was threaded on the 15 pound mono, a bead, swivel, then 15 inches of 15 pound braided terylene and a strong hook (size two) was tied close to the hook. I was balancing the bait when a ominous sound of crunching gravel invaded my privacy, surely not an angler? I daren't even look up in case whoever it was caught my eye and this gave them a pretext to enter into conversation. With eyes firmly rooted to the ground I hoped and prayed that the malevolent crunching would carry on past the gap that led to the lake, but no – like a shot to my heart it stopped and I then knew that whoever it was, was now heading towards me. I looked up and who should I see but my old chum Chris Ball. With relief I said "hello mate", his reply was "what the hell are you doing here?" I was about to reply when he went on: "If I had known you'd be here I wouldn't have bothered coming" and he then proceeded to whinge on like a menopausal matron for the next five minutes, eventually I had to stop him: "Look I know you're overwhelmed to see me, but I've got a feeding fish here and I must get on". I told him that I had baited my 'spots' and he went off to look for fish. With everything ready I slowly got myself into position. The fish was still feeding, in fact it had now taken most of the bait and was quite high on the shelf. I could now see it was one of the good ones which went thirty-plus. Because the fish never left the area once the started feeding positioning a hookbait was always precarious, you had to wait till the fish was looking away, then quickly but quietly lower the bait, next when the fish was unaware the bait had to be pulled into the exact position. I pulled the line, the bomb moved but the hooklink was over a sunken twig which was not only no good, but had to be removed and there was a possibility that the hook could snag on it with the resulting commotion ending my chances. So with heart in mouth I slowly retrieved the tackle amazingly the gods smiled and I had another chance. The procedure was repeated – this time the bait ended up in quite a good position but not really good enough. I wanted the bait on one shelf about six inches from the corner with the bomb on the shelf above. I lifted the bomb and put it on the top shelf which caused the bait to move to about three or four inches

Heart-tail from Longfield at 31lb 12oz

from the crease, did two inches matter? Of course it did. I found on this lake everything mattered, but with only eight to ten baits left I had to go with it. The fish carried on picking up the baits getting ever higher until it was just inches from the hookbait, it was motionless for a while then its gills flared and I knew it was about to test the bait. It sucked, then partially closed its mouth – my bait was in its lips but the hook wasn't – it blew the bait out again but didn't move. The procedure was repeated a couple more times with the same result, it really did require nerves of steel to remain calm, but I had seen this performance many times and knew what to expect. Then that moment had arrived, I know it sounds daft but I knew it just had to test the bait in its mouth. It moved gently forward, sucked and let the whole lot into its mouth – at that very moment I pulled the line between reel and first eye and set the hook.

The fish tore off under the bush, I pushed the rod deep into the water up to the reel and started to play the fish, a shout had Chris by my side in a second. The fight was short but eventful with Chris netting the fish first time in a masterly fashion. We laid it out on the grass behind us and admired an obviously big fish. Now Chris knows everything there is to know about carp fishing. If you want to know how many blades of grass there are in the *Willow* pitch ask Chris. If you want to know the most obscure fact about any part of our sport not only will he know, but he's probably got a photograph of it too. But I had caught him out a week earlier when I had caught a very large and distinctive fish again from Longfield, of which he had no history (that fish was *The Parrot* – now everybody knows the fish). So, when the question was posed again to a negative response. I said but you *must* know which one this is look it's got a heart-shaped tail, and so another fish gets a name.

Apparently it hadn't been caught for a very long time (actually *The Parrot* hadn't been caught for three years prior to my capture either, last caught by the very man who gave me my 'spots' the amiable John Allen). On the scales *Heart-tail* went 31lb 12oz. It felt strange just the two of us photographing and slipping the beauty back on that water where everything you did was usually under the glare of at least half a dozen pairs of eyes, but we celebrated in our own way, after which we carried on doing circuits of the lake for maybe another hour, Chris going one way, me the other crossing at regular intervals. It was fruitless and besides I had to be away. I said farewell to Chris on the ruin. His reply was "goodbye and I won't see you tomorrow or all week will I?" I said I was busy "well goodbye and I won't see you tomorrow" and so the protracted farewell went on and I was beginning to get a bit peeved as you do. Eventually as I strode off to the car park a sudden fit of mischief came over me. I stopped, turned and said "hold on a minute Chris tomorrow's Wednesday, I usually go fishing Wednesdays". He dropped everything and in a split second was eyeball to eyeball already hyperventilating and in a gush explained that I had too much work to do and that I should keep my commitments and really I shouldn't even have been there that day. I mulled over each point till the blood vessels on his neck were fit to burst and eventually agreed and so I turned to head for home with a final "bye Jan and I won't be seeing you tomorrow" ringing in my ears. Actually I was as jealous as hell because I was convinced that Chris would tear the place apart with this golden opportunity, every time the phone rang my heart skipped a beat. When I contacted Chris at the end of the week, he told me that no fish visited the margins. Ironically the lack of anglers' activity obviously allowed the fish to lay up in the middle of the lake unhindered, so on reflection I suppose the consistent pressure on the lake was a mixed blessing from a stalking point of view, coupled with the generosity of the regulars who let me fish the margins unhindered. On three acres preventing someone stalking fish is the easiest thing in the world.

Though I had only a morning's fishing that week fate had chosen to deal me one chance and that was all I needed, and to be fair to Chris in the hour of need he was magnanimous considering I had stalked a 35 and a 31 under his nose in a week, on that water which was *as difficult as sainthood, yet easy as breathing.*

BROMAGES 75
(FISHING TACKLE) LTD
Phone: 081-590-3521   666 GREEN LANE, GOODMAYES, ILFORD, ESSEX

**STOCKISTS OF
NUTRABAITS BAITS, OILS AND ADDITIVES
AND
S.B.S., PREMIER, ZENON
and other leading carp baits**

Boilies, Tigers, Peanuts etc

SPECIALIST TACKLE FROM
FOX · KRYSTON · DRENNAN · NASH
WYCHWOOD · KJB · EUSTACE GOLD LABEL
COLEMAN · GARDNER etc

RODS FROM
SPORTEX · NWB · ARMALITE
TRICAST · DAIWA etc

ACCESS/VISA welcome   Interest free credit
                            (ask for details)

ALSO AT

AVENUE ANGLING LTD
22A Woodford Avenue, Gants Hill,
Ilford, Essex. Tel: 081-550-7815

NEW 'Twi-Lite' Nite Marker Float
Send S.A.E. for details

A1 PICTURES

- *Photo enlargements – any size*
- *Slides duplicated*
- *Prints from slides*
- *Watercolour paintings*
- *Photos lightened or darkened*

We can get the best quality from your negs and slides, because all the work is hand printed with the greatest of care. Being a carp angler myself, I know just what you want.

Two people who know what quality is and won't accept anything but the best:

Geoff Bowers (Premier Baits) –
"Great pictures, done by an expert".

Steve Briggs –
"The best pictures I've ever had from anywhere".

**MARK DEAN
071-231 2507**
Please ring after 6pm

SOUTHEND ANGLING CENTRE

5/6 Pier Approach, Western Esplanade, Southend
Tel: (0702) 611066   Fax: (0702) 611066

CARP RODS

CENTURY COMPOSITES — Century

ARMALITE RANGE

Britain's best selling carp rod range

12' 2lb	£148.00
12' 2¼lb	£148.50
12' 2½lb	£150.00
12' 2¾lb	£155.00
13' 2¼lb	£151.40
13' 2½lb	£153.30
13' 2¾lb	£156.80
13' 3lb	£162.30
13' 3½lb Top Gun	£167.60

Century Black Max range available to order

Daiwa CARP RODS

AMORPHOUS RANGE

All with SIC Rings

AKN 125 Dictator+ 12' 2¼lb	£210.00
AKN 2SU Dictator+ 12' 2½lb	£215.00
AKN 122H Dictator+ 12' 2¾lb	£215.00
AKN 13S Dictator+ 13' 2¾lb	£220.00
AKN 13H Infinity+ 13' 3lb	£225.00

WHISKER KEVLAR RANGE

All with Fuji Rings

WKN 2200 Dictator 12' 2lb	£140.00
WKN 2214 Dictator 12' 2¼lb	£150.00
WKN 2212 Dictator 12' 2½lb	£150.00
WKN 234H Infinity 12' 2¾lb	£155.00
WKN 3214 Dictator 13' 2¼lb	£155.00
WKN 3212 Dictator 13' 2½lb	£160.00

NEW DAIWA POWERMESH CARP RODS

This new range provides amazing value for money. Very tight, very slim, very strong and very sensibly priced

Powermesh Carp 12' 2lb	£85.99
Powermesh Carp 12' 2¼lb	£89.99
Powermesh Carp 13' 2¾lb	£105.00
Powermesh Specimen 12'6" 1¼lb	£84.99

We are a Daiwa Premier Dealer. Send S.A.E. for 1992 Catalogue.

North Western CARBON & CARBON/KEVLAR

KEVLITE RANGE

12' 2lb Multi-Range	£129.00
12' 2¼lb Multi-Range	£129.50
12' 2½lb Multi-Range	£132.50
12' 2¾lb Multi-Range	£137.50
13' 2½lb Long Range	£142.50
13' 2¾lb Long Range	£145.00
13' 3lb Long Range	£147.50

SHIMANO CARP RODS

Twin Power Carp 12' 2lb	£112.00
Twin Power Carp 12' 2¼lb	£117.00
Twin Power Carp 12' 2½lb	£123.00
Diaflash Carp 12' 2¼lb	£174.00
Diaflash Carp 12' 2½lb	£179.00
Diaflash Carp 12' 3lb	£183.00

VITESSE CARP RODS

Not everyone's an expert. This range of rods gets you started at a budget price. Light and very strong with a no-quibble guarantee, and ideal purchase for the beginner

Vitesse Carp Short Range 11' 1¾lb-2lb	£49.95
Vitesse Carp Medium Range 11' 2-2¼lb	£54.95
Vitesse Carp Long Range 11' 2¼lb-2½lb	£59.95

CARRIAGE ON RODS – 3 DAY £5   OVERNIGHT £8

CARP REELS

SHIMANO

SHIMANO BAITRUNNERS

The first, and to many people still the best, baitrunning carp reels available

Aero 3500GT 2 spools	£89.90
Aero 4000GT 2 spools	£96.90
Aero 4500GT 2 spools	£99.90
Aero 3500	£64.90
Aero 4000	£69.90
Aero 4500	£74.90

Spare spools available on request

DAIWA BR REELS

New Bite-N-Run reels with free spool system. A quality alternative to the Shimano Baitrunners at a very competitive price. Very big seller last year

BR2050 2 spools	270m x 10lb	£69.99
BR2650 2 spools	270m x 14lb	£74.99
BR2050X	270m x 10lb	£49.99
BR2650X	270m x 14lb	£54.99

DAM CD350 FS

A brand new free spool carp reel for 1992. Different to othre baitrunner-type reels in that the free spool system is contained in the spool. The carbon body makes this reel much lighter than its competitors and features long tapered spool and 3 ball bearings.
Used to great effect in the Andy Little videos

CD350 FS 2 spools	£69.99

SILSTAR GXB50 BAITFEEDER

A very reliable budget reel for the beginner

SPECIAL OFFER PRICE	£39.99

TAURUS SL40 CARP REEL

A standard carp reel for the beginner providing exceptional value. Graphite body, rear drag, ambidextrous and supplied with 3 long nosed spools

Taurus SL40 3 spools	£34.95

EXTREME RANGE REELS

DAIWA SS300 TOURNAMENT CARP REEL

The ultimate long distance carp reel. This reel features a compact body, 35mm long stroke mechanism, large capacity coned spool with 3 degree taper for perfect line lay and 5 ball bearings. Simply the best

SS3000 Tournament	£175.00

DAIWA PM4000H

A less expensive extreme range reel of similar design to the above reel

PM4000H	£85.99
Also available – PM7000H large capacity	£89.99

SHIMANO BIOMASTERS

Two more excellent long range reels of high specification with cross-wind line lay

Biomaster 7000 GT	£96.90
Biomaster 8000 GT	£104.90

SHIMANO AERLEX 8000GT FB

Budget version of above reels

Aerlex 8000GT FB	£64.90

RYOBI PROJECT 7000GT

For the occasional long range carp angler. This reels provides a sensible budget option with its compact lightweight body, 2-speed line lay and long tapered spool. This reel defies the saying "you get what you pay for."
Supplied with 2 spools

Ryobi Project 7000 GT	£39.99
Ryobi Project 8000GT	£42.50 (larger model)

PADDED REEL CASES

Standard, large or small, green or black	£3.95
Aero Baitrunner shape, green or black	£4.95
Padded Opti-Pouches	£2.95

ALL REEL ORDERS POST FREE

BITE ALARMS

OPTONIC

NEW!! SUPER XL OPTONIC

£77

- Extra loud – 100 decibels at 1 metre
- Improved battery circuit, uses less milliamps at full volume than all modified indicators
- Wide frequency tone and volume switches, frequency range greater than any other indicator
- Externally mounted GPO 13T speaker
- 10 second green latching LED
- Supplied with stormproof ears
- On/off Switch • Supplied with soft pouch

OPTONIC New Super XL	£77.00
Super Special Compact	£66.00
Special Compact Hi or Lo	£55.00
Compact Hi and Lo	£39.95
Magnetonic Hi and Lo	£49.95
Basic Hi and Lo	£32.95
Optonic Extension Leads 5m Special	£7.95
7.5m Special	£8.95
Sounder Box 2T	£27.95
Sounder Box 4T	£69.95

BITECH VIPER

ELECTRONIC BITE INDICATOR
- Unique Sensitivity • Tone Control
- Superior Rod Support • Low Battery Consumption
- Mega Bright Latching/Flashing LED's
- LED's above the rod • Water Resistant
- Balljoint • Extension Socket
- Massive Volume Range • Complete with Pouch

ONLY £49.95

ELECTRONIC SOUNDER BOX

- Tone Control • Volume Control • Latching LED's
- Works with other bite indicators • Accepts 3 Rods

ONLY £35.00
Extension Leads £4.50

NEW!! DIAWA SENSITRON BITE ALARM

- Sensitivity Control • Extra load volume
- Variable tone control • Improved battery life
- 10 second latching LED • Futuristic appearance

DAIWA SENSITRON ALARM	£76.99

ACCESSORIES

Opti Polo	£2.95
Opto Fork	£2.25
Opti Pouch	£2.95
Opti Bolt and Nut	£2.15
Bite Alarm Bolt and Nut	£1.99
Twitcher Wheel	£2.15
Caps Ears	£2.10
Optonic Vee Betalights	£2.01

SUIT AND BOOT OFFER

"Efgeeco Silcatex heavyweight one-piece". Quilted 100% waterproof with hood **£79.95**

"Efgeeco Polar, super heavyweight one piece". Fleece lined 100% waterproof with hood **£94.95**

With every Efgeeco one-piece suit comes a free pair of hot foot boots worth **£34.95**

Deluxe thermal one piece suit, heavy pile, super quality, in blue **£24.95**

★ SPECIAL DISCOUNTS ★

For non-credit buyers only
Buy 2 or more rods, reels or bite alarms
GET 10% OFF

For credit terms see bottom of opposite page

SOUTHEND ANGLING CENTRE

5/6 Pier Approach, Western Esplanade, Southend
Tel: (0702) 611066   Fax: (0702) 611066

FREE CREDIT UP TO 9 MONTHS

OPEN 7 DAYS · CALLERS WELCOME
WE BUY AND SELL
SECONDHAND TACKLE

Kevin Nash Hooker Holdalls
All with reel pockets
Standard	12'		£49.97
	13'		£52.10
Deluxe	12'		£87.93
	13'		£89.47
Stalker Sling			£18.35
Deluxe Stalker Sling			£22.11

Kevin Nash Rucksacks and Bags
Hooker Rucksack	£84.99
Specialist Rucksack	£59.47
Carp Carryall	£35.49
Carp Carryall Specialist	£44.93
Stalker Bag	£25.85
Monster Specialist Carryall	£56.20
Pursuit Rucksack 60	£89.18
Pursuit Rucksack 90	£98.75
Pursuit Rucksack 120	£125.39

Kevin Nash Brolly Overwraps
Lightweight Overwrap 45"	£52.54
Lightweight Overwrap 50"	£59.37
Zip Wrap 45" Nylon	£78.43
Zip Wrap 50" Nylon	£88.65
Zip Wrap Oval	£97.36
Zip Wrap Canvas 45"	£98.75
Zip Wrap Canvas 50"	£125.39
Oval Umbrella	£97.28
Brolly & Brollywrap Oval	£188.73
Mini Side 50"	£27.66
Mini Side Oval	£29.67
Brolleywrap 50"	£41.46
Lightweight Ground Sheet 50"	£11.69
Oval Ground Sheet	£26.86
Lightweight Oval Ground Sheet	£13.63
Ground Sheet Bag	£3.90
Swival Storm Caps	£9.66
Bivvy Stick 26"	£9.45
Bivvy Stick 36"	£9.91

★ NEW FOR 1992 ★
KEVIN NASH TITAN BIVVY
Probably the ultimate carp bivvy	£185.00
Titan Carp Brolly	£141.00
Titan Side Wrap	£52.98
Hooker 56/112lbs. Scales	£50.39
Hooker Scale Pouch	£7.70
Avon Scales 40lb	£36.73
Carp Unhooking Mat	£12.10
Monster Carp Unhooking Mat	£16.07
Standard Boilie Bag	£5.99
Jumbo Boilie Bag	£7.99
Special Boilie Bag	£16.99
Rod and Lead Bands	£3.81
Velcro Rod Straps	£2.60
Fox Bag Cover and Mattress	£60.32
Deluxe Fox Bag Cover	£28.25
Deluxe Breathable Fox Bag Cover	£48.81
Fox Deluxe Wellie Wipe	£8.83
Sleeping Bag Kit Bag	£9.85
Standard Bedchair Cover	£22.00
Fox Bedchair Cover	£24.58
Fox Mattress	£43.50
Bedchair Kit Harness	£9.85
Bedchair Bag	£26.42

Kevin Nash Landing Nets
Standard Landing Net 42"	£48.45
Standard Landing Net 52"	£55.50
Hooker Landing Net 42"	£56.95
Hooker Landing Net 52"	£59.82
Arms 42"	£15.11
Arms 52"	£15.50
Standard Pole	£19.28
Hooker Pole	£24.72
Nylon Spreader Block	£3.52
Standard Mesh Net 42"	Only £16.55
Standard Mesh Net 52"	Only £19.43
Hooker Mesh Net 42"	Only £17.91
Hooker Mesh Net 52"	Only £20.54
Landing Net Bag	£4.13

Kevin Nash Carp Sacks and Slings
Sack 3' x 4'	£8.83
Sack XL 3' x 5'	£9.99
Sack XL + Extension Cord	£12.55
Big Sack 4' x 5'	£11.18
Zip Sack 50" x 30"	£10.12
Zip Sack + Extension Cord	£13.70
Sack Clip	£2.07
Sack Extension Cord	£3.20
Standard Sling	£7.45
Big Sling	£8.60
Specialist Sling	£8.60
River Sling	£4.45
Monster Carp Sling	£15.45
Hooker Sling Sack Combo	£12.95
Wet Sling Sack Bag	£3.90

SOLAR TACKLE

Buzzer Bars
2 Rod 6"/8"/10"	£8.95
3 Rod 12"/15"	£10.95
3 Rod Adjustable Front	£21.50
3 Rod Adjustable Back	£21.50

Extending Banksticks
12"	£12.25
16"	£13.25
20"	£14.25

Needle Systems
2 Rod	£19.95
3 Rod	£23.95

The Satellite
4 Rod	£40.95

NEW Lite-Flo Bobbins
Yellow, blue, green, red	£5.95

Accessories
Guy Ropes	£4.95
Bivvy Pegs	£10.95
Stabiliser	£5.50
Adjustable Stabiliser	£6.95
Stainless Coin Optonic Bolt	£2.95
Stainless Lockey Back Rest	£4.95
Carp Sack Pegs x2	£4.95

Savay Seed Mix
	1kg	3kg
Red Mix	£7.45	£18.95
Yellow Mix	£6.95	£17.95
Spiced Seed Mix	£6.95	£17.95
Quench Mix	£6.95	£15.95
Neptune Mix	£6.45	£15.95

Savay Mix Masters 100ml
Squid/Octopus Koi Rearer	£8.90
White Chocolate	£6.50
Golden Plum	£4.50
Esterblend 12	£4.90
Stimulin Amino Comp	£4.90
Stimulin Amino with Garlic	£4.90
Liquid Candy Sweetener	£8.90

NEW MAINLINE RITCHIE McDONALD READYMADES
The highest quality readymades yet available. A big range of flavours and sizes. Available in standard and bulk packs. Please write or phone for details.

WYCHWOOD TACKLE
K2 Rucksack	£123.00
Kt Stalker Bag	£28.00
Ruckman Lightweight	£51.00
Ruckman	£76.00
Packer	£91.50
Carp Quiver	£25.51
Stalker Bag	£22.99

GARDNER ROD PODS
30"	£15.29
44"	£19.17
Mega Pod telescopic	£27.14
ProPod, completely folding into one unit to fit holdall	£35.76

Rollaball Baitmakers – Long Base
12/14/16/18/20/22/24mm	£7.52
Rolling Table, 12/16mm, 14/16mm, 20/22mm	£2.62
Rollaball with Table, 8mm	£5.22
Sidewinder Boilie Machine	£50.94
Sausage Gun (8 nozzels)	£8.87

COBRA THROWING STICKS
20mm Standard, 14mm boilies 90yds	£11.95
23mm Super, 18mm boilies 100yds	£13.95
23mm King, 18mm boilies 110yds	£16.95
29mm Jumbo, 20mm boilies 120yds	£18.95

BARNETT
Black Widow	£9.95
Diablo	£15.14
Spare Bands	£2.95

FOX INTERNATIONAL
Super Deluxe Bedchair	£189.90
Standard Deluxe	£139.90
Super Adjusta Chair	£74.90
Standard Adjusta Level	£49.90
Swingers	£11.90
Swinger Heads	£3.90
Adjustable Pod	£34.50
Non-Adjustable Pod	£26.50
Supa-Bivvy	£184.90

KJB PRODUCTS
Rod Stands
2 Rod	£61.25
3 Rod	£66.40
3 Rod Special	£71.50

STEADES WAVELOCK BROLLIES
45" Nubrolli Mk.2	£47.99
50" Nubrolli Mk.2	£52.99
50" Camouflage Nubrolli, Mk.2	£62.99

Accessories
PVA String	£1.73
PVA Bags	£173
Leger Booms	69p
Leger Stops – Mini	51p
Line Stops – Large	£1.01
Run Clips – pair	97p
5" Straight Forceps	£2.29
8" Straight Forceps	£3.32
12" Straight Forceps	£5.61
5" Curved Forceps	£2.29
8" Curved Forceps	£3.32
12" Curved Forceps	£5.61
Black Berkley Swivels –	
Size 10, per 100	71p
Size 10 per 50	£3.25
Size 10, per 50	£3.25
Starlit Blue	86p
Starlit Red	86p
Starlit Mini, pair	86p

Betalights – KJB Coloured
	Small	Large
Red	£1.95	£4.95
Green	£1.95	£4.95
Yellow	£1.95	£4.95

★ Carp Rig Wallets ★
20 Zip Pockets in each. External velcro seal. Keeps all your rig bits neat, tidy and dry
£7.95 each   2 for £15.00

KEVIN NASH
P.V.A. String – Quick Melt	£3.00
P.V.A. String – Slow Melt	£3.50
Large Bore Rig Beads	66p
Anti-tangle Bead and Tube	£1.10
Bolt Beads	£1.31
Swivel Beads	£1.37
Micro Swivel Beads	£1.37
Casting Booms	90p
Feeder Booms	85p
3/5/8mm Beads	86p
Knot Beads	66p
Rig Foam, black, orange, yellow	£1.35
Polypops	£1.12
Rig Rings	£1.00
Micro Rig Rings	£1.00

RICHWORTH STREAMSELECT
Full range of boilies

NEW FOR 1992 – ZENON BOJKO MAINLINE BAITS
After many years of experience, Zenon Bojko, one of the country's best known and most successful carp anglers has put together a range of baits set to create a buzz in the carp world. Already this season a large number of big carp have been caught on these baits, topped by the Snake Pit at 45lb+. Be in front of the rest, not behind using last year's baits.

FISHMEAL MIXES 1 kilo
Zen's Pro Fish Base Mix	£5.75
Zen's Pro Marine Base Mix	£6.50
Zen's Marine & Liver Base Mix	£7.50

BIRDFOOD MIXES
Zen's Yellow Seed Base Mix	£5.95
Zen's SUpreme Bird Blend	£6.50
High Leakage Base Mix	£4.95
New!! Multism 250ml	£7.95
New!! Met Mino 250ml	£9.95

SPECIAL OILS 500ml
Feed Inducing Fosoil	£5.00
Ultra Marine Oil	£8.95
Strawberry Fosoil Inducer	£6.95

BOOSTER DIPS
Strawberry Oil, Juicy Fruit Oil, Tutti Frutti Oil, Peach Melba Oil. Per pot, all at £2.75

FLAVOURS
Strawberry, Zing, Spice, Scopex, Tutti, Cream, Salmon & Shrimp. Per 50ml, all at £2.75

LINES

Sylcast Sorrell
6,7,8,9,11,13lb	250m	£4.25
7lb	1000m	£10.95
8,9,11,13,15lb		£11.95

Maxima
	100yds	o/shot	600m
6lb	£3.75	£6.99	£11.45
8lb	£3.95	£7.39	£11.90
10lb	£3.99	£7.65	£12.25
12lb	£4.14	£7.90	£12.75
15lb	£4.25	£7.99	£14.45

NEW!! Daiwa Tapered Carp Shock Leaders
A god send for long range carp anglers. No more untidy leader knots. Just join your mainline to simular strength leader end and wind onto your reels. Available in two types.
Medium length, 12lb-30lb. 5 per spool	£7.99
Long Length, 8lb-20lb. 4 per spool	£6.99

Amnesia
Black, 200ft. 20lb	£2.40
Green, 200ft. 20lb £2.40 30lb	£3.65

SUPERBRAIDS

Kryston
Kryston Silkworm, 20m
10lb, 12lb, 15lb, 25lb	£6.89
Merlin 20m, 8, 10, 12, 15lb	£6.38
Super Silk 20m, 14lb	£6.89
Multistrand 20m, 15lb	£6.89
No Tangle Fluid	£3.02

Kevin Nash
Finesse TG, 4, 10, 12, 15, 25lb x20m	£6.62
Finesse Hair Braid x20m	£1.90
Finesse Enticer	
4, 10, 12, 15, 25lb x20m	£6.62
Finesse Dental Floss	£1.50

HOOKS

Kevin Nash
Outpoint, sizes 4, 6, 8, 10, per 10	£1.15
Specialist	
sizes 2, 4, 6, 8, 10, 12, per 10	£1.15
Snag, sizes 2, 4, 6, 8, per 10	£1.15
Spec. Boilie, 4, 6, 8, per 10	£1.15

Drennan
Super Spec.
sizes 2, 4, 6, 8, 10, 12	£2.87 per 50
Boilie Hooks	
sizes 2, 4, 6, 8, 10, 12, 14	93p per 10
Starpoint, sizes 4, 6, 8, 10, 12	£1.55 per 10

DRENNAN CARP SYSTEM
Drennan brass rings, mini and small	82p
Sub-surface controller	£1.39
Surface Controllers	
5g £1.60 10g £1.65 15g	£1.70
Bait drill	£1.70
Bait Needle	87p
Stiff Anti-tangle tube	98p
Shock beads, 5mm, 8mm	72p
Link beads	67p
Hair stops – small, large	87p
Bolt Beads	87p
Anti-tangle beads	77p
Free-run beads	77p
Floater loops	77p
Boilie Bayonets	67p

★ INSTANT CREDIT AVAILABLE ★
ORDERS up to £100, 3 or 6 monthly payments. Orders over £100, choose 3, 6 or 9 monthly payments.
MAIL ORDER TERMS – divide cash total by number of payments chosen, add delivery charge (rods only) to first cheque and any odd pence, date other cheques at monthly intervals (round pounds only), write cheque card number and expiry date on back of first cheque and send ALL cheques with order. A telephone number is useful. SHOP CREDIT TERMS – Customers in shop must bring cheque and proof of address.

★ SPECIAL DISCOUNTS ★
2 or more rods, reels, bite alarms **10% DISCOUNT** (non-credit buyers only)
All other goods – orders over £250 **10% DISCOUNT** (non-credit buyers only)
Orders over £500 **10% DISCOUNT** and 3 months credit (if required)

CARRIAGE CHARGES – Rods: 3 day delivery £5   Overnight £8
Bait – £2 per kilo to a maximum of £8   All other goods carriage free

HOW TO ORDER: STATE NAME, ADDRESS AND REQUIREMENTS CLEARLY, ENCLOSING CASH/CHEQUE/P.O./ACCESS/VISA BY LETTER OR PHONE

GREAT EXPECTATIONS

MARK THOMPSON

Come-on, tarp-on, yelled Captain Jack. The sun was setting over India Key and the anticipation was high. Fishing with live mullet attached to 30lb BS line and waiting for a 'strike'. I could not have imagined how difficult a 'hook-up' with a big tarpon was but my thirteenth strike resulted in the capture of a massive tarpon. The 40 minute, mostly airborne, fight was behind me. "How big is it?", I screamed as Captain Jack unhooked the beast. "115- 120lb!"

Although the fish was immediately returned without an official weigh-in I had little doubt that these guys are able to pinpoint the weight of big fish to the pound.

The flight home saw me drift off into the land of make believe, 'what next I thought?'... An abrupt burp in my ear brought me to, Christ why do I always sit next to the drunk on these flights? I mean, my ear!

Half awake, my mind wandered back to meeting Paul Boote and being held in awe of his vivid accounts of mahseer fishing India. Here is a man who knows where he is at.

My plan was simple, once back home I'd contact Paul and hope to be put on the right track. Mahseer it would be.

Life of course is not that simple and unable to contact Paul (where are you?) I obtained a video of the Channel Four TV documentary with Paul and John Bailey mahseer fishing a tributary of the Ganges. I do not know what it was but I was not inspired. I mean I didn't drop everything to go catch a mahseer!

Slowly, over a period of 12 months, I established a framework of information on mahseer. Good starting points being John Wilson's *Go Fishing* programme and Dave Plummer's excellent video *Mahseer Hunt '91*. It was clear from these sources that the River Cauvery in southern India is 'the' place for the largest mahseer. I do not want to make the location issue over simplified but if anybody wants further information then drop me a line.

So what constitutes a 'big' mahseer?

One of the earliest on record, caught in 1870, weighed 110lb from the Cubbany river. In 1906, Mr C E Murray Aynsley, caught a 104lb mahseer from the Cauvery river near Sirangapatna.

A small number of other fish over 100lb had been recorded during this period with fish of 119lb to Major J S Rivett Carnac in 1919 and a 120lb fish to J Devet Van Lingen in 1945, both from the Cauvery river.

Since that time there had been no reports of fish over the magic 100lb mark. Until, of course, Steve Harper's magnificent 104lb fish taken in 1991. A number of anglers have reported fish in the 75lb – 90lb category during recent years and without doubt those to have caught a 100lb plus mahseer join a very exclusive club!

My own ambition at the outset was to catch a 50lb plus mahseer on this trip and look forward on my eventual return to a 75lb plus fish. (The best laid plans!)

In the fullness of time a trip was booked in late January 1992. Flight and itinerary details make for boring reading even when the flight is delayed for one day (in the case of Air India this was the norm – be warned!) re-routed and devoid on arrival of my baggage (left back at Heathrow!) the flight could have only further deteriorated by a refuel in Iraq!

7000 kilometres, via Delhi and Bangalore, is one hell of a journey and my first view of the awesome Cauvery river numbed my acute tiredness.

Plundering through the Indian jungle with a river bed strewn with rocks as large as a London bus the river is both

Typical fishing spot

considerable and intimidating. Clearly the 30lb and 40lb big game line will be a prerequisite for success.

The transport, a sturdy Morris Oxford lookalike, finally arrived at the camp following a two hour journey down through a variety of dusty tracks and crevices. Before arriving at the camp the last sight of civilisation was a small village – a dozen mud huts with straw roofs! Needless to say facilities at the camp are basic and, providing you like a curry (or two!) quite bearable for a couple of weeks. Those who like 'creature comforts' however will do as well to stay at home and go to Waveney instead!

Finally after what seemed like several lifetimes I was fishing for the mighty mahseer. I had been assigned a ghillie for my stay at the camp. His name was Anthony Cruz and he proved to be excellent company. Whilst somewhat lacking in technical skills this was overcome with a most intimate knowledge of the river and its inhabitants along with a genuine love and enthusiasm for the fish themselves.

"Mash-eer, mash-eer" Anthony would whisper, in the most pleasant pigeon English, before recounting the tales of the big mahseer captures he has been involved in.

The first evening was spent fishing *Tiger Pool*. My 11 foot salmon rod coupled with a Shimano 7000 GT and 30lb big game line sent the freelined 'ragi paste' into a relatively sedate pool. There are clearly a lot of small fish in the river as my touch legering revealed. It was however, some 30 minutes into the first session when the rod thumped over and a big fish was on – 40 yards, 60 yards, 80 yards of line disappearing from the spool with disturbing ease.

Thankfully the pool was relatively snag free and within ten minutes my first mahseer was banked. The fish was tied to a stringer by Anthony Cruz and cameras and weighing sling prepared. The fish was clearly big and I'd have guessed it to be about forty pounds. I have seen a handful of 40lb plus carp including a couple of 60's so I was somewhat surprised when the scales swing around to just 50lb!

Christ, I was over the moon. I mean my first mahseer was 50lb!

The fish was returned to its watery haven (all the mahseer are returned, although the smaller carp and catfish are doomed for the pot – have many of you guys tried 'Common Carp Vindaloo'? – you should try it sometime!). Then it was back to the camp to prepare for the following morning session.

A welcoming cup of tea at 6am and we were back on the bank searching for that king of fish, the mighty mahseer. Both the morning and evening session passed without major incident although a number of small mahseer to 12lb or so were landed. Back at the camp excitement was high as another member of the party had landed a monster of 66lb from a pool called *Balamudu*. The fish falling to 'ragi paste', a boilie type bait made with millet flour and spices and moulded around the size 4/0 hooks before casting.

That evening and after dinner, well into dark, a couple of hours were spent carp fishing in the camp pool and I connected with a 20lb plus mahseer which was rather lively on the carp gear!

Next morning and it was our turn on *Balamudu*. Anticipation was high and following a slow start I hooked a good fish that, following a great fight, proved to be a 'black' mahseer just under 30lbs. A most distinctive looking fish and big, as I understand, for its type. The morning session would finish at 10.30 and it would be back to camp for breakfast.

25lb golden mahseer

ARE YOU SICK TO THE BACK TEETH OF OPINION POLLS?

WELL HERE IS THE RESULT OF ANOTHER ONE

We asked a small unrepresentative sample of carp fishers why they will not vote for us. This is what they said:

"I'm not a real carp angler"

"I'd rather spend the £13 subscription on fags, booze, bait and the missus"

"I can pick up copies of Carp Fisher at the tackle shop for £7.50 instead of getting them for nothing"

"Who needs a free, quarterly 20 page newsletter anyway?"

"Why bother, the Conferences and Regional Meetings I've been to were so good I didn't really mind paying more than members to get in?"

Redmire Pool	*"I've no romance in my soul"*
Etang de Rouge	*"Never did trust foreigners. Their fifty pounders are bound to be extra slimy"*
Yew Tree Lake	*"Lifting a forty could give me a hernia"*
Marsh Lake	*"OK, so it contains a thirty-five pounder, but that doesn't mean it'll feed"*
Horseshoe Lake	*"I'll stick to Grimsby Brick Pond, thank you. Someone once told me of a man who'd seen a fully scaled mirror in there"*
Waveney D Lake	*"Thirties crashing all night just outside the window would keep me awake, and anyway I can always book another caravan on the lake for an extra £50 a week"*

"I'm not short of a few bob and don't mind paying full price for my Leisure Sport season ticket. Bait and tackle discounts are for the poor"

"I'd rather talk to the parrot, people in supermarkets, politicians and pollsters than befriend other carp fishers"

"I'm daft"

VOTE CARP SOCIETY

For our Manifesto contact Vic Cranfield
33 Covert Road, Hainault, Ilford, IG6 3AZ
Telephone 081 551 8250

Big fish (104lb)
being played from coracle

Black mahseer – almost 30lbs

Big fish is on!

At 10.15 I was more than content to call it a day and head back for the grub. I was persuaded, rather reluctantly, to send the 'ragi' once more in search of the mighty mahseer.

One more cast I thought and then it would be 'curried carp' or whatever else that can be curried. Quite a strange thought process is that. I mean what can be curried? Most things of course. So there I am wasting the final moments of an already successful session dreaming about curried eggs, curried toast, curried knickers (typical isn't it, two days into a session and I am thinking about knickers!)

The incidents that follow will remain with me for my time on this island earth. Round whacks the rod, strike, fish on. Christ, what have I hooked here? Some 130-150 yards of line have evaporated into the deep boiling pool. Anthony Cruz becomes extremely lively and launches the coracle (a small round boat) and instructs me to play the fish out from the coracle. Makes sense thinks I, looking at perhaps 10-15 turns of line left on the spool!

To be fair the fight was brutal. One sided to the extreme. We had little chance. The fish towing both ghillies and myself at random. A stroke of luck saw the fish move into a shallow pool on the opposite bank over a mile away from my original spot! I can well remember playing the fish from the bank. One of the ghillies with his arms around my waist for extra strength the other ghillie with two hands on the butt of the rod for extra leverage and boy we were getting nowhere!

Clearly the gods were on my side and with the fish wallowing some 15 yards out and ready to disappear on another 50 yard run, Anthony Cruz, as if like magic, slipped into the drink and embraced the fish whilst placing it on a stringer. I mean I blinked and it is was all over. The fish was mine.

It was like nothing I had seen before. Christ, it was massive! Both ghillies and myself, with the brute in tow, rowed over to the original bank and by now the news had spread and the other members of the party and all the staff from the camp were there to greet us.

The weighing and photo session seemed to last all day, it probably did, but suffice to say the fish weighed in at 104lbs and was certainly the largest fish ever recorded from that particular stretch of river and joins Steve Harper's fish as the largest caught anywhere for over 45 years.

I mean, life can be an absolute bitch but life can be so good, so bloody good. eh?

Not surprisingly I was relatively laid back for the remaining duration of the trip though that very evening I did manage to catch a mid-thirty to complete a rather special days fishing.

So what next? For me it will be to Lake Victoria for a big nile perch... and then what? Did I hear you carp boys mention the possibility of 100lb carp from Cassien or where was it?

Great Expectations, eh!

104lb mahseer

BOB FROST TACKLE
No.1 Mail Order Specialist

NORTH WESTERN KEVLITES

LNTH	T/C	FUJI BNHG-B	FUJI S.I.C.
12'	2¼lb	£105.00	£135.00
12'	2½lb	£107.50	£137.50
12'	2¾lb	£110.00	£140.00
12'	3lb	£112.50	£142.00
13'	2½lb	£115.00	£145.00
13'	2¾lb	£117.50	£147.50
13'	3lb	£120.00	£150.00

NORTH WESTERN KEVLARS

LNTH	T/C	FUJI BNHG-B	FUJI S.I.C.
12'	2lb	£90.00	£120.00
12'	2¼lb	£99.50	£129.00
12'	2¾lb	£99.00	£129.00
13'	2¼lb	£105.00	£135.00
13'	2¾lb	£110.00	£140.00

NORTH WESTERN CARBONS

LNTH	T/C	FUJI BNHG-B	FUJI S.I.C.
12'	2lb	£80.00	£110.00
12'	2¼lb	£82.50	£112.50
12'	2½lb	£85.00	£115.00
12'	2¾lb	£87.50	£117.50
13'	3lb	£90.00	£120.00

ARMALITE

LNTH	T/C	FUJI BNHG-B	FUJI S.I.C.
12'	2lb	£115.00	£145.00
12'	2¼lb	£117.00	£147.00
12'	2½lb	£119.00	£149.00
12'	2¾lb	£120.00	£150.00
12'	3lb	£120.00	£150.00
13'	3lb	£130.00	£160.00
12'	3½lb Top Gun	£13.00	£160.00
12'	4lb Top Gun	£135.00	£165.00
13'	3½lb Top Gun	£140.00	£170.00
13'	4lb Top Gun	£140.00	£170.00

SPORTEX KEVLARS

LNTH	T/C	FUJI BNHG-B	FUJI S.I.C.
12'	2lb	£130.00	£160.00
12'	2¼lb	£140.00	£170.00
12'	2¾lb	£145.00	£175.00
13'	2¼lb	£150.00	£180.00
13'	3lb	£155.00	£185.00

ROD BUILDING SPEC

Rods are finished with abbreviated super slim Duplon handles, NPS reel seats, Duplon torpedo butt grips. Jet black whippings with one coat Epoxy resin. Complete with cloth bag.
2lb and 2¼lb rods have 7 rings plus tip (25mm butt ring) and 2½lb plus rods have long distance ringing i.e. 6 rings plus tip (30mm butt ring).
Full custom rod service available — name on rod — alternative rings — own ring spacings etc, etc.

Coloured tipped whippings   Add £3.00 per rod
Chevron butt and tipped whippings   Add £12.00 per rod
Full Duplon handle   Add £5.00 per rod

With over **25 YRS** professional rod building experience we guarantee the finest finish you've ever seen!!

REELS

SHIMANO BAITRUNNERS
- Aero GT 3500 .... £71.90
- Aero GT 4000 .... £77.50
- Aero GT 4500 .... £79.90
- Aero BTR 3500 .... £51.90
- Aero BTR 4000 .... £55.90
- Aero BTR 4500 .... £59.90

DAIWA FIXED SPOOL
- PG 1650 .... £37.95
- PX 1650 .... £31.95
- MG 1650 H £27.95
- EG 1650 X £21.99
- J 1650 X £14.95

LANDING NETS
- 36" complete + 6' handle £42.00
- 42" complete + 6' handle £44.00
- 50" complete + 6' handle £50.00
- 36" Arms only ..... £11.00   36" net only £9.25
- 42" Arms only ..... £12.00   42" net only £11.25
- 50" Arms only ..... £13.00   50" net only £16.25
- 6' handle only ..... £18.00   Spreader block £3.25

BITE ALARMS

OPTONIC
- Super XL £59.95
- Super Compact £58.00
- Special HI £48.00
- Magnotronic £44.00
- Standard HI £37.00

BITECH
- Viper Alarm £49.50
- Sounder Box £33.00
- 7m Leads £4.00

ACCESSORIES
- Optonic Pouch £3.35
- Brass Nut & Bolt £2.50
- Brass "U" Fork £2.50
- Twitcher Wheels x 3 .... £2.65
- Duracell Batteries £2.99

WYCHWOOD TACKLE
- K2 Rucksack £105.00
- Packer £83.00
- Ruckman £65.00
- Ruckman Lightweight £45.00
- Shoulder Bag £40.00
- Holdall Deluxe 12' £70.00
- Holdall Standard 12' £57.95
- System Select 12'/13' £54.50
- Spare Pouch £14.50
- Carp Quiver £23.00

WYCHWOOD CLOTHING

K2 ONE PIECE SUITS
Sizes: M/L/XL/XXL £110.00

FOUR SEASONS JACKETS
Sizes: M/L/XL/XXL £89.95

KRYSTON

SILKWORM 20MTS
4lb - 8lb - 10lb - 12lb - 15lb - 25lb £6.89

SILKWORM 40MTS
4lb - 8lb - 10lb - 12lb - 15lb - 25lb £11.19

MERLIN 20MTS
8lb - 10lb - 12lb - 15lb £6.38

MERLIN 40MTS
8lb - 10lb - 12lb - 15lb £10.47

MULTISTRAND
- 15lb x 20M £6.89
- 15lb x 40M £11.19

SUPERSILK
- 14lb x 20M £6.89
- 14lb x 40M £11.19

QUICKSILVER
- 25lb x 25 mtrs £10.17
- 35lb x 25 mtrs £10.68
- 45lb x 25 mtrs £11.19
- No Tangle Gel £3.00
- No Tangle Supergel £3.25

SOLAR TACKLE

BUZZER BARS
- 2 Rod 6"- 8"- 10" £8.25
- 3 Rod 12"- 15" £10.75
- 3 Rod Adjustable Front £20.75
- 3 Rod Adjustable Back £20.75

EXTENDING BANKSTICKS
- 12" £11.75
- 16" £12.75
- 20" £13.75

NEEDLE SYSTEMS
- 2 Rod £19.25
- 3 Rod £23.25
- 3 Rod Satellite £39.50

LITE-FLO BOBBINS
Red, Green, Yellow.
Size 40mm x 20mm £5.85

ACCESSORIES
- Stainless Backrests £4.85
- Guy Ropes £4.85
- Bivvy Pegs x 8 ..... £10.75
- Adjustable Stabilizer £6.85
- Spare Thumbscrews x 2 ..... £2.95
- Carp Pips x 3 ..... £2.95
- Locking Rings x 3 ..... £2.95

CATAPULTS
- Reddicat Long Range £5.99
- Reddicat Medium Range £5.99
- Spare Elastic £1.50
- Spare Pouch £1.50
- Spare Wedge x 2 ..... £0.50

FOX INTERNATIONAL

BEDCHAIRS
- Super Deluxe £169.50
- Standard Deluxe £119.50
- Standard Bedchair £89.50

SMALL CHAIRS
- Super Adjust Level £68.00
- Standard Adjust Level £49.50

BEDCHAIR ACCESSORIES
- Bedchair Support Tube £7.50
- Sleeping Bag/Foot Cover £44.90
- Carrying Strap £5.95
- Spare Feet £2.25

UMBRELLAS
- Supa Brolly £124.90
- Supa Brolly In-Full £54.90
- Supa Bivvy £145.90
- Specimen Brolly £72.95
- Tilt and Screw-in Pole £14.95
- Groundsheet £34.90
- Door Panel £19.90

TROLLEY
- Load Shift Trolley £94.90
- Trolley Strap System £9.90

SWINGER INDICATORS
- Standard Swinger £11.30
- Long Arm Swinger £12.60
- Red/Yellow/Green Spare Heads £3.75
- Add On Weights £3.75
- Swinger Set and Case £39.90
- Swinger Case £6.60

FOX PODS
- Adjustable 48" £32.50
- Non Adjust 30" £24.90
- Needle Bar System £8.60
- Needles x 3 ..... £7.75
- Needles x 2 ..... £5.75
- Rod Lok £6.40
- Scales Weigh Bar £5.35

SLEEPING BAGS
- Bob Frost — 5° £34.95
- Coleman Grey Fox — 10° £68.95
- Coleman Peakloft — 32° £116.95
- Fox Holofill — 10° £99.00
- Fox Quallofill — 30° £129.00

COOKING STOVES
- Coleman Peak 1 Unleaded £39.50
- Camping Gaz Bluet 206 ..... £18.99
- Camping Gaz Globe Trotter £28.99
- Camping Gaz Rando 360 ..... £34.99

UMBRELLAS

STEADE-FAST-WAVELOCK
- 50" Camouflage Nubrolli £59.99
- 50" Nubrolli £49.90
- 45" Nubrolli £44.99
- 50" Tilt £39.99
- 45" Tilt £34.99
- 50" Nubrolli with Velcro Fitted £67.99
- Umbrella Conversion Kits £8.45
- Umbrella Guy Ropes x 2 ..... £2.35
- Umbrella Bag £7.25

BLACK CARP LEADS

CARP BOMBS
- 1¼ oz per 5 ..... £2.35
- 1½ oz per 5 ..... £2.45
- 1¾ oz per 5 ..... £2.55
- 2 oz per 5 ..... £2.65
- 2¼ oz per 5 ..... £3.00
- 2½ oz per 5 ..... £3.20
- 3 oz per 5 ..... £3.30
- 4 oz per 5 ..... £3.70

FLUTED RISERS
- 1½ oz per 5 ..... £2.45
- 2 oz per 5 ..... £2.85
- 2½ oz per 5 ..... £3.00
- 3 oz per 5 ..... £3.50
- 4 oz per 5 ..... £3.70

ANTI-TANGLE BOMBS
- 1¼ oz per 5 ..... £2.75
- 1½ oz per 5 ..... £2.85
- 1¾ oz per 5 ..... £2.95
- 2 oz per 5 ..... £3.10
- 2¼ oz per 5 ..... £3.40
- 2½ oz per 5 ..... £3.50
- 3 oz per 5 ..... £3.70

TAIL BOMBS
- 1¼ oz per 5 ..... £3.10
- 1½ oz per 5 ..... £3.20
- 1¾ oz per 5 ..... £3.30
- 2 oz per 5 ..... £3.40
- 2¼ oz per 5 ..... £3.60
- 2½ oz per 5 ..... £3.80

- 2¾ oz per 5 ..... £3.90
- 3 oz per 5 ..... £4.10

BALL BOMBS
- 1 oz per 5 ..... £2.55
- 1½ oz per 5 ..... £2.65
- 1¾ oz per 5 ..... £2.75
- 2 oz per 5 ..... £2.90
- 3 oz per 5 ..... £3.40
- 4 oz per 5 ..... £3.95

DRILLED BALL BOMBS
- 1 oz per 5 ..... £2.65
- 1½ oz per 5 ..... £2.85
- 1¾ oz per 5 ..... £2.95
- 2 oz per 5 ..... £3.10
- 3 oz per 5 ..... £3.65
- 4 oz per 5 ..... £4.20

CAMMO LEAD COATING
- Green and Brown £2.50
- Sand and Brown £2.50

GARDNER TACKLE

BUZZER BARS BLACK
- 2 Rod — 8" Push On £3.05
- 2 Rod — 11" Push On £3.25
- 2 Rod — 8" Screw-in £3.62
- 2 Rod — 11" Screw-in £3.80
- 2 Rod — 15" Adjustable £4.72
- 3 Rod — 13" Push On £4.10
- 3 Rod — 13" Screw-in £4.25
- 3 Rod — 16" Screw-in £4.45
- 3 Rod — 20" Adjustable £5.40

BUZZER BARS STAINLESS
- 2 Rod — 6½" Screw-in £5.25
- 2 Rod — 8" Screw-in £5.80
- 2 Rod — 11" Adjustable £6.20
- 3 Rod — 11" Screw-in £6.00
- 3 Rod — 13" Screw-in £6.20
- 3 Rod — 16" Screw-in £7.05
- Buzzer Bar Spacers — Short £0.96
- Buzzer Bar Spacers — Long £1.15

BANKSTICKS — BLACK
- 10" Extending £3.55
- 20" Extending £4.00
- 30" Extending £4.55

BANKSTICKS — STAINLESS
- 10" Extending £4.65
- 20" Extending £5.85
- 30" Extending £7.05
- Bankstick Stabiliser — Black £2.46
- Bankstick Stabiliser — Stainless £3.55
- Hammer Head £1.25

MONKEY CLIMBERS
- 24" Windbeater £2.35
- 36" Windbeater £2.75
- Orange/White/Yellow
  — Spare Bodies £0.95
- 24" Grease £4.10
- 36" Grease £4.75
- White/Yellow — Spare Bodies £1.15
- 24" Trigger £4.55
- 36" Trigger £5.20
- White/Yellow — Spare Bodies £1.50
- 24" G.T. Standard £6.70
- 24" G.T. Large £7.35
- 36" G.T. Standard £7.35
- 36" G.T. Large £7.99
- 19mm or 25mm — Spare Bodies £4.00
- Pro-Pod — Adjustable £35.75
- Rod-Pod 30" £16.00
- Rod-Pod 44" £19.10
- Rod-Pod Aerial £5.65

AERIAL NEEDLE HOLDER
- 2 Rod £5.65
- 3 Rod £7.80
- Adjustable Line Clip £1.15
- With Terry Clip £1.35
- Brolly Pole — 29" £7.80
- Brolly Pole — 35" £8.99
- Bait Rocket £3.35
- Magic Markers £1.50
- Suspender £2.25
- Mixer Fixer £2.25
- Rig Bins £4.55
- Hair Needle £0.85
- Mini Hair Needle £0.85
- Stringer Needle £1.25
- Braided Hair Needle £1.10
- Needle Guard £1.05
- P.V.A. String £1.65
- Rod Rest Heads "U" £0.50
- Rod Rest Heads "V" £0.50
- Rod Rest Heads Push On £0.60
- Head Studs £0.50
- Camera Adapter £1.35
- Betalights — Round £3.45
- Betalights — Flat £3.45
- Betalights — Square £6.25
- Betalights — Mini x 2 ..... £3.85
- Back Leads — Standard £1.90
- Back Leads — Heavy £1.90
- Helicopter Bolt Beads £2.30

JOHN ROBERTS TACKLE

Semi Fixed Lead Rigs	£0.90
Helicopter Rigs	£1.30
Quick Change Beads	£0.99
Leger Stops Small	£0.55
Leger Stops Large	£0.55
Line Clips per 2	£0.90
Run Clips per 2	£0.90
Link Leger Beads	£0.60
Feeder Booms per 3	£0.80
Hook Knot Tester	£0.95
Hook Floatant Foam	£1.10
Butt Grips	£1.50

HOOKS

Mustad O'Shaugnessy (34021)
Sizes: 4, 6, 8 or 10 per 10	£0.70

Kamasan (B980)
Sizes: 4, 6, 8, 10, 12 per 10	£0.65

Kamasan Bent Hooks (B810)
Sizes: 6, 8, 10 per 25	£1.99

Au Lion D'or (1534)
Sizes: 4, 6, 8, 10 or 12 per 20	£0.90

Au Lion D'or Barbless (1542)
Sizes: 4, 6, 8, 10 or 12 per 20	£0.90

Jack Hilton
Sizes: 4, 6, 8, 10 or 12 per 25	£2.80

Jack Hilton Barbless
Sizes: 4, 6, 8 or 10 per 25	£3.10

BIVVIES

50" Camouflage	£95.00
50" Nylon	£79.95
45" Nylon	£64.95
Gardner Pop-Up	£129.95

STORMSIDES

50" Stormsides & Door & velcro	£68.50
50" Stormsides & Door	£51.25
40" Stormsides & Door	£38.80
45" Stormsides & Door	£46.95
45" Stormsides	£36.75
50" Mini Stormsides & Velcro	£33.75
50" Mini Stormsides	£23.50
45" Mini Stormsides & Velcro	£32.75
45" Mini Stormsides	£22.50

BIVVIE AND STORMSIDE ACCESSORIES

50" Groundsheet	£22.50
45" Groundsheet	£20.50
Swivel Stormcaps Brass x 2	£9.75
Stormcaps x 2	£4.10
Storm Rods x 2	£4.10
Bivvie Sticks Long x 2	£14.50
Bivvie Sticks Short x 2	£10.50
Velcro Pack 6M Both Sides	£10.25

WEIGH SLINGS

Small Sling	£6.25
Standard Sling	£7.25
Large Sling	£8.25
Pike Sling	£10.25
Zipped Sling	£11.25

RETAINING SACKS

Standard 3' x 4'	£9.25
Extra Large 3' x 5'	£10.75
Big Carp/Pike 4' x 5'	£11.75
Zip Sack 4' x 32"	£10.75
Sack Clip	£1.85
Sack Clip & Extension Cord	£2.99

UNHOOKING MATS

Large Carp	£12.95
Large Pike	£12.95

THROWING STICKS

Cobra Std — 16mm Boilies	£10.99
Cobra Super — 18mm Boilies	£12.99
Cobra Jumbo — 24mm Boilies	£16.99
King Cobra — 18mm Boilies	£14.99
Deluxe Bait Pouch	£6.99

GENERAL ACCESSORIES

Deluxe Rod Sling	£19.95
Bechair Wellie Wipe	£8.25
Boilie Bags — Standard	£5.70
Boilie Bags — Large	£6.90
Boilie Bags — Extra Large	£8.15
Large Accessory Bag — Padded	£5.40
Small Accessory Bag — Padded	£4.35
Umbrella/Landing Net Bag	£7.25
Rod & Lead Bands x 2	£3.20
Deluxe Rig Wallet	£7.95
Gardner Rig Bins	£4.25
Forceps Straight/Curved 12"	£5.25
Forceps Straight/Curved 8"	£4.25
Forceps Straight/Curved 6"	£3.25
Tube Threader	£1.35
Boilie Needle	£0.90

Boilie Stops — Red/Yellow/Black	£0.65
Micro Beads	£0.55
Black Beads 3mm x 50	£0.80
Black Beads 5mm x 50	£0.80
Shocka Beads 5mm x 10	£0.70

BAIT PRESENTATION AIDS

Tungsten Putty	£1.45
Nut Drill	£1.60
Polypops	£1.00
Rig Foam	£1.00
Floater Controllers — Small	£1.65
Floater Controllers — Medium	£1.65
Floater Controllers — Large	£1.65
PVA — String	£1.20
PVA — Thread	£1.20
PVA — Tape	£1.50
PVA — Easymelt Heavy x 20 mtrs	£5.25
PVA — Easymelt Std x 20 mtrs	£5.25

RIG TUBING

Antitangle Tube & Beads Clear	£1.55
Antitangle Tube & Beads Black	£1.55
Antitangle Stiff Tube Clear	£1.15
Antitangle Stiff Tube Black	£1.15
Clear Boom Tube 1.5mm Dia	£0.85
Clear Boom Tube 2.0mm Dia	£0.85
Clear Boom Tube 3.0mm Dia	£0.85
Black Boom Tube 1.5mm Dia	£0.85
Black Boom Tube 2.0mm Dia	£0.85
Black Boom Tube 3.0mm Dia	£0.85
Clear Silicon Tube 0.5mm Dia	£0.80
Clear Silicon Tube 1.0mm Dia	£0.80
Clear Silicon Tube 1.5mm Dia	£0.80
Clear Silicon Tube 2.0mm Dia	£0.80
Clear Silicon Tube 3.0mm Dia	£0.80

BITS 'N' PIECES

Carp Ears	£1.75
OPTI — Polo	£2.45
Swivel Beads	£1.25
Impact Power Gum — 11lb	£1.99
Impact Power Gum — 22lb	£2.50
Split Rings per 10	£0.50
Brass Rings per 20	£1.55
Berkley Swivels size 10 per 50	£3.60
Mustad Swivels size 10 per 50	£2.60
American Snap Swivels per 50	£3.20
Snaplinks per 10	£0.55
Sliding Float Stops	£1.10
Marvic Boilie Punch	£2.50
Spare Foam	£0.85
Anglers Thermometer	£11.99
Depthometer	£9.99
Pocket-Mate Torch	£10.25
French Tackle Box 2 Tier	£18.50
Stewart Boxes — Large	£6.99
Stewart Boxes — Medium	£4.99
Rig Foam	£1.15
Cammo Lead Coating	£2.50
Spool Cases	£6.99

LINE

SYLCAST 1000 METRES
4lb	£9.25
5lb	£9.75
6lb	£9.95
7lb	£10.45
8lb	£10.95
9lb	£11.45
11lb	£11.95
15lb	£12.95

MAXIMA 660 YDS
4lb	£10.15
5lb	£10.50
6lb	£10.80
8lb	£11.20
10lb	£11.60
12lb	£11.95
15lb	£13.60

BERKLEY BIG GAME
10lb - 1500 yds	£15.99
12lb - 1175 yds	£15.99
15lb - 900 yds	£15.99

HAIR BRAID

Ideal Braided Hair Material
Green x 50 yds	£1.80
Brown x 50 yds	£1.80
Black x 50 yds	£1.80

EAGLE ECHO SOUNDERS

FISH I.D. 2
★ Ultra wide display screen
★ Displays fish in 3 symbol sizes
★ Curved screen to reduce glare
★ Five display models
★ Fish alarm
★ Chart alarm
★ Continuous depth readout
★ Five 200M-in ranges
★ Wide angle transducer

★ Back-lighted display
★ Totally waterproof
★ Portable unit has own battery pack and suction-cup transducer
★ Full 1 year warranty

FISH I.D. 2	£224.95
FISH I.D. 2 Portable	£259.95

MAGNA 2
★ Ultrawide display screen
★ High resolution display
★ Advanced fish I.D. feature
★ Six display modes
★ Continuous depth display
★ Feet/metric readout
★ Depth alarm
★ Fish alarm
★ Moveable zoom ranges
★ Backlit display
★ Totally waterproof
★ Wide angle transducer
★ Portable unit has own battery pack and suction-cup transducer
★ Full 1 year warranty

MAGNA 2	£263.95
MAGNA 2 Portable	£329.95

ENTICER BASE MIXES

	1KG	5KG
50/50 Protein Mix	£4.50	£20.00
Fish Meal Mix	£4.50	£20.00
Spicey Fish Meal Mix	£4.50	£20.00
Bird Food (Yellow) Mix	£4.50	£20.00
Spicey Bird Food (Red) Mix	£4.50	£20.00

★ BULK DEALS — PLEASE RING ★

ENTICER BAIT ADDITIVES

Mineral Supplement x 175gms	£1.99
Liver Extract x 100gms	£2.99
Multi Flavour Enhancer x 100gms	£2.60
Liquid Sweetener x 50mls	£2.60
Liquid Sweetener x 250gms	£10.50
Liquid Emulcifier x 50mls	£2.60
Powder Dyes x 50grms Red/Yellow/Orange/Black/White/Green/Blue/Brown	£2.99

PREMIER BAITS

	1KG	2KG
Fish Base Mix	£5.20	£10.00
Salmon Fish Base Mix	£5.75	£11.00
Spiced Fish Base Mix	£5.75	£11.00
Marine Mix	£5.75	£11.00
Fish Fodder	£4.20	£8.00
Supreme Fish Mix	£7.50	£14.50
Aquatic Formulae	£8.65	£16.50
Summer Pro 65	£6.90	£13.00
Winter Pro 90	£10.66	£20.50
Spiced Cypro Seed	£6.90	£13.00
Salmon Seed Mix	£5.75	£11.00
Fruit Seed Mix	£5.75	£11.00
Savoury Seed Mix	£5.75	£11.00

★ Bulk Deals — Phone For Prices ★

PREMIER FISH OILS

Fish Feed Inducing Oil	£5.50
Noddoil	£11.00
Pure Salmon Oil	£12.00
Facid Oil	£5.50
Crunt Oil	£5.50
Japanese Fish Oil	£5.50
P.D.F.A. Supplement Oil	£10.00

SOLAR TACKLE BAITS

SAVAY SEED MIXES
	1KG	3KG
Red Mix	£7.45	£18.95
Yellow Mix	£6.95	£17.95
Spiced Seed Mix	£6.95	£17.95
Quench Mix	£6.95	£17.95
Neptune Mix	£6.45	£15.95

MIX MASTERS
	100 MLS
Squid/Octopus/Koi	£8.90
White Chocolate	£6.50
Golden Plum	£4.50
Esterblend 12	£4.90
Stimulin Amino Compound	£4.90
Stimulin Amino/Garlic	£4.90
Liquid Candy Sweetner	£8.90

POWDERED ADDITIVES
	4 ozs
Candy Sweetner	£4.50
White Chocolate	£4.90
Fresh Fruit	£4.00

KRYSTON ADDITIVES

Ambio 125 mls	£3.50
Ambio 500 mls	£11.00

BAIT MAKING EQUIPMENT

Gardner Sausage Guns	£8.85
Spare Cartridge	£1.50
Gardner Deluxe Sausage Guns	£28.95
Long Base Rollaballs 12/14/16/18/20/22 or 24m	£7.50
Giant Rollaballs 21' x 15' 12/14/16/18/20/22 or 24m	£29.99
Measuring Pippettes x 3	£1.00
Poly Pops	£1.00
Atomizer Spray & Bottle	£1.75
Re-Sealable Boilie Bags	
Sizes: 1000 boilie x 10	£0.75
Sizes: 300 boilie x 10	£0.55
Bait Soak Tubs — Watertight	£0.75

ENTICER STANDARD FLAVOURS

Apricot Sorbet	Malted Hops
Bacon Grill	Maple Syrup
Banana Split	Marachino
Black Juice	Marzipan
Butyric Acid	Mezzo (Curry)
Canadian Maple	Mulberry Pie
Caribbean Fruit	Optimum
Cassia	Original Golden Syrup
Cognac	Peach Melba
Condensed Milk	Phenol
Corn-on-the-Cob	Red Berries
Creamy Butter	Sand Eel
Dairy Cream	Sticky Treacle
Eastern Spice	Strawberry Jam
Fresh Kiwi	Sweet Mango
Gorgonzola	Tahiti (Coconut)
Hazelnut Whip	Tigernut
Honeycombe	Toffee Fudge
Juicy Fruit	Tropical Fruit (Guava)
Kairo	Waldorf (Walnut)
Marac	Wasp Grub
Madura	Yackam (Pineapple)

50ML BOTTLE	£2.50
250ML BOTTLE	£10.00

ENTICER E.A. FLAVOURS

Tropical Fruit	Redcurrant
Huckleberry	Lychee
Medlar	Coco-De-Mer

50ML BOTTLE	£5.25
250ML BOTTLE	£21.00

ENTICER ESSENTIAL OILS

Geranium Oil per 20ml	£4.65
Bergamot Oil per 20ml	£4.65
Clove Oil per 20ml	£3.99
Cinnamon Bark Oil per 20ml	£3.99
Black Pepper Oil per 20ml	£7.85
Peppermint Oil per 20ml	£4.65
Juniper Berry Oil per 20ml	£4.99
Nutmeg Oil per 20ml	£4.65
Rosemary Oil per 20ml	£3.99
Sage Oil per 20ml	£4.99
Spearmint Oil per 20ml	£3.65

MAESTRO BOILIES

STANDARD RANGE - 200 x 14mm
Cream Continental	£4.35
Pina Colada	£4.35
Tropicana Oils	£4.35
Yellow Bird Spice	£4.35
Honey Syrup	£4.35
Strawberry Oil	£4.35
Tuitti Fruitti	£4.35

PROFESSIONAL RANGE - 18mm
Cream Continental	£10.99
Pina Colada	£10.99
Tropicana Oils	£10.99
Yellow Bird Spice	£10.99
Honey Syrup	£10.99
Strawberry Oil	£10.99
Tuitti Fruitti	£10.99

BULK PACKS - 1000 x 14mm
Cream Continental	£18.50
Pina Colada	£18.50
Tropicana Oils	£18.50
Yellow Bird Spice	£18.50
Honey Syrup	£18.50
Strawberry Oil	£18.50
Tuitti Fruitti	£18.50

★ Large Bulk Deals — Please Phone ★

DON'T PAY A PENNY FOR 90 DAYS!!
NO DEPOSIT REQUIRED — UP TO 48 MONTHS TO PAY
PLEASE WRITE OR PHONE FOR DETAILS
Available on all orders over £250 — Licensed Credit Broker

CARRIAGE TERMS

All orders over £15.00	Add £3.00
All orders under £15.00	Add £1.50
Base Mixes 1-30 kilos	Add £3.00
Boilies 1-50 bags	Add £3.00
48 Hour Service	Add £5.50
24 Hour Service	Add £8.00

23, Bath Street, Leamington Spa, CV31 3AE
Telephone: (0926) 832328 Fax: (0926) 313117

NUTRABAITS

BAIT CATALOGUE AND NEW PRODUCTS FOR 1992

BAIT 1992-93
THE OFFICIAL PUBLICATION OF NUTRABAITS
Available 1st May 1992

120 pages of field testing reports, detailed product information, superb colour and black and white photographs and our up to date stockist list, in addition to contributions from the following:

Brian Skoyles	Baz Griffiths
Russ Widgington	Julian Cundiff
Dave Moore	Dave Colledge
Tony Hamshaw	Graham Slater
Kim Ludbroke	Dr Rex Elgood
Lee Jackson	Ken Townley
Tim Paisley	Joe Bertram
Kevin Green	Bill Cottam
Richard Skidmore	Andy Pratt
Cliff Roberts	Arnout Terlouw
Ian Selby	Mark Pidgeley
Richard Bourne	Richard Harris
Rob Ness	Dave McMillan
Andy Lovel	Hugh Parkin

THE ELITE RANGE
★ Cream
★ Peanut
★ Liver
★ Maple
★ Salmon
★ Saffron

THE COMPLETE FOOD OIL
As Formulated by LEE JACKSON

BULK FOOD OILS
NOW WITH ADDED ANTI-OXIDANTS

THE CAJOUSER RANGE
★ SPICE
★ FRUIT
★ SWEET

THE NUTRAFRUITS
★ Tropical
★ Apricot
★ Pineapple

MULTIMINO *with* **PPC**

PRICE £3 plus £1.00 p&p

BAIT 1992/93 can be obtained directly from us or from any NUTRABAITS stockist

Nutrabaits, 25-27 Fife Street, Wincobank, Sheffield S9 1NN

For Further Details Telephone 0742 422611

THE BIG CARP LIST

CHRIS BALL

The full 40lb-plus list and a review of last season's biggies, every single one over FORTY pounds in weight!

Chris Yates eventual record carp at 40lb exactly in 1972

Well... What a tremendous carp fishing season it's been, with so many huge carp coming to the bank. All told at least 26 carp all over forty pounds in weight have been recorded. Several of these carp have never been caught before over forty pounds and at least one fish is a complete newcomer to the *Big Carp List*, so all bodes well for the future.

As usual the start of the season saw a rush of outsized carp, the first of which came from Leisure Sport's Horton carp syndicate lake near Heathrow Airport. John Moult, the angler concerned, was double-quick off the mark, the fish coming out just 20 minutes after the start. Weighing a mighty 44lb 4oz this old campaigner looked in great condition (the fish as well as John!). The very next day far away in Essex a new *English Record common carp* of 45lb 12oz was caught by Damian Clarke. What a fantastic looking fish, and really a dream come true for young Damian who had set his heart on this carp for some time. June also saw long time carpman Bruce Ashby capture the best carp of his career with his first, and I'm sure not the last, forty pounder. Bruce's mirror went 40lb 10oz and came from 'you know where', (Harrow) in the Colne Valley.

Yateley, that marvellous complex of gravel pits on the Surrey/Hants border, as usual is never out of the carp limelight for long, in June carp fanatic Don Orriss of nearby Camberley really set the carp world alight with the North Lake monster. This fish, which is still (after ten years!), the largest known carp alive, came out at it's best ever weight – 46lb 1oz. That makes Don the sixth man ever to catch TWO different carp each over forty pounds in weight... Phew! Yateley scored again, within a week of Don's fish, when a young lad named Adrian Furze landed the Pad Lake whopper, this time a little smaller than usual, not that Adrian was complaining at 40lb 2oz.

Next, a magical 40lb fish came from a big gravel pit in Gloucestershire. The angler was carp specialist Mike Willmott, one who made his name by catching most, if not all of the famed Ashlea Pool carp. Mike's monster weighed 43lb 8oz and proved what many people knew about this exciting gravel pit – it contained whoppers! Before the month of June was out that famous Colne Valley gravel pit, Harrow, produced two *forty pounders*, Ray Sherrat and Graham White were the lucky anglers.

July saw the earlier Gloucestershire carp on the bank again, Lee Tomlinson banked the beauty at 42lb 12oz and made Rob's *Big Carp* front cover.

July also saw an extraordinary carp caught. Yes Wraysbury, that huge ultra-hard gravel pit in Middlesex gave up a fish to its most successful carp angler. Peter Springate, with help from Richard Skidmore, brought to the bank an unknown monster weighing 45lb 6oz. A totally staggering carp...
I'm lost for words!

Horton's biggest carp (*Jack*) made a mistake *twice* during July, first to Matthew McKeown (he'd already caught it before from Longfield, making him the first angler to catch the same forty from two different waters!). Later in the month Phil Thompson added this carp, at 42lb 6oz, to his considerable list of big fish.

Duncan Kay's big carp water at Higham Ferrers near Northampton was unfortunately closed the year before, but Duncan made sure the carp had a good new home only just down the road. It was from this water that long time carp angler Malc Rooker caught the biggest carp from its new home at exactly 40lb. Horton provided a new forty pounder in August, *The Parrot* – always tipped as a true

63

Right:
The classical big carp,
Don Orriss with the
Yateley North Lake mirror at 46lb 1oz

Below:
Andy Little makes history
with Norfolk's first recorded 40lb carp

BIG CARP LIST
Copyright Chris Ball

FORTY POUND PLUS CARP

Left hand letters indicate repeat captures

	WEIGHT	CAPTOR	LOCATION	DATE		WEIGHT	CAPTOR	LOCATION	DATE
A	51-08-0 (M)	Chris Yates	Redmire Pool	June 1980		41-12-0 (M)	Thomas Gelston	Hainault	November 1985
O	46-12-0 (M)	Richard Lloyd	Surrey Pond [*]	March 1990	N	41-12-0 (L)	Robin Dix	Yateley Car Park Lake	June 1985
B	46-02-0 (L)	Pete Richards	Erehwon	August 1989	D	41-12-0 (M)	Dave Whibley	Longfield	1989
C	46-01-0 (M)	Don Orriss	Yateley North Lake	June 1991	K	41-12-0 (M)	Alan Taylor	Mid-Northants	June 1990
C	45-12-0 (M)	Ritchie McDonald	Yateley North Lake	October 1984	I	41-12-0 (M)	Martin Gardener	Horton	November 1991
F	45-12-0 (C)	Damian Clarke	Snake Pit	June 1991	C	41-10-0 (M)	Jan Wenczka	Yateley North Lake	August 1981
C	45-08-0 (M)	Tony Moore	Yateley North Lake	July 1990	R	41-10-0 (M)	Chris Boland	Herts Club Water	January 1992
	45-08-0 (M)	Albert Romp	Savay	June 1990	M	41-09-0 (M)	Ritchie McDonald	Yateley Pad Lake	March 1991
	45-06-0 (M)	Peter Springate	Wraysbury No. 1	July 1991		41-08-0 (M)	Andy Grant	Herts Club Water	October 1990
	45-04-0 (M)	Peter Davis	Herts Club Water	November 1991	F	41-08-0 (C)	David Westerman	Snake Pit, Essex	June 1988
B	45-02-0 (L)	Ray Stone	Erehwon	December 1986	J	41-08-0 (M)	Kevin Nash	Silver End Pit	June 1985
	45-02-0 (M)	Ray Sherrat	Herts Club Water	June 1991		41-08-0 (M)	Alan ?[***]	Stanstead Abbot	December 1989
O	45-02-0 (M)	Richard Lloyd	Surrey Pond	July 1991	F	41-08-0 (C)	Phil Harper	Snake Pit, Essex	September 1989
B	45-00-0 (L)	Mark Fitzpatrick	Erehwon	June 1989		41-08-0 (M)	Andy Little	Yew Tree Lake	January 1992
B	45-00-0 (L)	Mark Fitzpatrick	Erehwon	July 1989	C	41-05-0 (M)	Chris Riddington	Yateley North Lake	October 1980
B	45-00-0 (L)	Ray Stone	Erehwon	July 1987		41-04-0 (M)	Andy MacTavish	Colne Valley Club Lake	October 1990
B	44-14-0 (L)	Ray Stone	Erehwon	November 1986	I	41-04-0 (M)	Matthew McKeown	Horton	July 1991
B	44-12-0 (L)	Keith Longden	Erehwon	August 1987	L	41-04-0 (M)	Jonathan Leigh	Lyne Lake	October 1978
C	44-08-0 (M)	Graham Mountain	Yateley North Lake	March 1989	B	41-00-0 (L)	Mark Fitzpatrick	Erehwon	September 1984
C	44-08-0 (M)	Nick Lee	Yateley North Lake	1989		41-00-0 (M)	Peter Wilson	Withy Pool	June 1990
	44-06-0 (M)	Ray Greenwood	Henlow Grange	June 1984	K	41-00-0 (M)	?[****]	Mid-Northants	June 1990
C	44-08-0 (M)	Gary Pails	Yateley North Lake	June 1984	K	40-12-0 (M)	Dave MacIntyre	Mid-Northants	October 1989
D	44-04-0 (M)	Steve Allcott	Longfield	December 1989	N	40-12-0 (L)	Don Orriss	Yateley Car Park Lake	October 1989
C	44-04-0 (M)	Dave Baker	Yateley North Lake	1985		40-12-0 (M)	Steve Hale	MOD Aldermaston	1987
I	44-04-0 (M)	John Moult	Horton	June 1991		40-12-0 (M)	Wayne Harris	Leicestershire Water	August 1991
O	44-02-0 (M)	Richard Lloyd	Surrey Pond	July 1990	M	40-10-0 (M)	Jock White	Yateley Pad Lake	1989
B	44-00-0 (L)	Mark Fitzpatrick	Erehwon	June 1987	H	40-10-0 (M)	Jon Holt	Longfield	1982
	44-00-0 (C)	Richard Walker	Redmire Pool	September 1952		40-10-0 (M)	Bruce Ashby	Herts Club Lake	June 1991
I	44-00-0 (M)	Steve Burgess	Horton	June 1990	K	40-10-0 (M)	Steve Gombocz	Mid-Northants	March 1992
	43-13-8 (C)	Chris Yates	Redmire Pool	August 1972	G	40-08-0 (M)	Kevin Clifford	Sandholme Pool	1983
C	43-10-0 (M)	Terry Pethybridge	Yateley North Lake	August 1991	A	40-08-0 (M)	Eddie Price	Redmire Pool	September 1959
C	43-09-0 (M)	Wayne Dunn	Yateley North Lake	October 1991	H	40-08-0 (M)	Colin Swaden	Longfield	October 1980
Q	43-08-0 (M)	Mike Willmott	Frampton	June 1991	F	40-08-0 (C)	Zen Bojko	Snake Pit, Essex	1988
B	43-08-0 (L)	Ray Stone	Erehwon	September 1985	E	40-08-0 (L)	Bernie Stamp	Herts Club Water	July 1987
E	43-08-0 (L)	Keith O'Conner	Herts Club Lake	October 1984	D	40-08-0 (M)	Matthew McKeown	Longfield	July 1989
C	43-08-0 (M)	Brian O'Bourn	Yateley North Lake	1989		40-08-0 (M)	Dave Cumpstone	Wraysbury No 1	June 1990
C	43-04-0 (M)	Steve Brown	Yateley North Lake	October 1989	I	40-08-0 (M)	Geoff Ball	Horton	September 1990
C	43-04-0 (M)	Adrian Tilbury	Yateley North Lake	July 1984	N	40-08-0 (L)	Ritchie McDonald	Yateley Car Park Lake	March 1991
B	43-04-0 (L)	Gary Morgan	Erehwon	August 1986	D	40-04-0 (M)	Robert Stock	Longfield	1985
C	43-04-0 (M)	Sam Fox	Yateley North Lake	September 1984	D	40-04-0 (M)	Richard Johnson	Longfield	1985
C	43-04-0 (M)	Ray Fuller	Yateley North Lake	July 1987		40-04-0 (M)	Steve Kearvell	Pit 2	June 1988
G	43-04-0 (M)	Clive Gibbins	Sandholme Pool	1984	G	40-04-0 (M)	Kevin Clifford	Sandholme Pool	1984
	43-04-0 (M)	AN Other [**]	Kingsmead	July 1990		40-04-0 (M)	Nick West	Wraysbury No 1	1980
M	43-01-0 (M)	Peter Bond	Yateley Pad Lake	November 1990	J	40-04-0 (M)	Phil Harper	Silver End Pit	1984
B	43-00-0 (L)	Keith Longden	Erehwon	August 1986	E	40-04-0 (L)	Lee Jackson	Herts Club Water	1983
	43-00-0 (M)	Graham Mountain	Tri-lakes	1983	K	40-04-0 (M)	Alan Taylor	Mid-Northants	January 1989
L	43-00-0 (M)	Jonathan Leigh	Lyne Lake	July 1980	K	40-04-0 (M)	Kevin Maddocks	Mid-Northants	January 1990
C	42-12-0 (M)	Kerry Barringer	Yateley North Lake	1985	K	40-04-0 (M)	Dave Willet	Mid-Northants	July 1990
	42-12-0 (L)	Martin Symonds	Waltham Abbey	September 1976	A	40-03-0 (M)	Jack Hilton	Redmire Pool	July 1972
I	42-12-0 (M)	Bernard Blight	Horton	August 1990	H	40-03-0 (M)	Colin Swaden	Longfield	November 1980
Q	42-12-0 (M)	Lee Tomlinson	Frampton	July 1991	E	40-02-0 (L)	Paul Fickling	Herts Club Water	1985
	42-08-0 (M)	Nick Peat	Yateley North Lake	1985	D	40-02-0 (M)	John Allen	Longfield	July 1988
P	42-08-0 (M)	Bob Copeland	Herts Club Water	June 1990	D	40-02-0 (M)	Neil French	Longfield	December 1988
I	42-08-0 (M)	Phil Thompson	Horton	July 1991	R	40-02-0 (M)	Allan Partridge	Herts Club Water	September 1990
B	42-06-0 (L)	Vic Bailey	Erehwon	June 1985	M	40-02-0 (M)	Adrian Furze	Yateley Pad Lake	June 1991
	42-04-0 (M)	Clive Percival	Herts Club Water	June 1990	I	40-02-0 (M)	Richard Howell	Horton	August 1991
	42-04-0 (M)	Max Cottis	Savay	June 1990		40-02-0 (M)	John Meecham	Harefield	February 1992
B	42-04-0 (L)	Mark Fitzpatrick	Erehwon	October 1984		40-00-8 (M)	Ron Groombridge	Boxmoor	June 1966
B	42-04-0 (M)	Ray Stone	Erehwon	July 1986	B	40-00-0 (L)	Ian Longden	Erehwon	September 1984
	42-04-0 (M)	Mick Dorton	Herts Club Water	September 1990	A	40-00-0 (M)	John MacLeod	Redmire Pool	July 1972
D	42-00-0 (M)	John Allen	Longfield	December 1987		40-00-0 (M)	Henry Weeks	Peckham	July 1972
	42-00-0 (M)	Ray Clay	Billing Aquadrome	September 1966	D	40-00-0 (M)	Clive Williams	Longfield	August 1988
	42-00-0 (M)	Ken Hodder	Yateley Car Park Lake	October 1979	P	40-00-0 (M)	Graham White	Herts Club Water	June 1991
E	42-00-0 (L)	Zen Bojko	Herts Club Water	1984	K	40-00-0 (M)	Malc Rooker	Mid-Northants	August 1991
D	42-00-0 (M)	Terry Dempsey	Longfield	September 1989	I	40-00-0 (M)	Dave Lane	Horton	September 1991
D	42-00-0 (M)	Jon Holt	Longfield	August 1987	K	40-00-0 (M)	Steve Gombocz	Mid-Northants	February 1990
	42-00-0 (M)	Peter Holmyard	Horton	August 1991					

[*] Illegally caught
[**] Will this angler come forward?
[***] Alan .... who?
[****] Who is this angler?

CHRIS YATES – First angler to catch TWO different carp over 40lb (Redmire 1972 and 1980)
RITCHIE MCDONALD – First angler to catch THREE different carp over 40lb (Yateley 1984 and 1991)
KEN HODDER – Largest floater caught carp 42lb (Yateley Car Park Lake (1979)
MATTHEW MCKEOWN – First angler to catch the same 40lb from two different waters (Longfield 1989, Horton 1991)
HERTS CLUB WATER – First UK water to produce FIVE different forties

Hounslow Angling Centre

Ritchie McDonald available in the shop for advice and sales, every Thursday, Friday and Saturday.

KEVIN NASH
NEW Titan Carp Dome...............£211.92
NEW Titan Carp Bivvy...............£185.40
(Available June 1992)
BROLLY WRAPS
Brollywrap 50"............................£41.46
Happy Hooker Special 50"...£67.37
Happy Hooker Special Oval.£76.13
BROLLY OVERWRAPS
Nylon 45" MKII (zig)....................£52.54
Nylon 50" MKII (zig)....................£59.37
Canvas 45"................................£122.94
Canvas 50"................................£128.84
Happy Hooker Special 45"...£52.54
Happy Hooker Special 50"...£67.37
Happy Hooker Oval....................£79.36
UMBRELLAS
Oval..£97.20
Brollywrap Special 50"............£168.19
Brollywrap Special Oval..........£188.73
HOLDALLS
11' Std (with pouches)..............£44.17
12' Std (with pouches)..............£44.79
13' Std (with pouches)..............£47.86
11' Deluxe (padded with pouches)...£71.11
12' Deluxe (padded with pouches)...£72.41
13' Deluxe (padded with pouches)...£73.99
RUCKSACKS
NEW! Hooker Pursuit Rucksack..£99.00
Hooker Rucksack......................£84.99
Specialist Rucksack..................£59.47
Carp Carryall.............................£55.49
Carp Carryall Special................£44.93
Stalker Bag................................£25.83
Monster Specialist Carryall..£56.20
Full range of Kevin Nash products available on request

FOX INTERNATIONAL
BEDCHAIRS
NEW Ultra Deluxe D/Chair........£219.90
Super Deluxe...........................£189.90
Std Adjustable Level................£139.90
NEW Standard Bedchair............£99.90
CHAIRS
Super Adj. Level Hammock.......£74.90
Standard Adjustable Level........£49.90
NEW Lightweight Adj. Level......34.90
NEW! BIVVY SYSTEMS
Super Bivvy.............................£154.90
Super Brolly............................£131.90
Super Brolly In Fill....................£54.90
ACCESSORIES
NEW Super Pod..........................£47.50
Rod Pod Telescopic..................£34.50
Rod Pod Standard....................£26.50
Swinger Bite.............................£11.90
Spare Colour Heads (red, yellow, green)...£3.90
Sleeping Bag and Foot Cover...£48.99
Deluxe Bed Cover.....................£48.99
Load System Trolley.................£97.27
Load System Straps...................£9.90
Jekk Shelter 50"........................£81.64
–30° Sleeping Bag..................£134.00
–20° Sleeping Bag...................£89.90
–10° Sleeping Bag...................£49.90
NEW Rollerpault Catapult..........£12.90

H.A.C.
Rod Pod (black), folding and adjustable complete with Bank Sticks........£42.00

RODS
DAIWA AMORPHOUS
13' 3lb Test..............................£225.00
13' 2⅔lb Test............................£220.00
12' 2¾lb Test............................£215.00
12' 2½lb Test............................£215.00
12' 2¼lb Test............................£210.00
SPORTEX CARBON REGULAR
Full range Armalites...............P.O.A.
All less 10% for pair

REELS
Shimano Baitrunners
Aero 4500..................................£74.90
Aero 4000..................................£69.90
Aero 3500..................................£64.90
Aero 3000..................................£59.90
Aero GT 4500............................£99.90
Aero GT 4000............................£69.90
Aero GT 3500............................£89.90
Buy pairs P.O.A.
SS 3000 Tournament..............£175.00
Daiwa Baitrunner 2050X...........£49.99
PM 4000H..................................£85.99
Ryobi Project GT 8000..............£42.00

BITE ALARMS
OPTONICS
NEW Super XL............................£77.00
Plus full range P.O.A.
BITECH VIPER
Bitech Alarms...........................£49.95
NEW Bitech Sounder Box..........£34.95
Leads..............................Each...£5.00
Brass Bolt for Viper....................£4.50
Viper Ali Bolt/Dome...................£4.50
NEW!! DAIWA Sensitron............£71.74

STEADEFAST
Nu Brollie 50" Bivvy (with holdall, stormrods & cap fittings)......................£150.00
Nu Brollie MKII 45"....................£48.00
Nu Brollie MKII 50"....................£53.00
NEW! Nu Brollie
Storm Tent................................£99.99

E.T. TACKLE
Bivvy Dome (Best winter bivvy)...£99.90

ROMART
NEW Inflatable Carp Mat
The best there is!.....................£31.95

K J B PRODUCTS
2 Rod Pod..................................£62.95
3 Rod Pod..................................£66.95
3 Rod Pod (wide bar).................£69.95
Intruder Bivvy/Tackle Alarm......£41.00
NEW Bite Alarm (2 Rod).............£99.99
NEW Bite Alarm (3 Rod)...........£119.99

MAGNUM STAINLESS STEEL
Rod Pod with Bank Sticks.........£75.00
Buzzer Bars.....................from...£7.50
Needle Systems..............from..£21.00
Adjust Bank Stick...........from..£14.25
Stabiliser Bar..............................£7.50
Bivvy Pegs x 8..........................£12.00
Opti Polo Back Rests Full range available.......P.O.A.

BAITS
Full range boilies, flavours, ingredients, mixes, oils etc.
Richworth...............................P.O.A.
Premier...................................P.O.A.
Colne Valley...........................P.O.A.
Nutrabait................................P.O.A.
Ritchie McDonald..................P.O.A.
Zenon Bojko..........................P.O.A.
KMM..P.O.A.
Solar.......................................P.O.A.
Kryston Ambio.......................P.O.A.

WYCHWOOD TACKLE
NEW K2 Quiver..........................£31.50
NEW K2 Stalker.........................£29.50
Carp Quiver..............................£27.50
Carp System Select (11", 12", 13")...£65.50
Additional Pouches..................£18.50
Insider (12', 13')........................£69.50
Insider Deluxe (12', 13')............£84.50
K2 Rucksack...........................£129.95
Packer Rucksack......................£96.50
Ruckman Rucksack..................£79.50
Ruckman Rucksack (Lightweight)...£53.95
Stalker Bag...............................£29.50
NEW Redicat Boilie Pult..............£6.95
Reel Pouches.............................£5.25
Sack Weigh Sling.....................£13.95

COLEMAN PRODUCTS
Lamp (Unleaded) Twin Mantle...£49.95
Stove (Unleaded).....................£41.95
Stove (Multifuel).......................£55.95
Generator 550/550A/550B.........£6.50
Generator 508/700.....................£7.00

OWNER/HOOKS/KINRYU
NEW Eyed Owner Super Strong
(Special Point)..............(10).....£4.50
NEW Kinryu Size 4 to 15.............£1.98
NEW Owners Size 4 to 15...........£1.98
Ritchie McDonald Size 8/6/4.....£4.50
Drennan Starpoint 12 to 4.........£1.65
Barbless 12 to 4.........................£1.65
Partridge Full range..............P.O.A.

TORCHES
Petzel.......................................£18.50
Bivvy Lamp................................£4.75
Maglite Full Range.................P.O.A.

NEW TENT (2 MAN)
1861 DOME WITH EXTENSION
Size: 205 x 205 x 110 . Weight: 3.8kg
ONLY £90.00
(An improved model Dome Tent – front extension of 130cm shock corded fibre-glass rods)

SLEEPING BAGS
German Mummy Bag (with arms)........£25.00
Commando Bag (w/proof base)...£31.00
British SAS Bag (58" down filled)...£32.00
Israeli Mummy Bag..................£25.00
Coleman –20°..........................£99.00
Plus Fox range

ZENON BOJKO
RITCHIE McDONALD
READY MADE BOILIES
Shelf Life or Freezer Packs
14mm (Handy Packs).................£2.30
18mm (Handy Packs).................£2.30
20mm (Handy Packs).................£2.40
14mm (Standard Packs)............£4.85
18mm (Standard Packs)............£5.00
20mm (Standard Pack)..............£5.25
14mm (Bulk Bags)...................£18.35
18mm (Bulk Bags)...................£19.35
20mm (Bulk Bags)...................£20.35

NEW WYCHWOOD Boiliepult.......£6.95

Andy Little • Kryston • Big Game
Amnesia • Maxima • Drennan
Solar Stainless • E.T.
Barnett Black Widow
Cobra Throwing Stick • Fox • KJB
Terry Eustace • Gardner
Kevin Nash • Ivel Full Range
Rod Hutchinson • Water Edge
Tackle Rite • Shimano • Daiwa
DAM • Shakespeare • Optix
Plano Box's • Coleman Fuel
Swiss Army Knives • Glowbait
Books, Magazines and Videos
SOLAR TACKLE
Full range available
NEW Pod in stock......................£89.95

WHAT YOU CAN'T SEE WE CAN GET – OR HAVE! PLEASE RING

FREE CREDIT CHART
OVER £50 TO £100 UP TO 3 MONTHS TO PAY
OVER £100 UP TO 6 MONTHS TO PAY

HOW TO PAY
Choose period of payment using the chart on the left. Send full amount for goods ordered with the amount divided into equal payments. Cheques should not exceed £50.00 each and must carry customer's cheque card number and expiry date on each cheque. All goods advertised are available at either of our two branches for callers, with cheque card and proof of address.

MAIL ORDER FROM HOUNSLOW ANGLING CENTRE ONLY
— ESTABLISHED 25 YEARS — IMMEDIATE REFUND IF NIL-STOCK —

HOUNSLOW ANGLING CENTRE
MAIL ORDER DEPT, 265/7 BATH ROAD, HOUNSLOW, MIDDLESEX. TEL: 081-570 6156 and 081-570 8885

RICHMOND ANGLING CENTRE
360 TWICKENHAM ROAD, TWICKENHAM, MIDDLESEX. TEL: 081-892 4175

leviathan – finally made the grade and was caught by Peter Holmyard at 42lb.

Terry Pethybridge – a man with a mission – after spending three years in search of the Yateley North Lake monster... caught it. No one can deny Terry this fish and at 43lb 10oz he was all smiles.

Leicestershire came bursting onto the scene in August, young angler Wayne Harris hooked a 40lb 12oz mirror from a lake in the county.

The Horton biggie *Jack* yet again made a mistake, twice! First to Richard Howell and secondly to Dave Lane who finally got in front of this big carp with a piece of Chum Mixer. It should have been me... only joking Dave.

Wayne Dunn, the lad from up north who has been running amok down south, hit the jackpot when he caught the Yateley North Lake carp at 43lb 9oz. An angler to watch...

I know it's boring... but Horton's *Jack* made yet another visit to the bank in November when persevering carp angler Martin Gardener caught the fish at 41lb 12oz. Shortly after, in fact on bonfire night, Peter Davis landed a perfect monster from Harrow, it weighed 45lb 4oz... quite a fish.

That was the last forty pounder caught in 1991, but shortly after the new year Harrow yet again stamped its authority on the big carp scene with another huge carp weighing in a 41lb 10oz, the angler concerned Chris Boland had beaten his personal best by several pounds.

Shortly after this my old mate and ace carp angler Andy Little recorded a Norfolk record of 41lb 8oz as well as his first English carp over forty pounds! The fish came from the Carp Society's Yew Tree Lake... The lake's owner Norman Symonds tells me it might be a fish he stocked some six years ago... not one that was stocked – if you believe the rumours – a few hours before!

Into February and up pops Harefield lake in Middlesex with it's long awaited monster carp. It was the much loved fish named *Nelson* that finally pushed its weight over 40lb, with two ounces to spare. The equally famous Johnny Meecham was the angler who landed the carp.

The last forty pounder of the season came on 6th March and was caught from the well known Mid-Northants fishery run by Duncan Kay. It was *Two-Tone*, a fish already caught earlier in the season at exactly 40lb, however this time Steve Gombocz skillfully landed the whopper at 40lb 10oz. Incidentally, two winters ago Steve latched into the same fish, again it was a forty pounder.

One fish is missing from the list of big carp captures of last season, that's the Ehrwon leather, *Pinky*. I believe it's been caught twice, but as *Big Carp* went to press I've still not got my hands on the full details. No doubt these will follow soon.

As the season closed, we can look back on a vintage year, with the most carp *ever* recorded over forty pounds, where will it all end...

If you spot an inaccuracy in the Big Carp List or you have additional information on carp I don't have recorded, please contact me through the magazine.

The *Erehwon Leather*, Ray Stone with the beauty in December 1986 weighing 45lb 2oz

67

SOLAR TACKLE

BUZZER BARS
2 Rod 6" 8" 10"	£8.50
3 Rod 12" 15"	£10.95
3 Rod Adjustable Front	£20.95
Back	£20.95

EXTENDING BANKSTICKS
12"... £11.95 16"... £12.95 20"... £13.95

NEEDLE SYSTEMS
2 Rod ..... £19.50   3 Rod £23.50

THE SATELLITE 3 Rod   £39.95

INDICATOR BODIES (SOLAR BORE)
3/4" & 1" Acetol		£2.25
PTFE Flip Top	Small	£3.95
	Medium	£4.25
	Large	£4.50

All above available in Gardner bore

Guy Ropes	£4.95
Bivvy Pegs x 8	£10.95
Stabilizer	£5.50
Carp Sack Pegs x 2	£4.95

SAVAY SEED MIX
	1kg	3kg
Red Mix	£7.45	£18.95
Yellow Mix	£6.95	£17.95
Spiced Seed Mix	£6.95	£17.95
Quench Mix	£6.95	£17.95
Neptune Mix	£6.45	£15.95

MIX MASTERS
	100ml	500ml
Squid/Octopus		
Koi Rearer	£8.90	£34.00
White Chocolate	£6.50	£25.00
Golden Plum	£7.50	£15.00
Esterblend 12	£4.90	£17.00
Stimulin Amino Comp	£4.90	£17.00
Stimulin Amino w. Garlic	£4.90	£17.00
Liquid Candy Sweetner	£8.90	£34.00

NEW LITE-FLO BOBBINS
Yellow, Blue, Green, Red
Small and Large   £5.95

NEW PRODUCTS
Stainless Opti Bolts	£2.95
Stainless Backrest	£4.95
Adj Stabiliser	£6.95

KRYSTON

Ambio	125ml	£3.53
	500ml	£11.29
Merlin 20m		
8lb 10lb 12lb 15lb		£6.38
Silkworm 20m		
4lb 8lb 10lb 12lb 15lb		£6.89
Silkworm Ultra Soft	12lb	£6.89
	25lb	£7.40
Super Silk	14lb	£5.99
Multistrand 75ft	15lb	£6.89
No Tangle Gel		£3.02
Superstiff		£3.25
Quick-silver — Snag Shock Leader		
	25lb	£10.17
	35lb	£10.68
	45lb	£11.19

SYLCAST SORREL LINE
1000m spools
6lb	£10.25	7lb	£10.75
8lb	£10.95	9lb	£11.75
11lb	£12.25	13lb	£12.75
15lb	£13.25		

250m one shot spools
6lb, 7lb, 8lb, 9lb, 11lb & 13lb   all £4.05

Sylcast Specimen also available in bulk spools

MAXIMA
660yd
6lb	was £13.50	now £9.90
8lb	was £13.99	now £10.40
10lb	was £14.45	now £10.90
12lb	was £14.99	now £11.40
15lb	was £16.99	now £12.40

HOOK-LENGTH MATERIAL
Drennan Braid	£6.19
Drennan Dacron	£2.00
Gama Braid	£5.95
6, 8, 10, 12, 15, 25 All breaking strains	
Gardner Dacron	£6.00
Multiple Fibre	£5.00
The Edge 6lb,10lb, 15lb per spool	£7.99

RIG BITS
ET All sizes Silicone Tube	99p
Drennan Rig Tube	77p
Putty	£1.05

HOOKS
Hutchie
OW	£3.80
WW	£4.60

Partridge
WS	£1.80
Jack Hilton	£2.90
Piggy Backs	£1.80
Ritchie Macs	£4.50
ET Helicopter Beads	£1.45
Nash Floating Beads	£0.80
Shock Beads (Rubber)	£0.70

BAIT BITS
KJB Stainless Gun	£30.00
Gardner Gun	£8.99
NEW Gardner Supa-Roller	£29.99
Long Base Rollers	
12, 14, 16, 18, 20- 24mm	£7.65
Waters Edge Super Roller	£45.00
Side Winder	£48.00
Poly Pops Nash	£0.99
Poly Pops KJB	£1.50
Nash Rig Foam	£0.99
Marvic Boily Punch	£1.40
Spare Foam for above	£0.99
Jumbo Boily Bags	£5.00
Camo Boily Bags	£5.50

UNHOOKING MATS
Romart Deluxe	£30.00
Nash Carp	£10.71
Nash Monster	£12.80
ET Carp	£11.87
Ritchie Mat	£10.79
Hutchie Carryall/Mat, both sizes	£62.00

NEW PEAK STOVE
Runs on unleaded petrol
£39.50

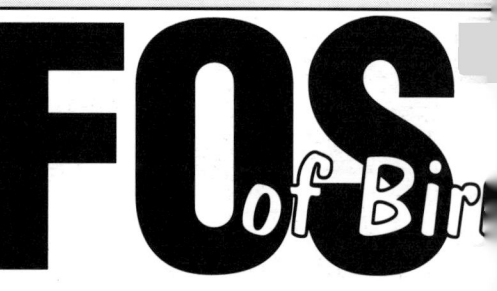

FOS of Bir

4 months Interest Free Credit

Over night carriage £10

266 KING'S ROAD, KINGST
TEL: 021-355 333

Why not take advantage of our Four Months Interest Fre
cheques, the first dated with order and the balance sprea

Roach
Quality Bivvies and Stormsides
45" Brolly Wrapover	£63.95
50" Brolly Wrapover	£73.95
45" Wrapover/Stormside Groundsheet	£19.25
50" Wrapover/Stormside Groundsheet	£19.25
50" 'Camouflage' Wrapover	£94.75
50" Deluxe 'Camouflage' Wrapover	£120.95
45" Stormsides	£33.95
45" Stormsides with door	£43.75
50" Stormsides	£37.75
50" Stormsides with door	£47.05
50" Stormsides with door (with Velcro sewn on Stormsides and included to sew to umbrellas)	£66.95
45" Mini Stormsides	£21.95
45" Mini Stormsides (with Velcro sewn on Stormsides and included for sewing on to umbrella)	£30.25
50" Mini Stormsides	£22.95
50" Mini Stormsides (with Velcro sewn on Stormsides and included for sewing on to umbrella)	£31.45

BIVVY DOMES
Hutchie	£149.90
ET	£99.00

Supa Brolly In-Fill	£54.90
Supa Bivvy	£145.90
Specimen Brolly	£72.95
Jekk Shelter to fit 50" umbrella	£79.90
Super Brolly	£124.90
Storm Pole Attachment for Fox	£6.50
Storm Pole Attach. for non-Fox	£6.50
Power Spike	£14.95
Tilt Mechanism	£8.95
Nylatec Repair Kit	£4.95
Groundsheet	£34.90
All-Season Door Panel	£19.90

GARDNER POP-UP BIVVY
NEW can be assembled in 10 seconds
Lightweight – one of the best on the market   £130.00

SLEEPING BAGS
Hutchie Bag	£135.00
German Army	£30.0
Fox -30° C rated	£129.90
Fox -10° C rated	£99.90

FOSTERS HAND-BUILT RODS

As you will see below, a huge range of makes are offered (many more in stock).
Please phone for your choice of rods, handle type, rings and whipping colour.
You may also like your name on the rod or test curve in italic lettering.

ARMALITE
11'	1 1/2 lb	
12'	1 3/4 lb	
12'	2 1/4 lb	
12'	2 1/2 lb	Phone
12'	2 3/4 lb	for
12'	3 lb	quote
13'	2 lb	
13'	2 1/4 lb	
13'	2 1/2 lb	
13'	2 3/4 lb	
13'	3 lb	

North Western
CARBON & CARBON/KEVLAR
		Blank	Built
11'	1 1/4 lb	£69.00	£90.00
11'	1 1/2 lb	£69.00	£90.00
11'	1 3/4 lb	£69.00	£90.00
11'	2 lb	£69.00	£90.00
11'	2 1/4 lb	£75.00	£105.00
11'	2 3/4 lb	£75.00	£105.00
12'	1 1/4 lb	£72.00	£93.00
12'	1 1/2 lb	£72.00	£93.00
12'	1 3/4 lb	£72.00	£93.00
12'	2 lb	£72.00	£93.00
12'	2 1/4 lb	£78.00	£105.00
12'	2 3/4 lb	£78.00	£105.00

Add £28.00 for silicon rings

ARMALITE TOP GUN
		Blank	Built
12'	3 1/2 lb	£94.75	£185.00
12'	4 lb	£97.95	£139.00
13'	3 1/2 lb	£101.75	£144.00
13'	4 lb	£102.75	£144.00

NEW! BLACK MAX
12'	2 1/2 lb	£123.00	£179.00
12'	3 lb	£132.80	£189.95
13'	3 lb	£135.52	£194.00
13'	3 1/2 lb	£139.35	£196.00
13'	4 lb	£139.80	£196.95

ERS
ngham

NG, BIRMINGHAM, B44 0SA
AX: 021-321 2023

Order by phone using Access/Visa or send POs, cheques or cash

heme on orders over £30.00? Spread the cost over four
months post dated. (Or we post date your Access/Visa).

POSTAGE
Under £30 - £1
BAIT - £2.50 per kg
5kg+ - POA
Rods - £3

SPECIAL OFFER
SUNDRIDGE SUPER XL OPTONIC

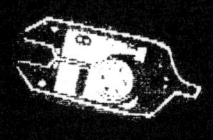

Was £77.00
OUR PRICE £58.00
Order now while stocks last

Rod HUTCHINSON
IMX RODS — THE BIZZO

12ft	2lb	£187.00
12ft	2¼lb	£187.00
12ft	2½lb	£197.00
12ft	3½lb	£197.00
13ft	2½lb	£197.00
13ft	3½lb	£215.00

GREY SHADOW RODS

12ft	2¼lb	£124.00
12ft	3½lb	£125.95
13ft	3½lb	£132.00

High Protection H/all 12'	£85.95
Puka Rucksack	£99.95

CYCLONE

One-piece (state size)	£185.95
Coverall	£82.95
Sleeping Bag	£135.00
Carryall & Unhooking Mat	£59.95
Dreamaker T-shirts	£7.95
Lift Bobbin (small)	£4.25
Lift Bobbin (large)	£5.25
Rod's annual catalogue	£2.95
New Hutchie Bivvy	£149.95

NEW Hutchie products available soon

NEW HUTCHIE HORIZON
12' 2½lb
Blank ... £68.60
Built by Fosters ... £99.90

SPORTEX
CARBON KEVLAR RODS

	Blank	Built
11' 1lb tc Tench/Barbel	£57.70	£113.95
11' 1¼lb tc LtCarp/Bar.	£66.70	£117.00
11' 2lb tc Med. Carp	£78.10	£128.00
11' 2¼lb tc Range Cp	£80.25	£134.00
11' 2¾lb tc Ext. Carp	£89.70	£143.00
12' 1lb tc Tench/Barbel	£70.20	£130.00
12' 1¼lb tc Lt. Cp./Bar.	£78.95	£135.00
12' 2lb tc Med Carp	£86.00	£141.00
12' 2¼lb tc Range Cp	£87.90	£155.00
12' 2¾lb tc Ext. Carp	£100.30	£160.00
12' 6" 3¼lb tc Pred Pike		£170.00
13' 2¼lb tc Range Cp	£105.48	£167.00
13' 3lb tc Ext. Carp	£108.60	£180.00

Silicon Carbide Rings - phone for price

VIDEOS

Carp Fever 1, 2 & 3	each £14.95
Cat Fever	£19.95
Carp in Session at Birch Grove 1 and 2	each £14.95
The Catfish Expedition	£23.50
The Carp Experience	£23.50
La Carping *Andy Little*	£16.25
Carping on Particles *Andy Little*	£19.95
Bait *(Angling Publications)*	£16.25
Carp From the Start 1 & 2	each £15.99
Euro Carp Quest	£17.99
Yately Ya-Hoo Video	£17.99
Startin Carpin Parts 1 and 2	£15.95
Gravel Pit Carping *Andy Little*	£19.99

CARP OUTFITS

OPTION 1 Rod Pod, 2 12' rods, 2 reels, assorted bits, line/rings etc. **£160**
OPTION 2 1 rod, 1 reel plus above **£100**
OPTION 3 Abu Cardinal DM5 £33.99, Silstar 3512 £34.99, Rig Bits, Nashy etc £15.00 Total £83.98 **£73.98**

BOOKS

The Deepening Pool *Chris Yates*	£15.95
Big Carp *Tim Paisley*	£17.95
Tiger Bay *Rob Maylin*	£15.95
Fox Pool *Rob Maylin*	£18.95
Carp Now &and Then *Rod Hutchinson*	£18.95
Carp in Focus	£16.95
For the Love of Carp *The Carp Society*	£15.95
Carp Quest for the Queen	£17.95

BEEKAY SPECIALIST TITLES
Catfish, Tench, Carp, Eels, Pike, Bream each £10.95

Pike In Pursuit of Esox Lucius	£19.95
The Carp World Year Book	£9.95
Mega Pike *Eddie Turner*	£16.95

CARP IN DEPTH SERIES
Floater Fishing, Rigs and End Tackle, Carp Baits, Tackle and Tactics, Carp Waters all titles £5.95

Many more books and videos in stock

Wychwood Tackle

K2 Rucksack £110.00 →

K2 Stalker Bag	£27.50
Packer	£85.95
Ruckman	£69.95
Ruckman L/weight	£47.50
K2 Suits (all sizes)	£120.00
Holdall/Shoulder Bag	£42.50
Stalker Bag	£22.50
Carp Quiver	£23.00
System 11'/12'/13'	£55.85
Spare Pouches (as above)	£14.95
Wychwood Insider	£59.95
Insider Deluxe	£72.95

KEVIN NASH

Hooker Rucksack	£79.00
Small Rucksack	£52.00
Carryall Carp	£31.44
Specialist Carryall	£39.82
Stalker Bag	£22.91
Holdalls	
11', 12', 13' standard	£46.00
12' Hooker Deluxe	£75.00

KJB

2 Rod	£59.35
3 Rod	£64.85
3 Rod 'Special'	£89.95
Extension Legs (pair)	£7.95
Main Bar Conversion	£8.95
Buzzer Bar Sets 2 Rod	£15.95
3 Rod	£18.95
3 Rod 'S'	£21.95
Rod Rest Heads 'U'	£0.90
Indicator Needles (each)	£1.40

SHIMANO

Baitrunner GT 3500	Phone for quote	£81.90
Baitrunner GT 4000		£89.90
Baitrunner GT 4500		£91.90

SCALES

Happy Hookers 56lb	£47.00
Happy Hookers 112lb	£47.00
Avons	£25.00

FOX INTERNATIONAL

Super Deluxe Bedchair	£179.90
NEW! Std Deluxe Bedchair	£129.90
NEW! Supa Adjusta Level Hammock Chair	£69.90
NEW! Std Adjusta Level Chair	£49.90
Replacement Feet for Std and SDL Chair (per 4)	£3.60
Rod Lok	£6.40
Swinger Bite Indicator Mk2	£11.30
Replacement Swinger Heads Red, Yellow, Green	£3.75
3 in 1 Luminous Monkeys Red, Yellow, Green, Clear	£7.50
Fox Pod 30" Fixed	£24.90
Fox Pod 48" Adaptable	£31.90
Load Shift Trolley	£94.90
Specimen Brolly	£72.95
Jekk Shelter	£79.90
Storm Pole Attach. (pair) for Fox	£6.50
for non-Fox products	£6.50
Std Umbrellas	
Tilt and Screw Power Spike	£14.95
All-Season Door	£19.90
Groundsheet	£34.90
Weigh Bar	£5.35
Needle Bar System	£8.60
Stainless Needles	
2 pack	£5.75
3 pack	£7.75

STANDARD BEDCHAIR ONLY £99.99

BITE ALARMS

Optonics	
Super XL £77.00 SAVE £19.00	£58.00
Super Compact	£58.95
Special Hi & Low	£48.95
Magnetronic	£44.95
Std Compacts Hi & Low	£37.95
Hi-Tech Viper Buzzers	£49.95
Hi-Tech Sounder Boxes	£35.00
Deluxe 4 Rod Sounder	£39.95
m Leads	£4.50
Ghetto Blaster	£19.99
T Back Biter	
ingle Standard	£26.75
ingle Deluxe	£33.75
ouble Standard	£32.75
ouble Deluxe	£39.75

North Western
CARBON & CARBON/KEVLAR

Landing Net complete with mesh arms, spreader block handle

36"	£42.16
42"	£44.44
50"	£51.68
5' or 6' Handle	£18.95
Arms	
36"	£11.35
42"	£11.35
50"	£13.98
Spreader Block	£3.50
Meshes	

	Hex	Hex/Micro	Fast Flow
36"	£9.50	£11.90	£8.20
42"	£11.50	£14.90	£10.80
50"	£16.50	£18.70	£15.20

ESSEX
E S S A Y S

J T A Y L O R

In the autumn of '89, I decided to revisit an old flame just for old time's sake. The old flame in question lived out in Essex and still had a lot of secrets but was decidly not virginal! I was bored with my more local relationships getting nowhere, so a change was definitely in order. Initially, a reconnaissance trip was the best plan to check out what the locals were doing, try to get some ideas on baits and rigs and give the local ladies' water ski team the benefit of my advice. Sunday traffic up the M11 was very light and a bright sunny day was set off nicely by a light westerly. Due to the woods on the western side of the lake, the surface should be flat, calm, perfect: The lake, my old flame, looked good, the cafe looked better, so after a quick fried breakfast I took a long walk up to the top of the lake. Heavily weed-fringed and shallow, it looked good but all the old pads had died away which was a pity. There was no cover left except the reeds and it was difficult to spot fish 20 feet out with eight foot high reeds. No real signs up in the shallows, so I made a quick check of the wetsuits and suntans on display next door at the ski club. Very nice! with a couple of beauties right in the edge... big thirties or low forties – lovely. Anyway back to the real world – all along the road bank, nothing was showing. By now the sun was well up, the natural smells of water and weed started to rise as well and everything slowed down for the midday heatwave. With all these warm springs we've had since about 1980 it can't be long before some real surprises show up ie Wraysbury? A 50lb from Staffordshire? Something like that.

I stopped for a chat with one of the locals whose rigs hung in

It was '83 when I first fished the lake

the butt rings, long links, hairs out of the eye, size sixes, no pop-ups. Those took me back to '83 when I first fished the lake! Having said that maybe he knew something I didn't, always best to keep an open mind!
"How's things?".
"Hard enough mate".
"Action at night still"?
"Yeah, very difficult this year. Most people have only caught one or two since July, just don't seem to be getting the pick ups. The boat (radio-controlled) helps get the baits (boilies) out to the middle or off the private point but even these areas are tough".

the hedge I heard a splash. Definitely carp. I ran to the field and looked out. Not more than 20 yards out was a big set of ripples, just past the end of a big old tree which had been blown in by the gales. Very interesting. Jumping fish middle of the day in a close area next to a snag. As I watched, up came another fish and tail-walked, a big common. Absolutely lovely. Did the chap on the corner cast to the fish, all of 45 yards? No! Almost unbelievable!

I sat on the tree and thought about it. About 15 feet in front of me, in 18 inches of water amongst the remnants of the

shot links seven... and neutral popped-up baits on size eight's. Experience had taught me these fish had soft mouths but I had not found a real solution. Some patterns worked better than others, top of the pile was the Au Lion D'or type, mimicked by the Drennan boilie. I preferred the Au D's. All packed and ready to go.

That first trip proved to be a real revelation. I arrived at the lake late Friday evening just after dark and found the spot occupied... typical. I decided to set up on the road bank and cast across to the pads. This I did, only to find the other angler,

"Nobody fishing particles"?
"Oh no, we've all agreed that particles ruin the fishing, so we're not going to use them".
"Ruin the fishing, crickey! Do the fish get ill or just die?"
"Well we think they get ill. Full of hard peanuts or maples, they spend all their time trying to digest the particles, get tired and don't feed on the boilies. They are losing weight because two guys used sacks full of tigers and caught some but feed all the rest for June and July".

Was this guy for real? I knew some of the locals were short on experience but this was a joke. I excused myself and walked on into the field. As I walked down

old pads, something moved. I stood slowly and put on the glasses. Another fish, a big double by the look of it.

Twenty minutes later another fish rolled halfway between the tree and the pads. Now, I'm not brilliant but even I could see that this was a situation for the soft rods and some daylight effort on a 'night' water. The fish were dying for it!

Back home the next Wednesday, out come the... and pots and pans and I cooked up some carp food. Leaving it to soak I went to check the tackle. 12 feet one and a quarter test curve compounds, 15 pound line, two ounce leads, 12 pound Dacron

one of the largest blokes for miles, had an extra rod in the pads, oops! He disagreed with my tactics needless to say and called me all kinds of a stroke puller! This was amicably resolved. He told me to wind in and go away, or the Essex equivalent. Anyway he carried on and I fished somewhere else. In the morning I was in his swim as soon as he even thought of leaving. I even helped carry his gear.

As soon as he was gone, I had the rests in and carefully balanced two from the eye hook rigs. One went out next to the sunken tree where the fish jumped, at the bottom of a slight ledge.

Returning the sparsely scaled mirror

About ten yards. The next was swung out under the overhanging tree to the right in about two feet of water. Both lines were left slack with light indicators at the bottom of the needles. Three pouch-loads of tigers around each bait and the scene was set. The time was about 11am.

By 12.30 it was pleasantly warm and a couple of shadows had drifted in over the close rod and kept dropping out of sight. A take looked imminent! An hour later it still looked imminent! Nothing happened and the fish disappeared. I lost interest, things looking less promising by the minute.

By now it was 4.30pm and I wandered off to water a bush. As I wandered back the local boy racers roared past and disappeared into the gathering evening, leaving only the long steady tone of a Delkim, mine. The left hand reel was spinning steadily and I pulled into a strongly running fish. On and on for about 25 yards she went, past the tree and out in the lake, having gone left past the end of the tree, then round in a smooth arc back in front of me. No ripple as she came into the margin, normally a sign of a biggie for this lake. An abrupt about turn was fol-lowed by a vortex and me giving line.

The compound did its job and up she came, paddling round on her side. Unusually, a big miror. She weighed 112lbs plus. Maybe I should get a witness. A new set of scales might be an idea. I got both. Young Simon came along and we decided on 21lb 12oz. After a couple of photos and putting her back, Simon and I carried on chatting. His best so far was 13 or 14 pounds from a different lake and he was trying to work out how to catch from this lake. I took to him straight away as he never tried to get any exact information of what, where, how, etc. He volunteered his experience and invited discussion. I gave him some ideas and wondered if he thought anything of them. Little did I know that he was going to progress and experiment so quickly his results would be outstanding.

I cast out again, about 5.30 and sat back awaiting darkness when I thought about varying my approach; fishing at medium range with different boilies on various rigs, just for interest's sake, whilst concentrating on the daylight hours. Consequently it was a pleasant surprise to have another take, the indicator jabbing up end down as the reel spun. This fish went on short runs right and left but never really tried to get under the tree. At 18lbs, a nice common. With darkness falling, young Simon came round to say cheerio and ask if I was back next weekend. That was my plan so I told him so.

During the night nothing happened at all. No fish jumped close in or at range, and no fish were caught between the 18 rods being fished. I was knackered winding all that lot in! At 7am the close rods were out again and it looked like a nice sunny day. At 9am I was in the cafe having a quick fried breakfast, having left the rods in the care of big Andy, the guy I had the disagreement with the first night.

As soon as I was back in the swim I was in. 17lb 12oz common, it was going to be a lovely day! Two hours later the right hand rod was away then stopped. The line was tight and under the tree, there were little vortices appearing. A bit of pulling and tugging produced a bright golden common of 11lb. This was very entertaining as this was a growing fish, not one of the old stock and must have been bred in the lake. (Too small for anyone to 'stock'). Given the amount of stick the lake had taken from other sources, any successful breeding was a real miracle.Maybe there is hope for all lakes. As I slipped her back the left hand rod roared off. This fish ploughed around and generally wreaked havoc in the swim. I saw the fish quite clearly, a largish common with a half moon scar on its head. Right over the net, without being able to lift it, the hook pulled out. Oh well!

I knew that the swim needed time, so I checked both rods, put on new baits, got everything straight and cast out again.

Sitting in the sun, with a cup of tea, I wondered about the change in weather patterns. More mild winters, hotter, drier summers, falling water tables. This was October and it was 22C, sitting in shorts only, and wondering how much longer this could go on. In ten years time will we be sunbathing in November? Then December and moving the start of the close season back to

Long, and almost a leather

June? The answer? To go to the pub and have a beer or two because that's about as much as any of us can do to influence things and probably why a lot of older carp anglers drink a lot. On the other hand maybe they just enjoy beer!

Anyway, back in the lake the fish were moving again. A fish rolled out to the right, very close to the road bank reeds. Nobody moved or cast to it, despite 3 or 4 locals seeing the fish, and being within 60 yards or so. My confidence was not sky high as the swim had taken a beating and the afternoon was drawing on. The sun was dipping behind the trees and losing some of its warmth. Thinking about another cuppa did the trick and the left hand reel spun furiously, the rod top pulling round to point after the departing fish. Yet another I was thinking and the feeling that I could really murder them if I kept it up was getting stronger all the time. This fish, another good common, swam around a bit and I quickly netted her before she knew what was what. Looking inside the mouth the hook had been well back initially but had slid forward to the lip which gave me further concern about hooks pulling out of these soft mouthed fish. The peculiar thing was that some of the fish had much softer mouths than others. They appeared to be more of a spongy texture whereas the harder mouthed fish were smooth and polished. I can only assume that the differences were due to feeding habits or just inherited characteristics bodily differences, as in any other living thing. I ruled out some form of disease, as their mouths always healed quickly and perfectly.

On the scales she weighed 20lb 4oz and I consciously admitted that one of my goals had been realised. Another quick photo session with young Simon at the controls and I was about ready to make a move. The next weekend was to be full of sun, smiles and stupidity.

All too slowly Friday afternoon can round. I had a party to go to and ended up thoroughly enjoying myself. So much so that I slept off the effects and left at about 6.30am on Saturday morning. Even at this early hour it was obviously going to be a scorcher, so a quick check on the important items was in order. Sun tan lotion, comfy chair, towel, drink all OK. After a quick trip up the M11 I pulled up next to the hedge and walked down to *the spot*. There was Simon — but the look on his face was a picture. A mixture of surprise, guilt and pleasure. "I didn't know ... I mean ... sorry I ... er." "Don't worry Si," I said thinking 'what a star,' he's worried about jumping in 'my' spot. "You stay there matey, I'll fish off the platform in the reeds." Needless to say he was happy to do this but he offered to move twice more, an attitude which should be an object lesson to any angler young or old. If someone does some pioneering work in a new swim then the best thing you can do is be pleased for him and carry on doing your own thing. The very worst thing to do is jump straight into his swim, copy his methods and try to catch fish because of someone else's work. What do you learn by doing this? Nothing, except how quickly other anglers get pissed off! Ask yourself how often someone you meet comes onto one of the lakes you fish, does something totally new and catches lots of fish. Why did they catch them? Why did they leave? If you are honest, the

---

SOUTHERN ANGLING SPECIALISTS

CUSTOM RODS

Armalite
12' 2lb TC	£132.00
12' 2¼lb TC	£132.00
12' 2½lb TC	£134.00
12' 2¾lb TC	£138.00
12' 3lb TC	£143.00
13' 3lb TC	£148.00

Bruce & Walker Merlin Range
12' 2lb TC	£130.00
12' 2¼lb TC	£130.00
12' 6" 2¾lb TC	£135.00
13' 6" 3lb TC	£140.00

Tricast - Legend
12' 2lb TC	£142.00
12' 2¼lb TC	£142.00
12' 2½lb TC	£142.00
13' 3lb TC	£160.00

Romart
Unhooking Mat £32.00
Berkeley Big Game Line
10/12/15lb £15.99

HOOKS

Drennan Hooks
Super Specialist/10	£0.65
Boilie Hooks/10	£0.93
Starpoints/10	£1.85

Kevin Nash
Outpoints/25	£2.18
Mustad Carp/50	£3.25
Kamasan B175/25	£1.99

REELS

Shimano Baitrunner Aero
4500 GT	£91.99
4000 GT	£88.99
3500 GT	£81.99
Aerlex 8000 GT	£61.99

KRYSTON
Silkworm 20m 8/10/12/15lb	£6.89
Silkworm Ultra Soft 12lb	£6.89
Silkworm 20m 25lb	£7.40
Supersilk 14lb	£6.89
Merlin 8/10/12/15lb	£6.38
Multistrand	£6.89
No Tangle Gel	£3.02
Superstiff Gel	£3.02
Ambio 125mml	£3.60
Ambio 500ml	£11.20

OPTONICS
Super XL	£69.95
Super Compact	£59.95
Magnetonic	£44.95
Basic Compact	£29.95

WYCHWOOD TACKLE
K2 Rucksack	£123.00
K2 Stalker Bag	£28.00
Ruckman	£76.00
Ruckman Lightweight	£51.00
Packer	£91.50
Carp Quiver	£25.51
Stalker Bag	£22.99

SOLAR TACKLE
Full range of stainless steel products

Savay Seed Mix
Red Mix	£7.45
Yellow Mix	£6.95
Spiced Seed Mix	£6.95
Quench Mix	£6.95
Neptune Mix	£6.45

Mix Masters
Squid/Octopus/ Koi Rearer	£8.90
White Chocolate	£6.50
Golden Plum	£7.50
Esterblend 12	£4.90
Stimulin Amino	£4.90
Stimulin Amino/Garlic	£4.90
Liquid Candy Sweetener	£8.90

PREMIER BAITS

Base Mixes
Fish Base	£5.20
Marine	£5.75
Fish Supreme	£7.50
Summer Pro	£6.90
Spiced Cypro Seed	£6.95
Spiced Fish Mix	£5.75
Fish Fodder	£4.20
Aquatic Formula	£8.65
Winter Pro 90	£10.65
Salmon Fish Mix	£5.75

Oils - 500ml
Fish Feed Inducing Oil	£5.50
Salmon Oil	£11.00
Jap Fish Oil	£5.50
PDFA 200ml	£10.00
Nodd Oil	£11.00
Crunt Oil	£5.50

RING MICK OR STEVE FOR FRIENDLY ADVICE FOR ALL YOUR CARP FISHING PROBLEMS

MAIN STOCKISTS FOR:
NASH • FOX • GARDNER • WATERS EDGE • GOLD LABEL TACKLE • KJB
IVEL • NUTRABAITS • RICHWORTH • ROD HUTCHINSON and many more

MAIL ORDER WELCOME
2 Stockbridge Place, Stockbridge, Chichester, West Sussex
Tel: 0243 531669

answers are normally very revealing. Anyway enough lecturing, back to the lake.

I set up in the woods so as not to clump about on the platform, which was built out into the reeds on the opposite side of the bay to the snag tree. My plan was to fish just off the sides of the platform, next to the reeds, with the same rigs and bait despite the bottom being much more silty. I wasn't casting as far and the tigers would be just as effective in silt as on harder bottoms. I wedged a bank stick between the sleepers and propped the rods up. With my chair pointed directly at the sun I noticed a flurry of action opposite. Young Si was 'in'. He played it gingerly and didn't rush. I decided to wait until it was in the net before charging round with the camera. Then I saw what he had for a net. His mate pucked up an aluminium handled pan net and I cringed inwardly. Not the best tool for the job! Sensibly though this chap waded out along the tree so as to be netting in deeper water. I had apparently stumbled on a hot-bed of sensible young anglers in Essex of all places. Some of the older ones should take lessons in good sense and manners. A bit of pulling and scooping and an obviously large common was in the net. I decided to go round. I got there as the fish was put down after weighing. Simon was breathless. "I can't believe it, 24lb 8oz ... it's enormous, it's fantastic." I slapped him on the back and smiled. "Get hold of her and I'll take some pics." He did as he was told and there were smiles all round as the shutter clicked. Firmly but carefully he then put the fish back. As soon as the head was under water the half moon scar on top was clearly visibly! Simon you win and some you lose. Simon then proceeded to show me his rig which was a pretty fair buoyant hook rig with tigers, and he had come up with his own additives which were pretty good! I obviously had some competition.

Later that same day Simon bumped a fish off, (good match anglers term for setting the hook and then pulling it out again) and I caught a 15lb 12oz salmon. Well at least that's what it behaved like. Steaking off then lunging up out of the water, shaking its head, trying to jump into the reeds but never running hard like a 'real' carp. This fish behaved exactly like lots of trout I've caught from artificially stocked lakes, apparently not knowing what a hook and line mean at all, shaking their heads and rolling about, quite un-fish like really. This one fish proved enough for me and I left early having a Sunday meeting with someone from work and I left Simon to it, to catch some more. I expected a Sunday evening 'phone call and sure enough at about 9.30pm it came. "Hi, Si here, I caught another one, only 17lb though." "What do you mean only 17?" "Well, I caught another personal best common, only not as big as the last personal best: if you know what I mean." "Yeah I get it. Are you there next weekend?" "Yep." "OK see you then, bye."

Again the week dragged past, the tigers were done and tackle checked. Away from work as quick as possible and into the wilds of Essex once again. I felt good about this weekend, the weather was to be thundery but warm and any breeze was likely to be down into my corner.

Friday night I tried all sorts of tricks. Four pound line, close in rod, long rod, stringers, lots of bait, just hook baits, bent hook baits, Diana Rigg, anything I could think of. The end result was a good night's sleep. As I got up I remember thinking how good it all looked. Early mist curling through the reeds and flooding down across the margins. A barn owl drifting effortlessly down the pathway on silent wings, momentarily stilling the early chitterings in the hedgerows. A lone warbler pouring out fluid notes in a long continuous stream, ending abruptly, leaving a moment of pure silence.

After winding in the rods I went for a walk round to the road, along behind some other anglers past the reed beds to look up the lake. It was already warming up nicely and way out in the middle several dorsal fins made 'V's' in the flat calm surface, all heading towards my reedy corner. "Today," I thought, "we are really going to do the business." As I wandered back down the path to my swim. Simon turned up, driven by his father. After helping him carry his gear down to the corner we had a conversation which is still etched in my mind. In the light of subsequent events it brought home to me a couple of vital points which will become obvious. "Alright son how's it going?" "Not bad, nothing overnight but things look pukka for today." "Yeah I agree, I'm not sure where to fish though. Next to you or under the trees?" "Well, the big one is due to come out soon and it's either going to be here or under the trees. If you fish next to me, you may catch fish from the other side of the snag tree but my bet is if I catch from here it will push fish over to the reeds. I think they are there anyway. In fact that's probably the best place for the big one to be." "Do you think so?" "Yep. If I wasn't here that's where I'd fish." "OK sounds good to me," and off he went, all of 20 yards, to the small gap under the trees, looking almost directly into the reeds. None of the locals had fished this swim for at least a couple of seasons, but I had baited it since my first trip and fished it once for a couple of hours after having seen a couple of cruisers. It was cramped and awkward but the fish did go in there. I watched with interest as Simon tackled up and baited his swim. He had come such a long way. His confidence and general air of calm were beyond his years. We sat and had a cup of tea, I was constantly expecting something to happen with bubbles starting to come up all over the swim and the sun coming up over the trees. A flat spot appeared 5 yards past my left hand rod and Simon predicted a fish within half an hour. As the sun warmed Simon's bay a couple of fish drifted down the reeds opposite, and I started to wonder who had the best chance. A single bleep from Si's rod had us rushing over. Nothing had moved and we laughed at the anticipation we both felt. Three quick bleeps from my swim and we rushed back. By contrast my right hand rod was bent round, several floating pads cut from the bottom floated up, and the water rocked as a fish tried to dig itself into the bottom. As I pulled the line pinged up from pad to pad and eventually I was in almost full contact. With a bit of see-sawing the fish was free. Whilst it lunged about Simon brought the net out and after churning backwards and forwards across the top in she went. A mirror of about 15–16 pounds, a nice start. Simon commented that he had yet to catch a mirror over 11lbs from anywhere and really had his heart set on one of the lake's favourites, *Matey*, a big scaley mirror about 22lbs. I assured him it was on the cards, along with the big one. I chucked out again and we walked over to watch fish sunbathing in the bay. Would they go down on Simon's bait? Only time would tell. Forty five minutes later I was away again, This time a flyer, going arrow straight out into the lake.

As I picked up the rod the run stopped. Striking anyway, I got solid, pulsing contact. This fish charged about on short powerful burst but never with much direction. It shot straight past the snag tree and into the margins, making me think of re-naming the swim 'The Non-Snag Tree', not having had a single real problem with it as yet. Big swirls and boils were coming up behind the fish despite it being in only three feet of water. It stayed right on the bottom trying at times to ground itself under the tree to my right. Eventually a tail appeared, then a back and she rolled over and waddled into the net.

"Well blow me," exclaimed Simon. "Talk of the devil, it's *Matey* Jon." "That'll do nicely." I replied. Sure enough 22lb 4oz of solidly-proportioned mirror which had Simon moaning about 'foreign' anglers catching all the mirrors by pulling strokes. I told him he was an ignorant peasant who should come and fish some 'men's waters' in 'The Valley.'

After some serious 'I know what I'm doing' poses for the camera, Simon decided on a recast. As the sun was well up we decided to take the chairs over and sit in the sun behind his swim. We re-baited and shot out another couple of pouches of tigers. We sat debating for about twenty minutes as to whether the fish would feed in his swim until it was confirmed for us with a slow steady take on Si's rod.

His right hand rod was bouncing up and down as a fish went right out of the bay. Si pulled into it and a flat spot appeared 30 yards to the right followed by a swirl and a slowly kiting fish went under the trees between us and my swim. There were no snags so steady pressure brought her through and she swirled again before churning round and round until it was time for the net, I pulled back the mesh and there lay another lovely common, about 18lbs.

"Very nice, Si," I said, "if it was a bit fatter it would be...." Beeeep, off roared Si's second rod, with great composure Simon threw his first rod at me, and grabbed the other. As he struck everything went solid. I thought it was snagged on a lily root. Slowly a huge cloud of mud appeared. Then the line jagged twice and moved slowly towards the reeds to the left. As the line touched the reeds, everything stopped again. Simon didn't cram on pressure and I didn't offer any advice. I had a certain feeling. The fish then turned and swam away from the reeds out into the open water. Very quickly I sacked up the first fish and ran back. Just past the original mud cloud Simon stopped her and out of the water came a paddle, wavering about. "Now that's big," I thought, my feeling getting stronger.

Round and round plodded the fish, not taking or giving line. Steady pressure, line singing in the wind, creaking cork handle, all these things struck me, Simon stared fixedly out at the line. "Take your time Si, it's a big one."

"I can't believe how strong it is," replied Si. Eventually something gave and Simon gained a couple of yards. The line cut up through the water and a great golden head and bronzed shoulders turned over and came back towards us. "Keep it steady Si, it's the big one," my feeling now a certainty.

Later Simon told me he had no recollection of me saying anything, let alone "It's the big one." At the time I was concerned that he might panic and ease off rather than finish the job! Again she rolled, much closer, and side on, all scales and fins, I heard Simon gasp. I went out deeper in the silt, better wet and safe, than dry but sorry. Simon turned the fish again, just to my left and I could see her virtually touching the bottom. I pushed the net out and pressed the arms down onto the bottom." "Just play her over the net Si." Over she came, blowing bubbles, head half out, right over the net, Si stopped her. As she swung round I lifted. She gave a little shudder as the net touched and it was all over, "well done Si, very well done, it's the big common." "What?" "It's the big common, it looks nearly thirty." "No! You're joking! It can't be." "Look for yourself."

I held the net open and Simon nearly fell over. He didn't know whether to laugh or cry. I unhooked her in the net and with the other fish quite

THE NEW

DELKIM

BITE INDICATOR
ACTUAL SIZE
AVAILABLE CLOSED SEASON
Send S.A.E for details

Delkim Ltd
4 Gold Street
Walgrave
Northampton
NN6 9QE
TEL (0604) 781541

Catch 1
FISHING TACKLE

OXFORD'S PREMIER TACKLE DEALER

for all your carp requirements

• STOCKISTS OF •
Nutrabaits, Cotswold Baits, SBS Premier, Richworth, Terry Eustace Gold Label, Partridge, Drennan, Nash, Wychwood, Northwestern and Armalite Rods, Anchor Tackle and many more

REMEMBER
Don't go fishing unless you're going to

"Catch 1"

14 The Parade	Yarnton Nurseries	Bicester Garden Centre
KIDLINGTON	Sandy Lane	Oxford Road
OXFORD	YARNTON	BICESTER
(086575) 2066	OXFORD	Oxon
	(0865) 841345	(0869) 321010

"Look for yourself it's nearly thirty"

happy round the corner, put her back to have a breather. Well what a turn up! Si looked shell-shocked and I should have remembered to actually fish where I thought the big ones should be. I learnt the hard way, and since then I have always tried to go 'where no man has gone before.' It always pays off.

TRENT CARP

NEVILLE FLICKING

Everyone is talking about Trent carp at the moment, yet no-one seems to want to write anything about it. I am not a Trent carp expert, to qualify for that would require a lot more fishing effort. Because I like to fish for pike and zander along with stillwater carp, my Trent carp fishing is generally limited to about 15 to 20 days a year, however despite the small amount of effort put in I've had some nice fish to just over 20 pounds.

You only have to talk to any serious match angler to know that Trent carp are widespread. I was talking to a match angling mate of mine the other day. On two pound line and wasp grub he had hooked and landed an eighteen pound mirror from the tidal river. A considerable feat of skill considering the pace of the river. He, of course, was fishing for smaller species and this was an accidental capture. However such captures are regular along the Trent, a river which runs from the heart of the country in the midlands to the Humber. I cannot comment on the upper and middle river, because I have not fished it. However I am pretty sure that what applies down my end applies there too.

Firstly then, for those who have to know what they are fishing for, how big do Trent carp grow? Well, there have been authenticated thirty pounders, but generally these are rare. Twenty pounders are caught fairly often by those who fish for them and double figure fish are easy to catch in the right areas. I would say the overall majority of Trent carp are commons, with fewer mirrors and the very odd fully scaled mirror, linear or leather. In shape, they vary from really fat humpty-backed jobs to long torpedoes. You really cannot be

20lb 12oz common from the Trent

dogmatic about Trent carp when it comes to the shape and variety of fish. I suspect that the river is a bit overstocked with all fish species and that growth is slow, however we already know that species such as roach, bream, barbel and chub can reach quite respectable sizes, therefore it stands to reason that carp will also do well.

Where and how then do you catch them? The where is the difficult one. My experience of the Trent is confined to below the A1 road bridge near Newark. The fishing I have done on the non-tidal river between the A1 and Collingham Weir has shown that the nearer you get to the weir the more likely you are to catch carp. Unfortunately, the average size gets smaller! Most of the fish caught from the river around Winthorpe and Holme are of a high average size, that is they are usually doubles with the odd 18 pound-plus fish. When you get near to the weir in the famous *Weir Field* pegs, most of the carp are around six to eight pounds, but the odd much bigger fish turns up amongst them. Below the weir the average size is quite good, around ten to 12 pounds with the weirpool itself quite prolific on the right day. As you get further downstream on the tidal river it gets harder, but most fish are doubles and you would be unlucky not to catch an 18 pound-plus specimen with a bit of serious effort. The tidal produced a 30 pound-plus common (kept fairly quiet) a year and a half ago, while fish to 23 pounds have been caught by match anglers such as Terry Smith (Anglers World Holidays). Location on all of the river below Newark is rather hit and miss, but really your best friend is the match angler (bet you never thought that would happen!) and the match results in the angling weeklies. This is a good way to find hot pegs for carp particularly because just about every bit of the Trent has a white post with a number on it! Easy isn't it? Well not really, because some swims are consistent producers while other last only for a few weeks at a time. You have to fish them to find this out. Obvious visible features as to why one swim produces more carp than another are hard to find, unless you do some serious plumbing. Better still have a day with a boat and a sonar. What you are looking for is depth variation in an area plus snags and slack water swims. In contrast carp can also be found in white water swims under weir sills, so there is plenty to get you thinking.

I am inclined to be a bit dubious about anglers who say they can read the water and predict where they can catch carp. There may be something more to learn here, but until someone writes about it, I will remain convinced that location is hard work! What then about the how, and while we are at it when? The how is not that difficult, most stillwater anglers get the galloping willies when you mention running water. Why this should be I'm not sure, but fishing on the Trent is not ideal for those who like to get a good night's sleep. Being a bit older than most of the carp anglers around these days I have difficulty staying awake when carp fishing. However when fishing the Trent there's always something to keep you up, be it weed, chub or even carp! So if you are thinking of carp fishing at night and getting enough sleep to do a day's work, forget it. Because the Trent is in the Trent area of the NRA you are limited to two rods. Now I am all for fishing three rods even in the Trent area, but on the Trent itself it is not worth it. For one thing you are surrounded by match anglers who will complain to someone about carp anglers breaking the rules. Two rods are all you really need on the Trent, simply because you cannot cover all the river and a close in and middle rods gives you as good a chance as anything. (Anyway to keep the bait going into three separate spots may place a strain on resources!)

Rigs are not that important, a simple hair rig with a mono hooklink and a fixed lead is all you require for Trent carp. You are better off with flat leads of around three ounces and in weirpools you may need up to five ounces of lead to hold out. I make some very Mickey Mouse feeders out of sheet lead and plastic pipe. Because there are snags the hooklink is of a lower breaking strain than the main line (I usually use a fine diameter line such as 15 or 18 pound Daiwa Shinobi) and the lead or feeder also has a weaklink incorporated. Strangely in weirpools I have found running leads to be more effective, do not ask me why. Bite indication is by the usual methods, fishing off the baitrunner and I've thrown my monkey climbers away for those things that come in pretty colours and hang on bits of wire (Cliff Fox wouldn't give me any, so no publicity for him!) Sometimes it pays to fish with the rods up in the air to reduce water resistance, but this does make you liable to

Homemade feeders (stuff full of particles or boilies and breadcrumb) for snaggy swims plus flat leads

catch bats and boats. If you fish enough lead you can hold out OK. Rods – well they need to be two to two and a half pounds to cope with the lead being thrown around. I scrounged a couple of the Amorphous rods off Daiwa, having found my lighter rods (which I use on pits) to be a bit underpowered for big-lead work.

Bait choice depends on only one thing, cheapness, linked to deterent properties! In an ideal world we would all be on sweetcorn, but seeing as every other fish in the river eats it, you have to consider a more resistant bait. Tiger nuts spring to mind, though my particle-caught carp have been confined to maples and chick peas. Boilies are probably the favourite, around 16mm. Many anglers have chub trouble, but me, I've only had about five in four years, so I must be doing something right. (Sadly I've not figured out what!) Choice of boilies depends on your own taste. I would stay away from readymades because they are too expensive for Trent fishing. Though if you get them cheap (know what I mean...) they are as good as anything. Make you own up out of one of the cheaper mixes or make your own recipe. I'll give you a cheap one from Lucebaits guide to cheapo carp baits.

  6oz soya meal
  1oz gluten
  ½oz milk powder
  ½oz maize flour or
  fine breadcrumb

For harder baits add quarter of an ounce of egg albumin and one ounce of semolina. This makes a nice easy to roll bait, which you make up with eggs as normal. A classic HNV it isn't, but it's still food and carp love it! Alternatively our yellow seed mix which has its own flavour (a feed inducer used for calves) scored for me the first time I used it, so it is my standard bait on the river. Quantity of bait is a difficult one. You need at least five pounds of bait per session. If you were on a lot of fish ten pounds would not be too much. I fill the swim in to start with using around two pounds of bait around the two hookbaits. Then I top up depending on the amount of knocks I am getting on the rod top from nuisance fish.

As to when, well anytime, winter, summer, autumn, day or night. I have seen carp caught when the air temperature has been minus 13C. Most of my fish have been caught during the day, but nights are worthwhile where allowed. Night fishing and bivvies are dodgy issues on the Trent. The match anglers think they own the river so breaking the usual no night fishing rule annoys them when they cannot get to their swims (though *they* think nothing of arriving at 2am in the morning to grab a swim!). Tact is the best policy. If you do night fish, keep away from busy areas, do not set up a bivvy and do not look as if you have been there a week. Do not fill in a swim with bait next to a match angler and do not fish on a match stretch the night before a match (or at least clear off before the matchmen arrive).

Some idiots are doing all the things they are not supposed to do and I can see stretches of river such as Worksop and Districts Holme Marsh fishery being out of bounds to carp anglers before long. Lastly do not add to the litter problem! I do not mind if the Trent remains unfashionable as a carp water, but I am sure more and more anglers are going to enjoy getting to grips with it in the near future. You never know what it will turn up next!

Rods up in the air can attract unwanted attention ie this barge!

Dusk on the river

ANGLING CENTRE

NORTHAMPTON

Stockists for

- Solar Tackle
- Fox International
- Gardner Tackle
- Wychwood
- SBS
- Maestro
- Kevin Nash
- KJB
- Gold Label
- Nutrabaits
- Richworth
- Catchum

and others!

85 St. Leonards Road, Far Cotton
Tel: 0604 764847

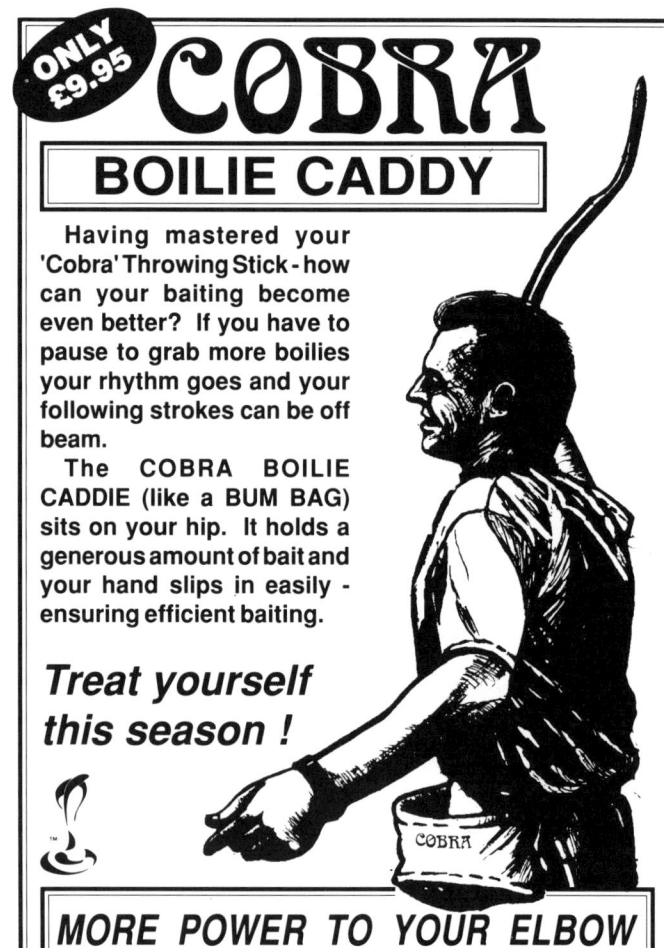

COBRA BOILIE CADDY

ONLY £9.95

Having mastered your 'Cobra' Throwing Stick - how can your baiting become even better? If you have to pause to grab more boilies your rhythm goes and your following strokes can be off beam.

The COBRA BOILIE CADDIE (like a BUM BAG) sits on your hip. It holds a generous amount of bait and your hand slips in easily - ensuring efficient baiting.

Treat yourself this season !

MORE POWER TO YOUR ELBOW

NEW CATALOGUE!
A COMPLETELY NEW FORMAT FOR 1992
LARGER AND BETTER THAN EVER BEFORE

Last year we changed printers and were very disappointed with the results, not only with the quality but also in the fact that we let many customers down due to the fact that the catalogue was late despite many promises from last year's printers.

If you were one of the people that had to wait last year we are SORRY.

This year we have gone back, tail between legs, to our original printers. We know where we stand and we know this completely new formatted catalogue will be available from mid-April.

WALKERS OF TROWELL
THE COMPLETE ANGLERS CATALOGUE
SPRING 1992 £1

If you ordered tackle from us last year, you will automatically receive a catalogue this year. If you aren't a customer of ours, but you would like a copy of our catalogue simply fill in the form below (or send us a copy of your address if you don't want to cut this magazine up) and send us £1.00. In return we will send you a catalogue as well as a £1.00 voucher. This voucher may be used on your first order to us over £5.00.

Our catalogue is a catalogue! Not a few A4 sheets stapled together like so many others.

WALKERS OF TROWELL
NOTTINGHAM ROAD, TROWELL, NOTTS.
Tel: 0602 301816/307799   Fax: 0602 440898

Name ....
Address ....
....
.... Post Code...........

BIG CARP

BITECH VIPER LTD

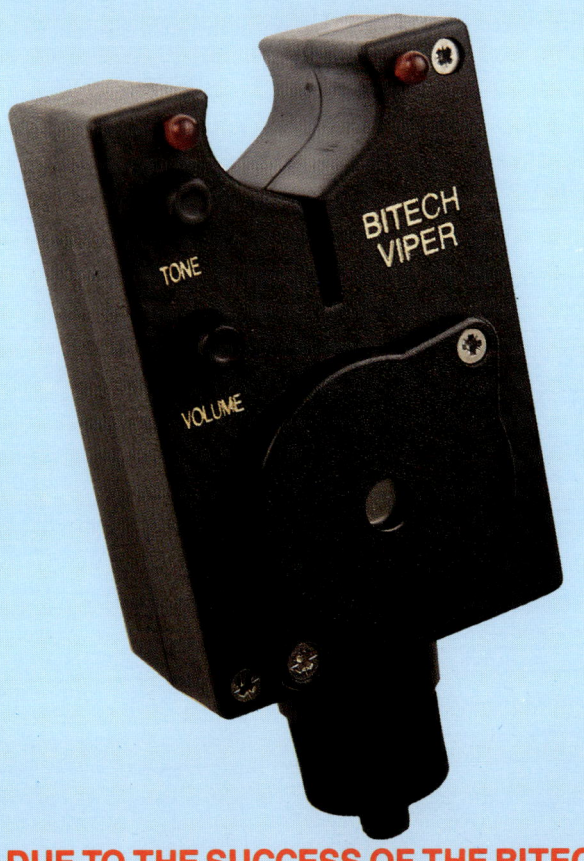

THE BITECH VIPER IS NOW FIRMLY ESTABLISHED AS A TOP QUALITY, MODERN BITE INDICATOR

The BITECH VIPER still costs just £49.95 which means that you cannot get better value for money anywhere, especially as it comes in a FREE top quality pouch and is FITTED with a Duracell Battery. The modern case design does not need carp ears or other gadgets.

The sensitivity is unrivalled and can be tested by comparing how many pulses are produced by the BITECH VIPER when a length of line is passed through it and compared to any other bite indicator. This extra sensitivity alerts you earlier and lets you decide when to strike and catch the fish as it eats your bait.

Independent TONE and VOLUME controls with NEW specially made knobs which are easy to adjust with wet or cold fingers.

The BITECH VIPERs unique LEDs will let you see them from any position and in any light. They are so bright that you can see them in full sunlight and they glow like torches at night.

High speed electronics give massive Audio/Visual output while consuming very little battery power. The BITECH VIPER should give a whole season of fishing on just one Alkaline battery.

DUE TO THE SUCCESS OF THE BITECH VIPER WE HAVE PRODUCED A MATCHING EXTENSION BOX TO COMPLETE THE SET.

As with the BITECH VIPER we have provided you with more features beautifully packed into a smaller overall size than ever before.

The EXTENSION BOX will take up to 3 rods and has a different colour latching LED for each rod. There is also a Red flashing run LED.

With independent TONE and VOLUME controls you can set the output to any level you want. If you can sleep through the loudest settings you should see your doctor.

The EXTENSION BOX has been designed to work with all known 2.5mm jack plug systems. Even if you haven't got BITECH VIPERs you can still use our EXTENSION BOX to upgrade your existing equipment.

The leads are 7 metres long and are sold separately to allow you to set up with plenty of space so that your swim is safe and tidy.

The EXTENSION BOX is small enough to fit into your hand and comes complete with a FREE Duracell battery. With our NEW specially moulded control knobs you will be able to adjust the TONE and VOLUME controls in the comfort of your bivvi.

The BITECH VIPER has U.K., European and U.S.A. Patents applied for and is available from all good tackle dealers! Guaranteed for 12 months against faulty manufacture.

TRADE ENQUIRIES WELCOME

Phone Bill Thurston on 0732 872048 or fax us on 0732 872052, or you can write to us at the address below

BITECH VIPER LIMITED, P.O. Box 928, Aylesford, Kent ME20 6XF

EIGHT NIGHTS IN FRANCE

DAVE MILLER

Early evening on Friday 13th September 1991 myself and friend Darren Roberts arrived at Newhaven in good time for the 18.45 Sealink ferry crossing to Dieppe. Friday 13th is not a good night to travel for the superstitious, which may possibly explain why the ferry was only about half full that particular evening. The journey passed by uneventfully save for myself and Darren trying to dodge the chap who was the compere for a Karaoke night that they were holding in the main lounge and bar of the ferry. Any poor victim that was unfortunate enough to get nabbed by the compere was unceremoniously hauled up to the microphone and then had to perform some dreadful song which had been designated to them. All this in front of dozens of fellow passengers. We (not surprisingly) kept a low profile by hiding rather furtively around a corner at the back of the bar. Eventually and with some relief we arrived in Dieppe around 11pm and drove off into the darkness of the French night.

A little after 4am we arrived at our destination and the long arduous journey had finally come to an end. Fox bedchairs were removed from the car and we attempted to snatch an hour or two of sleep before sunrise. Although I was desperately tired, having not slept for almost 24 hours, I was still unable to get even one minute of sleep. I was glad when dawn arrived, so we could go and have a recce at our chosen venue and hopefully spot some carp activity.

Several alternative venues in the same locality were also known to us, which gave us other options if the fishing turned out to be poor on on first choice water.

Our venue consisted of two fairly large expanses of water which were inter-connected by a half mile long channel. This channel had a uniform depth of eight feet and a fairly uniform width of some 60 yards and it was along here that we intended to fish. The channel was delightfully secluded and completely surrounded by a mass of thick woodland. Our nearside bank had about four large open areas where one could happily bivvy up and fish. The far bank however was densely wooded and very heavily overgrown along its entire length. A number of trees were dead and the whole margin of that far bank was festooned with a mass of tangled underwater branches and tree roots. Predominately and in typical fashion, the carp frequented this heavily overgrown far bank.

Saturday morning was hot and still and we did not relish the long hike from the car to our swims, with all the tackle and provisions along with the heavy buckets full of pre-soaked particle baits. Grudgingly we got on with the task and by midday were well ensconced in our chosen swims, with Darren set up about 30 yards away and to my left.

Our bait for the eight night session consisted of 50 kilos of peanuts and an additional 75 kilos of maize (50 kilos of which we purchased very cheaply in France). These particles were heavily flavoured with fruit essences and were taken out and scattered close to and along the far bank margin using an inflatable dinghy. The distance fished was too far for catapulting out bait, and spodding with a bait dropper would have been too tedious and time consuming even to contemplate, not to mention a little perilous with all the overhanging trees opposite us.

The reasons we had decided to use particle baits were threefold. Firstly, particles are very cheap and if the same weight in boilies had been used instead we would have needed to have taken out a bank loan to purchase them. Secondly, the small and innumerable poisson chats (a peculiar stunted species of catfish which infest 99 per cent of French waters) make a complete mockery of boilie fishing in the warmer months. They will devour any size/colour/flavour combination of boilie you care to throw at them. Thirdly, we simply believe that particle bait fishing is in most instances (except in winter), more effective than the use of boilie baits anyway.

Hookbaits would be either double peanuts or four grains of maize and used in conjunction with pieces of cork, thus creating either slow sinkers or else two inch pop-ups (aided additionally by a swan shot). Lightweight particle hookbaits can be prone to tangling, so to overcome this, large buoyant microwaved pop-ups were PVA'd to the hook on each cast. This eliminated any tangles and the pop-up would drift off as soon as the PVA had rapidly dissolved. Foolishly, I endeavoured to use an actual boilie hookbait on one rod, but I quickly changed it having caught four poisson chats within the first hour. Not surprisingly I never again used another boilie for the duration of the session.

A good deal of my summer fishing is done with particle baits, but clever and sometimes misleading modern day advertising hype would have us believe that expensive boilies or boilie mixes are the only commodities on which to catch carp. Personally I treat this hype with scepticism and with a little disdain, dismissing it for what it surely is – blatant commercialism.

Heavy tackle was required to extract any hooked carp from

Poisson Chat fortunately, the only one to pick up a peanut hookbait

the troublesome far bank snags. My set up consisted of the following items: Three, two and three-quarter pound test curve, through action 12 foot rods coupled with Shimano GT4000 Aero reels. Main line was 15 pound Berkeley Trilene and the ten inch hooklinks were made from 20 pound Cortland Micron with size two Drennan Super Specialist hooks. Three ounce in-line round leads were slid onto 15 inch length of stiff boom tube. The boom tube was affixed to the hooklink swivel by virtue of some two millimetre silicone rubber – creating a fixed lead presentation. Any items of tackle less substantial than those actually used, would have proved to be woefully inadequate. I used three rods for the entire session, whilst Darren using similar set ups to myself opted for four.

By late afternoon we had baited our swims heavily with a mixture of peanuts and maize and as we cast out our hookbaits, so the session commenced. Although night fishing is illegal in France, by remaining unobtrusive and tactful we did not envisage any problems arising from our fishing during the hours of darkness.

I did not particularly want any action that first night as I had not slept for a long time and really needed a full night's sleep. Mercifully the Optonics remained quiet all night, but at 7am I was awoken from my slumber by a slow, steady run on my right hand rod. A small common carp of around eight pounds was quickly and rather unceremoniously bustled in and unhooked in the water. It was not the size of carp we had anticipated, but nevertheless a bit of a confidence booster I guess.

No more action occurred until early on Sunday evening, when I received a fast take on my centre rod. I hooked and held onto the carp but was rather taken aback by the immense power of the fish. I was convinced something was going to break and so I relented and let the fish have two or three yeards of line, by back-winding on the reel. Sadly this turned out be be a bad move on my part as the carp was able to reach an underwater snag some five yards out from the bank, which I did not know existed at that time. Darren went out in the dinghy in an endeavour to free my line but alas everything had locked up solid and I was forced to pull for a break (not an easy task, I might add, with 15 pound Berkeley Trilene). I accepted the loss calmly and philosophically, but vowed not to let any more carp gain sanctuary in the snags.

It was several hours into the darkness of Sunday night when I once again received a slow but steady run on my centre rod. After making contact, I steadfastly refused to give the fish any line at all, indeed the clutches on all three reels had been screwed up tight since the beginning of the session. I could not believe the incredible power of the carp, but desperately I hung on with grim-faced determination and as a consequence was physically pulled along the ground as I held onto the rod, which was locked into full test curve. Surely the fish would relent and allow me to turn it – but no, it then gave the most stupendous and frightening surge of power I have ever experienced from a carp. Savagely the rod was wrenched downwards and much to my chagrin the carp had made the same troublesome solid snag that I had lost the previous fish on. In the reflection of the moonlight I could distinctly see my line pointing directly at the snag. What a bummer, I thought, as once again I pulled for a break. I was shell-shocked. What more could I have done I wondered? I felt thoroughly dejected and disillusioned and it would have been all too easy to have thrown the rod into the bushes and clambered back into my sleeping bag. However, I painstakingly and methodically re-threaded the rod, tied on some new terminal tackle and rebaited. I must confess that I recast back out rather gingerly, dropping a good ten yards or so short of the snag.

Eventually I returned to the sleeping bag but I did not get back to sleep for a long while as I lay there pondering those two lost carp. I know it sounds crazy, but I was actually dreading getting another take. I could not have handled getting steamed into that problematical and much maligned snag again by any more unseen monster carp. The far bank snags, along the treeline were both obvious and acceptable, but this additional snag which was smack in the middle of my baited area was beginning to annoy me intensely.

After what seemed an eternity, I drifted back to sleep, but not before I had thought out a new strategy. Hooking and holding tactics had so far proved unsuccessful, therefore I decided that for any future takes I would hook and heave – heave very hard at that.

There was just the faintest glimmer of daylight over to the east the next morning when I had a take on the rod that I had recast during the night, vindication I felt for my persistence. As per the plan, I really beefed into the carp, savagely pumping it into my own half of the swim. As the fish swung under the rod tip, I eased off the pressure and flipped the anti-

26lb linear mirror

reverse switch on the reel over, which would allow me to backwind to the fish once it was in the confines of my own margin. I was pleasantly surprised at the ease at which the carp had been pumped in, with the heavy pressure really working a treat. Predictably once under the rod tip the carp went beserk and shot off along my right hand margin. This area was to my knowledge snag free and so I was not duly perturbed. Five minutes of steady and firm pressure had the fish almost ready for netting, when to my horror, I could feel an awful grating sensation through the line. After several anxious seconds the carp rolled and I could see an old rotten piece of branch, about five feet in length had become ensnared on my line. I was unable to rid the offensive and relatively heavy object from my line, although slowly but surely I was able to swing the branch into my margin and snap most of it away, with the carp towing along about five yards behind. Unfortunately a piece of the branch, about a foot long remained attached to my line, too badly entwined to remove.

I could have hand-lined the fish in, but decided against it. There was only one other solution and that was to wind the offending object up into the tip ring, heave the carp up onto the surface and let Darren net the fish whilst I controlled it on a long line. The task was duly completed and a glorious linear mirror weighing exactly 26lb was my reward.

Late on Monday afternoon we once again baited our swims heavily with the mixture of peanuts and maize and then sat back in eager anticipation, contemplating the forthcoming night. Earlier in the day, I had managed to ascertain the precise location of the troublesome snag whilst out in the dinghy, and pinpointed its exact position with the aid of a polystyrene marker.

At 2am I had a slow, steady run, again on my centre rod. Brute force tactics, which unfortunately were my only option, had the carp under the rod tip in seconds but, to complicate matters, I was then away on the right hand rod. My reaction was to drop the first rod, disengaging the bail-arm and winch hard into the second rod. With some assistance from Darren, I was able to net both carp with relative ease. The brace consisted of a 16lb 13oz mirror and a 13lb 1oz common. Both fish were in absolutely pristine condition, neither having encountered a hook ever before.

So after the first three nights I had hooked six carp, whilst Darren was unfortunately yet to receive any action at all. It was perhaps significant that all the action I had received had occurred on my two rods fished furthest right and that additionally there appeared to be a disproportionate amount of carp activity down to the right of where I was fishing. Sensibly Darren decided to move swim, setting up about 150 yards to my right.

Exactly 24 hours after my previous takes, I was once again connected to a carp and with total confidence in my tackle, I nonchalantly heaved it in under my rod tip. Could be another 'patsy' I mused to myself (my rather tongue in cheek terminology for carp weighing less than 20lb). With that the carp shot off with tremendous power and I only just managed to turn it, some ten yards or so away from the far bank, from where I had only just extracted it in fact. I played the fish hard, my tackle was strong and the hookholds on all previous captures had been excellent. I maintained the upper hand right up to the latter stages of the battle, despite some periodical surges of frightening power from the carp, coupled with the added complication

37lb 3oz common

40 GOOD REASONS

RITCHIE MCDONALD 40LB 8OZ - YATELEY - TROPICANO

PETER SPRINGATE 45LB 6OZ - WRAYSBURY - BIRD FOOD BLEND

ALBERT ROMP 45LB 4OZ - SAVAY - BIRD FOOD BLEND

ANDY LITTLE 41LB 8OZ - YEW TREE LAKE - STRAWBERRY YOGHURT

For using Richworth

that it had also picked up both of my other lines. Eventually the carp was in the margins and presumably beaten; however it was intensely dark, the moon having by now sunk down below the far bank treeline, and the carp that I was attached to was a very long fish. As a consequence my first two attempts at netting it were abortive, and on both occasions the carp, feeling rejuvenated, had powered off again.

I began to grow tense and worried; my two other lines were still hooked around the line that I was playing the fish on, which was compounding the problem of getting the carp over the normally capacious 45 inch landing net arms. For the third time I had the carp beaten and swinging in towards me. I contrived to get it right this time and it was with some considerable relief that I lifted the net arms and the carp sank down into the folds of the net. Mercifully the carp was now mine and I bit through the line, leaving the fish in the landing net and still in the water. I tended to my two other lines which fortunately were not badly tangled at all.

What had I caught? I wondered to myself as I struggled along the bank with the heavy carp enmeshed in the landing net. Torchlight revealed an immensely long common carp and it was with a sense of excitement that I gathered my scales and weigh sling. The scales were suspended from a tree notch and zeroed to the weigh sling; then came the moment of truth. The needle spun round and settled at 37lb 3oz – the biggest common carp I had ever seen in the flesh, either on the bank or in the water. What a touch, I thought to myself as I sacked the fish up, ready for the early morning photographic session.

It transpired that Darren had hooked a carp at long last, down in his new swim, but his luck was just not in and he had lost the very powerful fish in some snags along his right hand margin.

The days remained hot, sunny and cloudless (very typical of most of my visits to France) and really a waste of time as far as daytime fishing was concerned. No carp would show on the top and no carp appeared in the near margins therefore floater fishing and stalking were not feasible options. The onset of evening however would renew your optimism and fill you with tense anticipation as to what the night ahead would bring forth.

Wednesday night held nothing in store for either of us, save for a number of hours of much appreciated sleep; broken sleep though for myself, disturbed by the incessant nocturnal activity of the rather considerable rat, coypu and hedgehog populations rustling and scurrying around outside my bivvy half the night.

Contrary to the first few nights spent at the water, a number of carp were now beginning to show to the left of where I was fishing and as a result Darren moved back hopefully into his original swim to try and intercept them.

Thursday night produced no action for myself, the Optonics remained silent for the second successive night. Darren had been briefly connected to a carp at dawn however, but his line had sheared on some unseen snag ten seconds after initial contact.

24lb river mirror

Onto Friday night, and periodically throughout the night I had heard heavy carp crash out close to our baits, and although I was expecting some action, nothing occurred on either mine or Darren's rods.

It was now Saturday morning and we were left in rather a quandary as to what our next move should be. We had one more night left but if we remained where we were it would have entailed an horrendously early pack up – if we were to make Dieppe for mid-day Sunday.

After some deliberation we decided to drive some 70 miles northwards and fish another water on which Darren had fished before and which would allow us to pack up later the following morning. As we neared our new destination we coincidently bumped into Geoff Shaw, who had just arrived in the locality with a party of half a dozen or so anglerss. Both myself and Darren had previously fished in France with Geoff and therefore he kindly gave us a good tip as to where it would be worthwhile fishing for just a single night.

We fished a backwater connected directly to a river and baited up the nine feet deep swims fairly lightly, as we only had some 14 hours in which to fish. I personally used just 100 catapult pouchloads of particles initially, far less than I would have used if the session was to be of a longer duration.

Around 11pm carp started to swirl tantalizingly over my baits and I sat up fully alert, willing one of them to pick up a hookbait. At 1am it finally happened and exuberantly I struck into a very powerful carp. Unlike on the previous venue, I could now afford the luxury of giving the carp line – it took it too and at a phenomenal rate of knots; probably around 80 yards on the initial run. After perhaps 15 minutes I was able to slip the net under the fish, having first negotiated the awkward ten feet high bank which I was perched upon. The mirror carp was truly a wild river fish weighing in at 24lb 2oz. I was delighted with this capture as I enjoy catching 20lb-plus carp from as many different and varied venues as possible and this was now the twenty-first different venue from which I had achieved this (18 in England).

I lay wide awake for the remainder of the night, excited and hopeful of more action. Meanwhile Darren's misadventures continued; fishing opposite me and about 100 yards to my left, he had hooked two carp that night but upon hearing the strangled curses in the still of the night, I knew he had lost them both. It transpired that both carp had shot straight towards a half submerged tree some 30 yards away from where he had hooked them and as he piled on the pressure to keep the carp away, on both occasions the hook had pulled out. I must confess that at the time I felt a mite sorry for him as his misfortunes had been so prevalent right through the week; although now in retrospect I find the whole episode highly amusing. Seriously though, I have had sessions in the past when I have landed nothing but had multiple losses of carp and it is not a pleasant experience.

No further action occurred and around 7am regretfully we packed up. An 8am departure from the water left us just enough time in which to return to the port at Dieppe. Arriving there we discovered that the crossing on which we had been booked had been cancelled due to technical difficulties with the ferry itself and we would have to wait an additional four hours for the next one. Tired from a sleepless night, dirty and feeling dishevelled from just over a week's fishing, it did not come easy killing four worthless and mind-numbing hours doing nothing. Finally we were all shepherded onto the next ferry along with all the passengers who had originally been booked on it. The ferry was absolutely packed; we had to stand up all the way as every seat had been taken and we certainly could not be bothered to queue for upwards of half an hour, just to purchase some vastly over-priced item of food or a drink. Nice one Sealink - not even an apology was forthcoming, which at least would have gone some way towards an appeasement.

So there it is, in spite of the return journey, one of the most enjoyable fishing sessions I had ever experienced, so different from fishing on the over pressured English carp lakes. I cannot wait for my next visit to France; work and finances dictate that it will not be until the spring of 1992 - but already I am counting down the days.

Carp Company Products

Chestnut, Sandy Lane, Send, Woking, Surrey GU23 7AP. Chris 0483 224168
3 Stroudes Close, Worcester Park, Surrey KT4 7RB. Bob 081-330 4786

Base Mixes
Neutral	£ 8.50	2k
Hemp	£ 8.50	2k
Fish	£10.50	2k
Birdfood	£10.50	2k
Milk	£10.50	2k
Mixed Nuts	£10.50	2k

All mixes are made with high quality human grade ingredients, and contain all the necessary elements to range them as H.N.V. baits. They roll and bind superbly, without the use of gluten. There is a built-in natural emulsifying agent, which disperses the fats and liquids in the base mix more efficiently and therefore positively influences its digestability.

A lot of work went into the taste of the base mixes, they will catch carp without the use of flavours and attractors, but the addition of these will enhance the mix and your confidence.

Oil Based Flavours
£2.90 per 50ml
Taste these flavours!

What you smell is what you taste. No burning, no chemical after-taste. The components used are of natural and nature identical origin. Nothing new there you may say, but what makes these special is the fact that those components are heat-stable and their solvent is a naturally derived oil rich in phospholipids. Not only does it make a good alternative to chemical solvents it has nutritional value on its own.

Mexican Vanilla, Cream of Creams, Coconut, Raspberry, Butter, Fish, Cheese, Capex, Fresh Herbs, Fruit Punch, Golden Nectar, Caramel, Oriental Breeze, Cool Mint, Hot Peppers

Ethyl Alcohol Flavours
£4.00 per 50ml
What can we say? Simply the best!
Apricot, Peach, Vanilla Bean, Pistache, Coco-Milk, Pure Chocolate

Propylene-Glycol Flavours
£2.90 per 50ml
Only three of the best
Fenugreek, Maple Dream, Maple

Appetite Stimulators
£3.00 per 50gr
Based on the latest research done by nutritionists
Fruit, Sweet, Savoury, Spice, Milk, Fish

Additives
Liquid Bio Emulsifier	£2.90	50ml
Liquid Sweetener	£2.90	50ml
Powdered Sweetener	£3.00	50g
Liquid Sweet Taste Enhancer	£3.00	50ml

HOW TO ORDER
Send cheque or P/O including P&P to one of the above addresses.
Up to 2kg - £3.00; 4k - £4.00; 6k - £5.00; Over 10k – FREE
PLEASE SEND S.A.E. FOR FREE CATALOGUE

SEARCH AND EMPLOY

Just about every item of specialist luggage available today is made from either PVC-coated fabric or nylon — or a combination of the two.

This has been the case for some years and although the materials now have a dated look and feel to them, they continue to be used as no alternatives are available.

WRONG

At **Wychwood** we are forever seeking out and evaluating new materials and components in a constant effort to improve the quality of the luggage we make for you.

Materials like **Cordura**, for instance, now feature prominently in our range. Cordura is the only material companies involved in the manufacture of mountaineering equipment will entertain due to its exceptional strength to weight ratio and proven all-weather properties.

And this year sees us introduce another brand new material after extensive testing — and, as yet, unnamed. Used for our standard range of rucksacks and specialist rod/reel holdalls, it's strong, exceptionally hardwearing, easy to clean — and most importantly in our opinion — very smart.

If you want to continue using luggage from companies who make do with the same, tired old materials, fine. If not, take a look at the new improved **Wychwood** range at your nearest stockist. You won't be disappointed.

Wychwood

Wychwood Tackle, Northwood Road, Windrush Industrial Park, Burford Road, Witney, Oxfordshire, OX8 5HB. Tel: (0993) 702975

The 'Sod' – A Pod for all angles. (Patent applied for.)

The Solar Pod or as we call it the 'Sod' is another precision machined, 100% stainless steel product developed by Solar Tackle.

It's taken us 18 months to come up with this totally unique, one piece practical design.

The Solar Sod Pod has fully adjustable legs and banksticks and can be extended to any length between a compact 22″ and 40.″ When set up, the 'Sod' is the most rigid and robust rod pod available and yet the whole thing weighs less than 3 lb.

We guarantee that the Solar 'Sod' Pod is the easiest, strongest, lightest, most compact, practical, precision-made, rigid, robust, piece of stainless steel that you could ever sit behind and cannot help but make even the scruffiest of anglers look the Absolute B*****ks.

Is this the best Pod in the world…

PROBABLY?

- Unique one piece, fully adjustable design.
- 100% stainless steel and yet weighs less than 3 lb.
- Unique centre boss locking system, which locks both the legs and banksticks in the optimum position for maximum rigidity.
- Due to the design of the Solar Pod the whole set-up is complete in a matter of seconds, as it has no separate 'Kit' type parts to assemble.  
- Extends to 40″ in length and shuts down to 22″ when packed.
- Adjustable pointed legs to give maximum grip, whatever the ground.
- Adjustable banksticks with coin slotted locking screws.
- Needle bar fitting allows for positioning of indicators anywhere along the length of the pod.
- The Solar Pod comes supplied in a protective tube and when packed in your tackle bag becomes a neat little Sod!

There is a full range of needle systems available for the Solar Pod which includes an adjustable and a 2 and 3 rod set-up, though if you already use a Solar Satellite system this will screw straight on.

A brochure is available with information on our full range of stainless products, baits, additives and articles. No charge, but please send a large S.A.E. Good luck.

All products available from 'Solar' stockists. Please contact us should you have any difficulty obtaining any items.

PRICES:	
Solar Pod	£89.95
Needle system, 2 rod	£13.95
Needle system, 3 rod	£18.95
Needle system, adjustable	£29.95
(Please note, Solar Pod does not include buzzer bars.)	

SOLAR TACKLE

35 Sutherland Road, Belvedere, Kent DA17 6JR. Tel: 081-311 3354.

BLACK COUNTRY HUNGER FOR A SOUTHERN BEAST

DAVE MALLIN

As I was looking through the Angler's Mail back in 1987 I came across the headlines "Ambush in a Bay". Three lads from Rotherham had taken an impressive catch from a very hard southern gravel pit, Wraysbury Number One.

The story and photographs of the fish kept playing on my mind so I decided to drive down and have a look for myself. It was August 1987 when I first set eyes on Wraysbury Number One. The pit was enormous –far bigger than anywhere I had ever fished before, 62 acres of windswept gravel pit. What surprised me most was how quiet and overgrown the place was... three or four anglers at most. The swims were few and far between and some a very long walk from the Douglas Lane car park. Having spent all day looking around the lake in all the nooks and crannies and noting all the likely looking places, I decided I would return the following weekend for a weeklong session. The week at work seemed to drag by, such was my enthusiasm.

When I arrived at Wraysbury I pulled into the Douglas Lane carp park to find three carp anglers already there. Two cockneys who were packing away, and a northerner. The two cockneys had been bivvied up there for a week and hand't had or seen a thing. The other angler turned out to be Dave Moore, the big common-tamer, who had arrived the previous night. I decided to drop into one of the swims vacated by the cockneys, in the hope that the carp, which hadn't been over the area the previous week might pass over it this week. It seemed logical at the time! The plumbing rod was cast out and it was soon obvious the area was weed-choked, with eight to nine inches of weed. However, I found a small gravel patch about three feet square at 30 yards range to which I 'pulted one hundred pure white, scopex, sense appeal boilies. The other two rods were fished 60 and 80 yards out using blatant pop-ups from the lead over the weed. One hour later the 30 yard rod belted off 'I nearly fell off me bedchair'. As I leaned into the fish, the tell-tale knocking on the rod top, told me it was a tench, 5lb 1oz.

The styles which Dave Moore and I were fishing were totally different. He was fishing at extreme range, using beefy rods and big Shimano reels. I almost felt inadequate with my old T24's. The week was uneventful, I did more looking and walking than actual fishing but didn't see any carp. I bade farewell to Dave, who had been really good company, and headed back north.

I decided to leave Wraysbury to the heroes of carp fishing, those who had managed to take fish from this ultra-difficult pit, until I felt ready.

Four years on, and after success at some very difficult Midland lakes, I knew I must travel to beat my personal best. Yateley immediately sprang to mind, as did Wraysbury. Three whole days spent round the two lakes in the close season felt rewarding as I started to get a feel for the lakes. The plan was made, Wraysbury would be visited first as it was closest (125 miles from home). Stalking tactics – just a rod and a bag of floaters. If no fish were spotted in the catchable areas, then I wouldn't fish. I would carry on to Yateley, to fish whichever of the three big fish lakes took my fancy. It sounded good in theory!

This start to the season was to be an exception, a laid back affair, different from the previous two seasons – sitting there for three days before 'the off'. My alarm went off at 6am on the 16th of June. I strolled downstairs and took my time which is totally out of character for me. I had breakfast, packed my gear in the car and set off at 7am. The drive was steady and relaxed, everything was going like clockwork and I had a strange feeling inside me, *hunger for a southern beast* from that moment *I knew.*

I arrived in Wraysbury village at 9am and purchased a season permit from the newsagents. I made my way straight to the area where I thought the fish might be, there was a lovely warm breeze into the bay – great. I crept through the undergrowth with a catapult and a bag of floaters to a point at the mouth of the bay. The water was gin clear and the bottom was clearly visible at five feet deep. I 'pulted six pouchfuls of floaters out on the edge of the ripple and watched eagerly as the wind took them out across the bay. Half an hour concentrating on the water and not a movement seen, I started to walk off to look at another fancied spot. I took one last glance back... a huge back broke the surface! I moved back and floated two more pouchfuls of floaters in. Six fish bow-waved together like dolphins. They began to pick at the floaters only ten yards out, the fish were clearly visible. Three commons and three mirrors. Two of the mirrors were over thirty pounds and one I thought was close to forty pounds. One common was a good thirty, (which I recognised as the one Dave Moore had taken in 1987), the other two commons were around the twenty five pound mark. I eased back from the water's edge shaking, and ran like a madman back to the car to get my rods. Minutes later I was pack at the point fumbling around tying a size four Super Specialist to my eight pound Maxima and my old faithful T24 rod. I watched and waited until they were having them well, but the big mirror just picked odd floaters off at random and totally refused some free offerings. I fancied the big common like hell but the mirror was *huge*. By then there were about one pouchful of floaters left so I decided it was time. I pushed two floaters, freelined, up the line and pulled them back to rest on the eye of the hook. I stood behind a small bush on the point and waited for the big one. Up he came greedily for the two floaters but turned away at the last minute, he had seen the hook. The big common repeated the procedure, as did another thirty pound mirror (a linear).

I reeled in and toyed with the idea of changing the hook to a size eight. Just then the big fella came bow-waving across the top. The fish knew where my hookbait was, and that it was unsafe, but what he didn't know was that I had reeled it in and pulled the two soggy floaters over the hook and punched the bait 15 yards out into his path. He approached the hookbait confidently and slurped it back.

Whallop, I gave him a good strike to set the hook as my T24's are quite soft. The rod was immediately bent to the butt... all I could do was hold on as the clutch was absolutely screaming, the fish was going so fast I had to keep feeding line to it with my left hand as it was bumping the rod tip down. This fish was obviously very angry with himself. Soon he had taken 80 yards of line and was near the margins at the end of the bay. I had kept the rod high to avoid the weed and snags, but now I bent into the fish, and with as much pressure as I dared I let the rod sap the beast of his energy. Fifteen minutes later the fish was ready for the net, *'come to daddy'* I thought to myself as I pulled him over the cord. There was a massive eruption as the fish found a new lease of life and powered off towards some snags to my left. I bent the rod round and pumped as fast as I could. *'please don't come off big fella'* he rolled on the surface exhausted and was lead to the net like a lamb, *'got ya'!* I lifted it up the bank and laid the net on the thick grass. I unhooked the fish and sacked it in the deep shady margin. I packed my rod up, ran back to the car and drove to the Douglas Lane car park to get somebody to witness the capture and take some photographs. The car park was full of cars and bivvies and as I approached the first bivvy, who should it be but Dave Moore. I told him my news and he told me there had also been a 39lb 4oz mirror out opening night to one of the Rotherham lads.

Dave, Richard Skidmore and John Hallet came round to the bay where we weighed the fish and photographed it. They even took some video film, these lads were excited as I was, well nearly!

The fish weighed in at 37lb dead, a new personal best. The rest of the fish had moved away with the wind change but who cares, what a result!

The next couple of trips to Wraysbury were frustrating as I spotted fish in various spots but they moved quickly, these fish are very nomadic.

I decided to put the second part of my plan into action and drove the extra 15 miles to Yateley. I decided on the Pad Lake. The first trip was in early July and the *Forty* had been out and all the other fish hooked and lost, needless to say I blanked. The next trip (my usual Sunday till Tuesday) was also a blank, though I felt I was fishing well. I was catching tench regularly so I knew the rigs and bait were working. A five inch, eight pound hooklink with a size eight Super Specialist hook seemed to be very effective. I also used a one and a quarter ounce lead for maximum indication. The tench seemed to prefer dead weight sinkers to pop-ups, so that was my set up. Third trip on August 12th I set up on the narrow path to the left of the weed corner, this being the best area to view the whole lake. My marker rod revealed a large gravel area at the end of a bar running down the middle part of the lake. Both rods were fished there. The first night was hectic and tiring, five tench were landed to seven pounds. I had worked the tench into a frenzy, using a three-bait stringer every cast and feeding a constant stream of boilies in every ten to 15 minutes. After landing another tench at 9.30am I recast to the 'hot area' when suddenly I had a blistering take, the rod was bouncing in the rests. I pulled into the fish and knew immediately it was one of the big two. The fish tested me and my eight pound line to the limit trying to power me into the marginal snags. To say I was relieved when I pulled the fish over the cord was an understatement. The 15 minute battle left me shaking uncontrollably. Micky Daly helped me weigh and photograph the fish, 33lb 8oz – great. I was walking on air! Incidently this carp was a male fish, *'take my word for it'*. The next morning again at 9.30am, another fast take, the rod hooping over as the fish started to power off, I

Chorley Anglers
SPECIALIST TACKLE DEALERS AND ROD BUILDERS

CENTURY ARMALITE, CONOFLEX, HARRISON, TRI-CAST, ETC.
BLANKS AND CUSTOM BUILT RODS A SPECIALITY

SHIMANO AUTHORISED DEALER • DAIWA PREMIER DEALER • WYCHWOOD • FOX • NASH
EUSTACE GOLD LABEL • KJB • GARDNER • DRENNAN • NUTRABAITS • RICHWORTH • ETC

NEW FOX INTERNATIONAL
Supa Brolly	£124.90
Supa Brolly In-fill	£54.90
Supa Bivvy	£145.90
Extra Storm Pole Attachments x 2	£6.50

REELS REELS REELS
DAIWA PM 4000H
Superb distance reel. Big spool with 6mm diameter shaft, unique line guard system and fast 5:1 retrieve. **£79.90**
SHIMANO AERLEX 8000GT
One of our staff has added a measured thirty yards to his casting by using this reel. Converted with a full bail arm. **£65.00**
SHIMANO BIOMASTER 3000X
Brilliant lure fishing reel. The ideal partner for our Lure Special. **£39.90**

BIG GAME LINE
Highly abrasion resistant and very supple. Breaks well over stated test. 4oz spools. 10lb/12lb/15lb **£15.95**

RODS RODS RODS
Armalite Express 12ft 3lb	£130.00
Armalite Express 12ft 2½lb	£125.00
Armalite C.P.T. 12ft 3½lb	£140.00
Armalite C.P.T. 12ft 2½lb	£125.00
Armalite C.P.T. 12ft 2¼lb	£125.00
Harrison Ballista 12ft 2¾lb	£99.95
Harrison Multi Range 12ft 2¼lb	£99.95
Harrison 11ft Avon	£75.90

Chorley Anglers 10ft Lure Special
At last, a rod designed for British lure fanatics! This rod has won a lot of friends since it was unveiled at the P.A.C. Conference. Handles lures from ½oz to 1oz-plus with plenty of power to set hooks at range yet retaining a sensitive tip. **£79.90**

FOX BEDCHAIRS IN STOCK!

ROD PODS
KJB 2 rod	£59.95
3 rod	£64.95
Fox Standard	£24.90
Extending	£32.50
Gardner Pro-Pod	£34.95

WYCHWOOD
K2 RUCKSACK
Huge capacity and carries like a true backpacker. Puts all other rucksacks in the shade. Worth every penny. **£120.00**
Carp Quiver	£25.48
Insider Holdall 12ft or 13ft	£65.89
Insider Deluxe 12ft or 13ft	£81.21
K2 Suit	£122.61

PREMIER BAITS
Booking NOW for bulk deals

KRYSTON PRODUCTS
NEW Ambio 125ml	£3.53
500ml	£11.20
Silkworm 20m 8lb/10lb/12lb/15lb	£6.89
Silkworm Ultra Soft 12lb	£6.89
Silkworm 20m 25lb	£7.40
Supersilk 20m 14lb	£6.89
Merlin 20m 8lb/10lb/12lb/15lb	£6.38
Multi-Strand 75ft	£6.89
No Tangle Gel	£3.02

12 Gillibrand Street, Chorley, Lancs, PR7 2EJ.
Telephone (02572) 63513
Open 9-5.30 Mon-Fri 9-5.00 Saturday (Closed Wednesday)

MAIL ORDER
Sorry we don't have a catalogue. Just phone to check your requirements and we will give you our best attention.

POSTAGE RATES PER ORDER
Small items 50p Large items £3 Rods £5

Wraysbury 37lb

was giving it line when the hook pulled out. To be honest I didn't care at the time but looking back it could quite well have been the *Forty*.

Two weeks laters one-eyed Jack had the brace in my absence, 36lb 8oz and 34lb, the *Forty* was down but what a brace, 'Well done mate'. I decided to pull off for a month to let the big 'un recover. During a couple of day trips to the crayfish pool at Kingsmead I managed to sneak a few out on floaters at 19lb and 23lb, the long scaley thirty managed to beat me twice, but that, as they say, is another story.

On my return to the Pad Lake I was told that three fish had been hooked and lost. I tried not to let this bother me and fished the first night, but when Craig lost a fish in the morning I didn't feel confident so decided on a move to the Car Park or the North Lake. I reeled in and walked round both lakes, and immediately fancied the North.

The wind was gale force ripping into the back bay and nobody else was there. I set up on the works bank at the mouth of the bay in the hope of ambushing the fish. I set my rods up in the water and angled them diagonally, casting behind the weed rather than over the top of it. The left hand rod was cast to the back of the island in the bay. The other rod was cast to the front of the little island on the mouth of the bay. These areas were baited very heavily as I was 100% confident the fish were there. That night my umbrella was gutted twice and I had to sleep with my arm through the brolly ribs. At 4am the left hand rod was bent round and the bobbin a blur. When I finally managed to hit the run the line was solid. For ten minutes I pulled, holding the rod straight, the eight pound line singing in the wind, 'til an enormous weight was coming towards me. Slowly, inch by inch I hand-lined an enormous piece of weed to my feet. Convinced it was a tench I hauled the whole mound into the net. I felt down in the net *'magic'* it's a carp, a long fish of about 18 pounds I thought. When I pulled the weed away, in the torchlight lay one of the prettiest long scaley mirrors I have ever caught. Was I pleased? I'll say not many – she weighed in at 26lb 4oz.

This brings me up to date, last trip on the Pad Lake was the end of October when I pulled out of another fish after I had managed to steer it out of the pads. The fairy tale ending wasn't to be. I'll be back in the new year after the birth of our first child. I'd just like to thank Julie (my other half) for being so understanding with my fishing.

Bye for now and good luck to all the lads who are fishing at Yateley.

Left:
Crayfish Pool 23lb

Below:
North Lake 26lb 4oz

93

Pad Lake - 33lb 8oz

Kent Particles

J. Bevan
40 Borkwood Way
Orpington
Kent, BR6 9PD
0689 850276

Access *VISA*

MAIL ORDER, CREDIT CARDS WELCOME

PREMIER BAITS

Fish Meals · Fish Base Mixes
Protein Ingredients · Oils · Flavours
Colours · Vitamins · Extracts · Bird Seeds
Bulk Orders

PARTICLES

Tiger Nuts · Moth Beans · Maples
Peanuts, Small Red, Large Pink · Hempseed
Tares · Dari · Groats · Rapeseed
Maize · Popcorn · Aduki (Adzuki) · Pinto
Mung · Butter etc · Chick Pea · Blackeye
Tic Beans · Yellow Peas · Cow Peas
Anything not listed please ask

TIGER NUT MEAL
Available soon

TIGER NUT BASE MIX
Available soon

BIRDSEEDS

Robin Red · Red Factor · Spicy Pepper
Nectarblend · PTX
Blue Maw · CLO · Cypryseed
Anything not listed please ask

COLEMAN
Sleeping bags · cookers

EPI Gas Lanterns
and cookers

KJB Tackle and Accessories (tubing etc) · Bob Frost Accessories · Wychwood Tackle · Romart
Magnum Stainless Steel · Bruce & Walker's Merlin Rods · Proteus Line
Reuben Heaton Scales, Weigh Bars and Tripods · Roach Tackle & Clothing available to order
D.M. Brolly Camps · Bivvy Domes · Kryston Silk · Easy Melt PVA
Weights · Catapults · Tubing · Rig Putty

Kettles (adonised) · Water Carriers (2½ gals) · Fuel Bottles
Torches · Roller Tables · Bait Guns · Wind Shield · Collapsible Washing Bowls

---

**Enquiries for A1 Enlargements, Slides, Water Colours etc or
Phone Mark on 071-231 2507 and ask for details**

HOW TO ORDER

Make cheques out to **Kent Particles** including postage and send to the above address or telephone 0689 850276.
Send an S.A.E. for price list

POSTAL RATES

1kg....£2.75   2kg....£3.50
Upto 4kg....£4.50   Upto 8kg....£5.50
8kg to 30kg....£6.50

GOOD DISCOUNTS FOR CARP SOCIETY MEMBERS

Kent Particles

BOUNTY HUNTER PUBLICATIONS

BIG CARP MAGAZINES

Issue 1: £3.75 – Still available
Issue 2: £3.75 – Still available
Issue 3: £3.75 – Still available
Issue 4: £3.75 – Still available   **Issue 5:** £3.75 – Still available
Issue 6: £3.75 – Still available

Subscribe to Big Carp Magazine: £22.50 UK, £28.50 Overseas, **POST FREE.**
For any back issues of Big Carp Magazine send £3.75 + 75p postage.

BINDERS NOW AVAILABLE – SEE BELOW

BIG CARP VIDEOS & BOOKS

YATELEY YA-HOO	CANARY'S CARPIN'	STARTIN' CARPIN' 1	STARTIN' CARPIN' 2	FOX POOL
£17.99 post free	£15.99 post free	£15.99 post free	£15.99 post free	£18.95 post free
Rob Maylin	Kevin Nash	Kevin Nash	Kevin Nash	Rob Maylin & The Famous Five

NEW BIG CARP OFFERS

Big Carp Annual – Available May 1st
Phone for information

BIG CARP BINDERS
Vol. 1 (Issues 1-6) &
Vol. 2 (Issues 7-12)
Top Quality Cordex Binders
£8.50 POST FREE

Zen's Rig Book – Available mid-May
Phone for information

HAREFIELD HAULIN'
Rob Maylin's Harefield Video –
Available July.
Please don't phone until July.

BIG CARP SPECIAL OFFERS FOR 1992

OFFER 1 – Binder Vol. 1 containing issues 1-6 £31.00 – BINDER VOL. 2 FREE!
OFFER 2 – 1 Year's subscription, issues 7-12 – ANY BACK ISSUES POST FREE!
OFFER 3 – 1 Year's subscription, issues 7-12 + Binder Vol. 1 £31.00 – BINDER VOL. 2 £5!

Big Carp Sportswear (NOW AVAILABLE IN BLACK)

Now is your chance to purchase Big Carp quality clothing. T-shirts, sweatshirts, polo shirts, jogging bottoms and baseball caps; all finished in Royal Blue or Black with the Red, Gold and Black Big Carp logo stylishly embroidered on each garment. These are not the usual cheap printed shirts, but are quality sportswear manufactured by Halken Hunt who make individual sportswear for such famous names as Paul Gascoine and Rob Maylin to name but two.

Product	Size	Price	P&P
T-Shirt (short sleeve)	M, L, XL	£10.00	£1.00
Sweatshirt (long sleeve)	M, L, XL	£15.00	£1.50
Polo Shirt (short sleeve, collared)	M, L, XL	£13.00	£1.00
Jogging Bottoms	M, L, XL	£19.00	£1.50
Baseball Cap (9oz adjustable)	One Size	£10.00	£1.00

Be the envy of all your friends, pull the girl of your dreams, be the best dressed carp angler in the pub. It's easy when you wear the fashionable Big Carp Sportswear.

<u>ALSO</u> **Personalise Your Sportswear** For an extra £3 you can have the name of your choice stylishly embroidered in gold thread under the Big Carp logo. Anything you like! Joe Bloggs, Carp Casualty, Tim Paisley, Master Baiter, The Darenth Hit Squad etc., either your name or the name of the group of anglers you fish with. You can look the absolute 'Dog's Knackers' with personally embroidered Big Carp Sportswear.

<u>NEW</u> **Big Carp Bum Bags – £8.99 + £1 p&p**

The new BC Bum Bag is finished in dark blue hard wearing fabric with red piping and the Big Carp logo. Money compartment, puff pouch, club card and licence compartment. Keep all your gear safe and look cool at the same time, no carp angler should be without one. Please allow 28 days for delivery if you require mega-fat size.

We realise that not all of our readers can afford £22.50 for a subscription, the simple answer is just to walk into your local tackle shop and ask him to order Big Carp Magazine from us, for you. There is no minimum order, tackle shops order what they want. Big Carp is not available in newsagents – only tackle shops.

For information on any of our products please phone **0525 715728** during office hours.
CHEQUES SHOULD BE MADE PAYABLE TO **BOUNTY HUNTER PUBLICATIONS** AND SENT TO:
65 THE QUANTOCKS, FLITWICK, BEDFORDSHIRE MK45 1TG

MY PASSION FOR CARP

SAVAY - AN OPPORTUNITY TAKEN

ANDY LITTLE

Because of the friendship that I struck up with Lennie Middleton and his little group of anglers, I was fortunate enough to be invited into the syndicate that was to be formed at Savay. It was Bob Davis, one of Lennie's friends, who I also became quite friendly with whilst fishing Darenth, who was trying to organise this particular project, along with Graham Rowles who was the fishery manager at the Redlands controlled water. I had known about Savay for several years and little snippets of information always managed to drift through on the carp angling grapevine. Although very little was ever publicised about the catches, I knew in great detail the sort of stocking that had taken place there over the years.

Very few people realise that Savay started out as a trout fishery and it wasn't until the Ruislip club took over the fishing rights in the late forties that it became a coarse fishery. It was in 1950 that Savay actually received its first stocking of 300 Leney strain carp. There had been other stockings since but it was this first influx of Leney fish that really interested me, for it was known that, given the right conditions, this very exceptional strain of carp could go on and do quite tremendous things. Famous waters such as Redmire and Billing Aquadrome have produced massive carp from this particular strain. So here we have this very rich southern gravel pit that had fortunately been stocked, in my opinion, with the best type of fish available.

As you can imagine, there was very little arm twisting when it came to me being offered a place on that very first syndicate. The carp anglers who were members of the Ruislip club did such a good job of keeping their catches quiet that other than a few anglers on the select grapevine that existed in carp angling very little was known about what was actually going on there. The idea of forming a syndicate was to ascertain the potential of the carp fishing at Savay. This, with hindsight, was a bit of a joke!

Obviously, Redlands were looking to produce some extra revenue from this stretch of water and they could see that if the carp fishing potential was good, then there may be a situation there that they could capitalise on. The problem was that the way it was described to us was that this was going to be a trial and very much a one off situation. There was a very good chance then that I would only be able to fish Savay for just this one season. The timing for this could not have been worse, for up until now I had been on shift work, which had enabled me to fish for quite extensive hours during the week, but I had recently been given promotion and I was back on the eight to five stint. It certainly posed something of a problem; if I only had this one season to fish then I obviously wanted to fish for as much time as possible.

Although Savay was some 65 acres or so in size, the syndicate was not allowed to fish all of it. In fact, I doubt if there was probably any more than about 40 acres for me to choose from. It was definitely no larger than anything I had ever tackled before. That, together with the fact that Savay is split up into many small bays by islands and long peninsulas, made it seem a much smaller water than in fact it really was.

I had to think of some plan of action to get the most out of the time I had available to me. What I had decided to do was to fish every night of my rota and the weekends. I had about six weeks holiday owing to me, so all of this time was going to be devoted to fishing at Savay. I did have a few other commitments on other waters, but some of these would have to go by the wayside. They could always be fished another day.

I often wonder, when I am looking back, what the original carpers of the Ruislip club must have thought of all this, for they had had this little piece of heaven to themselves for quite some considerable time and for sure, whatever happened once the syndicate went on there, it would never, ever be the same again. I suppose all they could hope for was for us all to fail miserably, for although there were substantial stocks at Savay, it was by no stretch of the imagination, an easy water. In fact, I do know that during this time some of the original members of the Ruislip club really struggled to catch fish there.

There were two rotas and it was almost like a Who's Who of carp fishing. Bob Davis had actually picked out, to my mind, some of the best carp anglers in the country. Now if these lads weren't going to catch from Savay, I'm sure no one was.

I was very fortunate to be on the first rota, so I was going to get first crack at fishing Savay. Rota one consisted of:

Derek Cunnington
Pete Ward
Graham Marshall
Malcolm Richardson
Andy Little
John Dunn
Bob Davis
Dave Beckett
Keith Gillings
Mike Wilson
Lennie Middleton
Rod Hutchinson
Kevin Maddocks
John Webb
Graham McCulum

Rota two was:

Paul Bray
Roger Smith
John Richards
James McCulum
Bob Harper
Sam Gates
Tony Howles
Keith Selleck
Geoff Kemp
Paul Allen
Albert Romp
Clive Dietrich
Bob Baker
Malcolm Winkworth

Certainly this was a force to be reckoned with and, in my opinion, I don't think any water, up until that time, would have had so much pressure exerted on it as these anglers were about to put on Savay.

By the time the rotas were drawn up and we'd had a couple of meetings for the rules and regulations and, of course, parted with our money, there was very little of the close season left and I felt there was much work to be done. I would just have to put myself out so every spare moment I had for the rest of the close season, was spent on the banks of Savay. The time was consumed by plumbing the depths and looking for fish and just gently trying to get to know the place. Although at first the sheer size of the water did not seem to be a daunting prospect, I found so many favourable areas that all of them could not be possibly covered.

From my close season observations, the same fish could be seen at one end of the lake one day and the opposite end the next day, so they were going to move around a lot. Although there were odd bands of residential fish, the bulk of them seemed to move on either because of weather conditions or bankside activity. This again, I thought may be something of a problem for suddenly, a water that had experienced very little pressure was about to be descended upon by a band of very proficient carp anglers. I'm sure there were many swims at Savay, prior to the syndicate, that had hardly seen an angler during the whole of the season.

I was confronted by some marvellous sights towards the start of the season. From vantage points high above the water, I observed two or three large shoals of carp, containing in excess of 50 fish. There were very few of these fish that looked under 20 pounds. In fact, I would have said the majority of them were over 25 pounds, with a lot over thirty. This, I had never seen anywhere before. I was spellbound, just watching these huge shoals of very large carp moving up and down this beautiful water.

It was very difficult making up my mind exactly how I was going to approach the water in terms of bait. I knew that in the past successful anglers such as Mike Wilson had had some tremendous catches by fishing on particles, obviously at very close range. There were a number of swims that actually screamed out at you that they were going to be good for this type of approach. My only problem was that in the back of my mind I kept thinking that all of a sudden there was going to be a great deal more bankside activity and would the carp respond in the same way? Of course, during the quiet of the close season, the fish were very much present in the margins and on the surface of it, this looked like the obvious place to fish, but after much wrestling in my mind I actually decided to do the opposite and try to find a couple of likely areas where I could fish at reasonably long range.

What I was hoping for was to try to get the edge over the other guys, remembering that they were all proficient anglers – so I had to do something completely different. I did know, after talking to one or two of them during the course of the close season, it was going to be a full frontal approach on the particles that most of them were going to adopt, so I sorted out three different areas in various parts of the lake that I could fish fairly comfortably at long range against particular features.

My favourite was along the first part of the Canal bank. There was a confluence of bars that all finished up on quite a large plateau just in front of an area known as *Alcatraz*. Now here the lake split into a Y – the right hand side of it going into the North Bay, while the left hand side went down through the channel and eventually ended up in Cottage Bay. Any carp moving up and down the lake would have to make up their minds which way they were going to go, either into the North Bay or into the channel and beyond. Therefore it seemed logical that this would be a good interception point.

As a back up, there was another area in the Cottage Bay itself. Here was a very large bed of zebra mussels, and I'm sure it was a natural feeding area as well as another stop off point on their way in and out of the Cottage Bay. At the other end of the lake, the southern end, there was a swim which came to be known as *The Birches*. Here the water narrowed down and there was another confluence of bars, ending up in quite a few dead ends. I was sure that with a good northerly wind blowing, the carp would end up down there. These then were really the three areas I was going to concentrate on, so regardless of weather conditions and bankside activity, I would have a choice.

The plateau out in front of the *Alcatraz* area looked to me to be the most favourable spot in all the lake, the problem being that there was no actual swim from which it could be fished. So, very carefully, I made myself a swim in the reeds, just enough for rods and bedchair. I could now set about a baiting up programme and for the rest of the close season, instead of walking the banks and doing any more plumbing, the time was devoted to rolling bait and actually baiting up.

The bait I was to use was going to be very similar to the one I had used at Darenth during the previous winter. The distance I would be fishing would be roughly the same so I knew that the mix and the size of the baits that I was rolling could easily cope with baiting up the *Alcatraz* area. I had slightly changed the original mix which was quite a good protein mix of casein, lactalbumin, calcium casinate and gluten etc. In the new mix I had substituted some of the lighter milk protein powder with semolina, so I ended up with the heavier casein, semolina

Tired and wet, but very happy

and gluten. This was bound together with eggs and could be made up to quite a solid bait which would stand being catapulted a considerable distance without flattening or breaking up. The attractor was again the maple – this was a marvellous flavour that I had great success on during the latter part of the winter at Darenth. I was using quite a lot, up to about 20ml in a ten ounce mix, and also quite a bit of sweetener; there was very little concentrated sweetener about at the time, but by diluting ordinary granulated sugar in a pan of boiling water I was able to get the concentrated solution and this I used to sweeten the mix.

It was quite funny really, because obviously there were a lot of the other syndicate members milling around during this latter part of the close season and, naturally, we discussed the sort of tactics that we were going to use. Although I kept a fair bit to myself, I did say that I was going to fish it at long range on boilies and most of them thought I was absolutely mad! Because they were all observing the fish in the margins and they had been caught there they wondered why on earth I was going to fish at long range, when they were seemingly so catchable in the margins. I was just hoping that I hadn't got it completely wrong and I was going to end up looking a right berk whilst everyone else was stacking them up under their rod tips.

There was an opportunity to go in with one or two of the other guys, but I opted to do my own thing. I did, however, keep having this inkling at the back of my mind that perhaps I had got it wrong. The rest of the

A superbly scaled whacker

ERIC'S (NEW) ANGLING CENTRE

ERIC & JOSIE WELCOME ALL CUSTOMERS TO THEIR NEW LARGER ANGLING CENTRE

SEE THE MOST EXTENSIVE STOCKS OF CARP, AND SPECIALIST TACKLE ON DISPLAY AT YORKSHIRE'S PREMIER TACKLE SHOP

MAIL ORDER A PLEASURE PLEASE RING FOR DETAILS ACCESS AND VISA ACCEPTED

401 SELBY ROAD · WHITKIRK · LEEDS LS15 7AY · TEL 0532 646883
YORKSHIRE'S PREMIER CARP SPECIALISTS AND TACKLE SHOP

PREMIER BAITS

QUALITY INGREDIENTS AND FLAVOURINGS

15 BLENHEIM CLOSE, PYSONS INDUSTRIAL ESTATE, BROADSTAIRS, KENT CT10 2YF
TELEPHONE: 0843 860850

1991 CATALOGUE 50p P&P

Jock White 36.12 Yateley

Don Orris 46.2 Yateley

FISH BASE MIXES

For best results add dry mix gradually to eggs/flavour/oil

Fish Base Mix	£5.20 per kg	£10.00 per 2kg
Salmon Fish Base Mix	£5.75 per kg	£11.00 per 2kg
Spiced Fish Base Mix	£5.75 per kg	£11.00 per 2kg
Marine Mix	£5.75 per kg	£11.00 per 2kg
Fish Fodder	£4.20 per kg	£ 8.00 per 2kg
Supreme Fish Mix	£7.50 per kg	n/a
Aquatic Formulae	£8.65 per kg	n/a

Use Fish Oil at 30ml per 6 eggs

FISH OILS

	per 500mlg	per gallon
Fish Feed Inducing Oil	£ 5.50	£35.00
Noddoil	£11.00	£70.00
Pure Salmon Oil	£12.00	£75.00
Crunt Oil	£ 5.50	£35.00
Japanese Fish Oil	£ 5.50	£35.00

Not to be used with Emulsifier

SUPPLEMENT

P.D.F.A. Supplement Oil £10.00 per 200ml

FISH BASE BULK DEALS

10 kilos of Mix + 2 x 500ml Bottle of any Fish Oil except Noddoil or Salmon Oil.
For 2 x 500ml bottle Noddoil or Salmon Oil add £10.00 to total price.

10kg Fish Base Mix + Oil	£50.00 + p&p	10kg Fish Fodder + Oil	£40.00 + p&p
10kg Salmon Fish Base Mix + Oil	£55.00 + p&p	10kg Supreme Fish Mix + Oil	£70.00 + p&p
10kg Spiced Fish Base Mix + Oil	£55.00 + p&p	10kg Aquatic Formulae + Oil	£77.50 + p&p
10kg Marine Mix + Oil	£55.00 + p&p		

PROTEIN MIXES

Summer Pro 65	£ 6.90 per kg
Winter Pro 90	£10.66 per kg

SEED MIX

Spiced Cypro Seed	£6.90 per kg

NUTRITIONAL SEED MIXES

These mixes contain the correct level of Noddoil Attractor, Sweetener and a unique blend of flavours already milled into the dry mix. Just add dry mix to eggs until the correct consistency is achieved. Boil for two minutes and allow to dry.

Salmon	£5.75 per 1kg	£11.00 per 2kg	£50.00 per 10kg
Fruit	£5.75 per 1kg	£11.00 per 2kg	£50.00 per 10kg
Savoury	£5.75 per 1kg	£11.00 per 2kg	£50.00 per 10kg
Neutral*	£5.50 per 1kg	£10.50 per 2kg	£45.00 per 10kg

* as other nutritional mixes, but without flavour so you can add your own.

DRY INGREDIENTS

	£/1kg	£/5kg		£/1kg	£/5kg
200 Mesh Casein	8.25	38.00	Salmon Meal	3.20	15.00
90 Mesh Rennet Casein	8.25	38.00	Anchovy Meal	3.20	15.00
80 Mesh Acid Casein	8.25	38.00	Sardine Meal	2.20	10.00
Lactalbumin (N.Z.)	8.25	38.00	Capelin Meal	2.20	10.00
Lactalbumin (W.G.)	8.25	38.00	White Fish Meal	2.20	10.00
Calcium Caseinate	8.25	38.00	Tuna Meal	2.80	13.00
Cypry Seed	2.00	9.00	Daphnia	8.00	37.00
Norwegian Seaweed Meal	4.00	18.00	Codlivine	3.00	14.00
Vitamealo	3.20	15.00	Robin Red	6.00	28.00
C.L.O. Bird Food	2.00	8.00			

Mark Dean 34.0

Lee Tomlinson 42.0

PURE EXTRACTS

Japanese Oyster Extract	£7.00 per 2oz
Atlantic Shrimp Extract	£7.00 per 2oz

VITAMIN

Nutra-Vit – £2.60 per 4oz pot
Colours – Yellow, Red, Brown, Blue £1.76 per 25 grams.

Now available Premier T-shirts featuring London, Paris logo
Only in Black – L, XL, FM – £5.00 + 60p P&P

FLAVOURS

	£/50ml	£/200ml		£/50ml	£/200ml		£/50ml	£/200ml
Anchovy Extract	n/a	2.75	Pistachio Nut	2.50	6.00	Pineapple Crush	2.50	6.00
Apricot	2.50	6.00	Shrimp Scampi	2.50	6.00	Raspberry Jam	2.50	6.00
Bun Spice	2.50	6.00	Tropical Fruit	2.50	6.00	Smoked Ham	2.50	6.00
Cinnamon	2.50	6.00	Victoria Plum	2.50	6.00	Chocolate Mint	2.50	6.00
Honey Special	2.50	6.00	Cheesecake	2.50	6.00	Condensed Milk	2.50	7.00
Kiwi	2.50	6.00	Clove	2.50	6.00	Lime	2.50	7.00
Maple Syrup	2.50	6.00	Cornish Cream	2.50	6.00	Mungo Juice	2.50	7.00
Melon	2.50	6.00	Garlic	2.50	6.00	Salmon	2.50	8.00
Passion Fruit	2.50	6.00	Ginger Root	2.50	6.00	Fresh Strawberry	2.50	8.00
Pear	2.50	6.00	Peach Melba	2.50	6.00	Liquid Sweetener	2.50	6.00

Premier Measuring Cylinders 25ml £1.50   50ml £2.50   25p P & P

★ PREMIER BAITS NOW AVAILABLE IN HOLLAND FROM: ★

PREMIER BAITS HOLLAND, POSTWEG 81, 3769 BW, SOESTERBERG, HOLLAND. TEL 034 63-51907
HENGELSPORT CENTRUM, WOUT VAN LEEUWEN, OOST HAVEN KADE 47, 3134NW, VLADRDINGEN
TEL: 031 104 343060   FAX: 031 104 356573

HOW TO ORDER

Make out cheque including postage payable to "PREMIER BAITS" and post to address opposite.
N.B. 500ml bottle Fish Oil weighs ½ kilogram.
We now accept most major credit cards.

POSTAGE & PACKING RATES

1 kilo	£2.50	Up to 5kg	£4.65
2kg	£3.15	Over 5kg	£5.50
3kg	£4.10	Over 50kg	P.O.A.

lads were certainly very good anglers and all, in their own right, had done exceptionally well on many waters up and down the country and I'm sure a lot of them were far more experienced than me. Anyway, I was now committed to doing my own thing and I would have to see it through, come hell or high water. Mapping out the water was a mammoth task; I did spend a lot of time with rod and reel, legerweight and float but it was so time consuming that I needed to do the job much more quickly. To be honest, although I probably shouldn't be saying this, I ended up getting in the water myself and in fact swam over most of it, feeling for the features with my feet. Of course, this was during the close season and I was doing it quite late in the evening, so I could not be seen. It was quite interesting and is one of the best ways of getting to know a water where you can actually do it. There are so many bars in Savay that a lot of the areas are just like a ploughed field, and the side of the bars are incredibly steep. The interesting thing was that many of the bars actually joined each other, so what you would have would be two bars running parallel to each other and then ending up in a V shape as they both joined together. Now this end of these long troughs, between the two bars that were joining, had to be a really good area because there was so much food that had accumulated there.

There was one of these in front of the *Reedy* swim, at about 50 yards, so there was a second area I could fish as well as the distant plateau. There were plenty of areas, however, where I just couldn't get down deep enough to find out exactly what was there, so I was still unable to cover the whole area, but I found enough of interest to suit exactly what I was going to do. These much deeper areas were of very little interest to me – at the start of the season anyway.

So, with the end of the close season rapidly approaching, I had done all the mapping out that I wanted to do and had got a fair number of baits introduced into the water. I'm glad to say the carp were already responding to my baiting up, which really started to give me a little bit of encouragement.

I was aware that there were more large carp at Savay than I had ever seen in my life, although of course I didn't know exact numbers. You have to remember that up until then, for the whole of my angling career, I had only caught five thirty pounders. I say only – I was very pleased with my results, but I had been used to fishing waters which, at best, had maybe one or two thirties and a handful of twenties. I was now confronted with a situation that there were many more twenties; I really didn't know how many, certainly many more than I had ever seen anywhere, and also there was a very large percentage of 30 pounders.

During my close season observations I had seen as many as maybe ten fish that could have possibly been over thirty pounds, so this was something quite exciting and incredible. I was aware of the potential and there were times that, just looking at the fish, I was shaking at the thought of putting a hook anywhere near so many large carp.

My first session on the water was on the first day of the season. As I said before, I was very lucky that I was on the first rota, so this was an opportunity I was certainly not going to let pass by. I had originally planned to start at Longfield with a friend of mine, Dave Reekie, and then move on to Darenth later on in the season but, of course, this had to go by the wayside – the call of Savay was just too great.

Lennie, for some reason or another, was not quite so optimistic as I was about Savay and he decided that he was going to start at Waveney and carry on his trials where he had left off at Darenth. Both Kevin and Lennie had done extremely well at the Waveney Valley complex a couple of seasons before and I think he really wanted to get himself in front of a lot of responsive fish, just to keep his experimentation going. You have to remember that there were very few people who knew what was going on, and I was very lucky to be part of this little band of very innovative anglers.

From what I could make out, there was probably going to be at least three-quarters of the rota there on the first day of the season. It was going to be quite interesting to see how they all fared.

Mind you, I really got stitched up that first day! Bob Davis told me that there was very little point in getting there until about 4pm on the 15th June as the gate would be closed and the lock that was on there would have a different key. So I thought rather than waste a day, I would actually do a day's

It just got better...

work, therefore giving myself another day later in the season. I suppose it was somewhere around half past three, quarter to four when I arrived at Savay on the afternoon of the 15th and to my amazement, I found the gate open. I was even more amazed when I drove down to the car park to find it almost full!

You can imagine the sort of things that were going through my mind at that point. With so many people there, I really wondered if I would get a swim in any of the three areas I had in mind. I could see that one of the swims over on the Cottage bank had already been taken, so there were only the other two areas which I fancied, that might be free. It was quite a long walk round to the Canal bank, so I thought I might as well load up my gear and take it anyway. There were sure to be one or two spots down there, even if I couldn't get my little *Reedy* swim.

As I made my way past *Alcatraz* I could see that Bob Davis and Keith Gillings were already set up. As I turned the corner into the North Bay, the Norfolk lads were making themselves comfortable, so at least this would mean there would be less people down on the Canal bank, so I felt that I had a chance.

There was no one at all along the Canal bank adjacent to the North Bay, and it wasn't until I reached Mike Wilson's swim that any other spots had been taken. Now Mike's was a swim to end all swims – he had been fishing here for two or three seasons and he had really made it comfortable for himself. He had nice cover in front with some beautiful iris, duck boards which were put down to stop him getting muddy feet, and the rest of the swim was turfed and cut. Mike's set up had to be one of the best prepared that I had ever seen; rods were all set out perfectly, rod mats and indicators, spare rods to the side and landing net positioned. If that wasn't bad enough, he had already got a very professional looking two and a quarter square camera set up on a tripod stand. He was obviously going to do the business! I was very much aware of the sort of success that Mike had had previously. In fact, during our one or two meetings throughout the close season, he had been quite open about his tactics and the sort of fish he had caught. He had been using particles, mainly maize, and using this as a carrier for some very special flavours he had been playing about with.

He obviously knew the topography of Savay very well, because we had quite a discussion about many of the features that abound within this lake. In fact, his own swim, which was on the east bank of the North Bay, looked perfect. There was a small island to the right, with a long bar leading off it, and a plateau some way to the left. All of this was only a few rod lengths out from the bank. These features acted as a natural funnel for fish moving in and out of the North Bay, so to my mind, he had chosen this spot very well.

I had a quick chat with Mike, but he could obviously see that I was itching to get started. He gave me the good news that there was no one in the little *Reedy* swim, so I could breath a sigh of relief. Just as I approached the swim the heavens opened, so it was up with the umbrella and on with the kettle. Mike came along for a chat and we sat there under the umbrella and, while sipping our tea, talked about the many different lakes that we had fished over the years. Eventually, we got around to Savay itself and just how I was going to approach it. He looked at my set up, with my two ounce leads and fast taper rods and was quite mystified about the whole thing – remember, he had been quite open about his method and I suppose he was wondering why I wasn't following suit. When I showed him the thousands of three-quarter inch diameter boilies that I was about to use, he was completely horrified.

The rods were basically the same as those I was using at Darenth the season before. All I had done was that I had changed over from the original green Clooper blanks from Going Brothers, to the newer, slightly more upmarket black Conoflex Cloopers. These were still very fast taper jobs, ideal for this distance fishing that I was doing. By then I had gone on to the Cardinal 66X reels which, at the time, I honestly believed were the best available. The problem was that these came in a peculiar bronzy brown colour with a cream flier to the spool. This was, of course, during the ultra cult period and this just would not do, so these were painted matt black to match the rods. The spools of the Cardinals were overfilled with eight pound Sylcast line. This I used straight through the hooklink as well, for I was positive they could not be tackle-shy fish. A two ounce lead and a size six Au Lion d'Or hook completed the

An incredible fish caught on maple flavour

Penge Angling

FREE CREDIT!!!
UP TO NINE MONTHLY PAYMENTS AT NO EXTRA CHARGE
Three Shops Covering London, Kent & Essex

ROD HUTCHINSON TACKLE

Rod HUTCHINSON FISHING DEVELOPMENTS LIMITED

MAIN DEALER
Penge Angling are delighted to be chosen as one of the few dealers able to offer the whole range of this exclusive tackle.

ROD HUTCHINSON DE-LUXE I.M.X. CARP RODS
Rod assures us that they are far in advance of any other carp rods now available. They are fitted luxuriously with deluxe silicon rings and all black deluxe F P S reel fittings and fitted carbon line clips.

Rod's advice is that all carp anglers fishing long range on big lakes will be after the 3.5lb models in both 12' and 13'. These are for extreme range fishing.

The 2.5lb models will in the right hands cast 150 yards, although your average angler will be casting more in the 120 yard range.

The 2lb and 2.25lb models are the ultimate in all round carp fishing and both will still easily cast 100 yards. These are more suited to the smaller type of water. All are terrific products but it has to be said the buzz around the carp world is for the 3.5lb rods.

12' x 2lb TC	197.75	12' x 3.5lb TC	208.00
12' x 2.25lb TC	197.75	13' x 3lb TC	208.00
12' x 2.5lb TC	203.00	13' x 3.5lb TC	225.00

All rods are guaranteed against breakage during fishing or casting.

SHIMANO

SHIMANO CARP RODS
Powerloop
11' 1.5lb	82.00	12' 1.5lb	92.00
11' 1.75lb	82.00	12' 1.75lb	92.00
11' 2lb	82.00	12' 2lb	92.00

Diaflash
12' 1.75lb	163.00	12' 2.5lb	179.00
12' 2lb	169.00	12' 3lb	183.00
12' 2.25lb	174.00		

AIKEN

VECTOR XT SPECIMEN SERIES
A revised and updated series for the new season featuring all the most popular models demanded by carp and specimen anglers with an extremely high quality of design, construction and finish. The rods feature single leg lined carp rings with a three leg butt. Fine quality cork is used to make the abbreviated handles in all cases which look very well with the graphite reel seats. The rods are spigoted for a reliable and efficient joint and finished with wine tyings. The range gives a wide range of options for the modern carp angler.

XT SPECIMEN 12' 2lb Med. action	£68.95
XT SPECIMEN 12' 2.25lb Med. action	£72.95
XT SPECIMEN 12' 2.5lb Med. action	£74.95
XT SPECIMEN 12' 2.75lb Med. action	£79.85

VECTOR XS SPECIMEN SERIES
Almost identical in design and concept to our XT specimen series, the XS features an 80% carbon cloth in place of the 96% of the XT series.
This means the rods are slightly heavier and slightly thicker in blank diameter but, with a Carp rod, this is not so relevant as the power level is still maintained and the rod is available at a more reasonable price.

The XS series utilises single leg lined intermediates and a three leg butt ring, abbreviated cork handles and a graphite reel fitting. The rods are attractively finished with blue whipping and are spigoted for maximum performance.

XS SPECIMEN 12' 2lb Med. action	£49.75
XS SPECIMEN 12' 2.25lb Med. action	£52.85
XS SPECIMEN 12' 2.75lb Med. action	£55.50

CENTURY COMPOSITES
ARMALITE RANGE *Century*

Our best selling specialist carp rods.
All finished rods supplied with SIC rings.

	Blank	Rod		Blank	Rod
12' 2lb	94.70	192.40	13' 2.2lb	100.20	198.15
12' 2.25lb	96.14	194.10	13' 2.5lb	103.28	203.65
12' 2.5lb	99.58	197.50	13' 2.75lb	105.57	205.25
12' 3lb	105.66	205.35	13' 3lb	111.74	211.60
12' 3.5lb	108.39	208.10	13' 3.5lb	115.88	215.60

SPORTEX
The Woven Kevlar Range which proved very popular last season is extended to include new stalking rods.

	Blank	Rod
12' 2.25lb	98.40	169.78
12' 2.75lb	111.28	174.87
13' 2.25lb	116.01	183.16
13' 3lb	119.43	186.58
10' 2lb Stalker	75.28	131.84
10' 2.25lb Stalker	84.74	135.71

S.I.C. Rings on Sportex Rods add 35.00

Daiwa
COMMITTED TO TOTAL QUALITY

DAIWA CARP RODS
These new carp rods by Kevin Nash are brilliant.
With this sort of power and action at you disposal you can start to appreciate such names as Dictator, Infinity Etc.

AMORPHOUS RANGE All with S.I.C. Rings
AKN116 STALKER 11'6" 1.5lb	199.99
AKN12S DICTATOR+ 12' 2.25lb	210.00
AKN12SU DICTATOR+ 12' 2.5lb	215.00
AKN12H DICTATOR+ 12' 2.75lb	215.00
AKN13H INFINITY+ 13'3lb	225.00
AKN13S DICTATOR+ 13' 2.75lb	220.00

WHISKER KEVLAR Full Fuji Rings
WKN2134 DICTATOR 12' 1.75lb	135.00
WKN2200 DICTATOR 12' 2lb	140.00
WKN2214 DICTATOR 12' 2.25lb	145.00
WKN2212 DICTATOR 12' 2.5lb	150.00
WKN234H INFINITY 12' 2.75lb	155.00
WKN3200 DICTATOR 13' 2lb	150.00
WKN3214 DICTATOR 13' 2.25lb	155.00
WKN3212 DICTATOR 13' 2.5lb	160.00

DRENNAN

DRENNAN SPECIMEN RODS
12' Specialist 1.25lb 3-7lb lines	95.66
12' Light Carp 1.75lb 6-12lb lines	137.42
12' Medium carp 2.25lb 7-14lb lines	137.42
12' Distance Carp 2.5lb 8-14lb lines	137.42

All the Carp Models have S.I.C. Rings

BAITS & INGREDIENTS

MISCELLANEOUS
Arouser 25ml	1.67	N-Butyric Acid 25ml	2.64
Sweet Cajouser 50ml	3.52	Nutramino 250ml	5.20

PREMIER BAITS
Base Mixes
	1kg	2kg
Fish Base Mix	5.20	10.00
Salmon Base Mix	5.75	11.00
Spice Fish Base Mix	5.75	11.00
Marine Mix	5.75	11.00
Fish Fodder	4.20	8.00
Supreme Fish Mix	7.50	N/A
Aquatic Formulae	8.65	N/A
Summer Pro 65	6.90	N/A
Winter Pro	10.66	N/A
Spiced Cypro Seed	6.90	N/A

NEW Nutritional Seed Mixes
These mixes contain the correct level of Noddoil Attractor, Sweetener and a unique blend of flavours already milled into the dry mix. Just add dry mix to eggs, boil for two minutes and allow to dry.
Salmon, Fruit, Savoury .... All 1kg - 5.75, 2kg - 11.00

SHIMANO

SHIMANO REELS
Baitrunner Aero Range
The country's top selling carp reels.
Tapered spool, free spool feature and twin drag system.

Model		Capacity	Spools	Price	S/Sp
Baitrunner Aero	GT3500	280ydsx10lb	2	89.90	4.76
Baitrunner Aero	GT4000	260ydsx12lb	2	96.90	5.29
Baitrunner Aero	GT4500	280ydsx15lb	2	99.90	5.29
Baitrunner Aero	3500	280ydsx10lb	1	64.90	4.76
Baitrunner 4000		260ydsx12lb	1	69.90	5.29
Baitrunner 4500		280ydsx15lb	1	74.90	5.29
Biomaster 7000GT			1	96.90	
Biomaster 8000GT			1	104.90	
LX4000		285ydsx14lb	1	23.00	
SGT X 3000		215ydsx10lb	1	39.90	
SGT X 4000		285ydsx14lb	1	44.90	

DAIWA REELS
New Bite-N-Run reels with free spool system, and the new SS3000 which Kevin Nash says "will cast over the carp anglers horizon. It will handle anything that swims".

Model	Ratio	B/Bearings	Capacity	Price	S/Sp
BR2050	4.9:1	3	270mx10lbs	69.99	10.00
BR2650	4.9:1	3	270mx14lbs	74.99	11.00
BR2050X	4.9:1	1	270mx10lbs	49.99	10.00
BR2650X	4.9:1	1	270mx14lbs	54.99	11.00
SS3000	4.2:1	5	300mx15lbs	175.00	35.00

ROD HOLDALLS
KEVIN NASH		WYCHWOOD	
Standard Hooker 11'	48.58	System Select 12'	61.35
12'	49.94	13'	61.35
13'	52.10	Insider 12'	61.25
De Luxe Hooker 11'	86.60	13'	65.95
12'	87.93	Insider De Luxe 12'	74.50
13'	89.47	13'	81.25
Stalker Sling	18.34		
De Luxe Stalker Sling	22.11	**ROD HUTCHINSON**	
Savoy Rod Hod 11'	75.25	High Protection 12'	85.95
12'	78.88	Holdalls 13'	87.95

RUCKSACKS AND BAGS
KEVIN NASH		WYCHWOOD	
Hooker Pursuit R/sk	99.30	K2 Rucksack	123.00
Hooker Rucksack	84.99	K2 Stalker Bag	28.00
Specialist Rucksack	50.47	Lugger Bag	32.20
Carp Carryall	35.49	Ruckman	76.00
Carp Carryall Spec	44.93	Ruckman Lightweight	51.00
Stalker Bag	25.85	Packer	91.50
Monster Sp. Carryall	56.20		

ROD HUTCHINSON
Pukka Rucksack	99.95
Carryall/Unhooking Mat	65.95

UNHOOKING MATS
Rod Hutchinsons
Carryall/Unhook Mat	65.95
Nash Carp U/Mat	12.09
Monster U/Mat	16.07

New! ROMART Blow Up
Unhooking Mat 32.00

WEIGH SLINGS
Kevin Nash
Standard Sling	7.45
Big Sling	8.59
Specialist Sling	8.59
Monster Carp Sling	15.43
Sling/Sack Combo	12.93

BETALIGHTS
Green
Mini-to Fit Alarms	1.40
/' x /' Flat 350ml	3.95
1" x /' Round 200ml	3.95
1" x /' x /' Sq 475ml	6.95

KJB Coloured
	Small	Large
Red	1.95	4.95
Green	1.95	4.95
Yellow	1.95	4.95

Premier Fish Oils 500ml
Fish Feed Inducing Oil	5.50	Facid Oil	5.50
Noddoil	11.00	Crunt Oil	5.50
Pure Salmon Oil	12.00	Jap. Fish Oil	5.50
P.D.F.A. Supplement Oil			200ml - 10.00

MARTIN LOCKE SOLAR BAITS
	1kg	3kg
Quench Mix	7.10	18.34
Neptune Mix	6.59	18.29
Spice Mix	7.10	18.34
Yellow Seed	7.45	19.25
Red Seed	7.98	20.33

SOLAR FLAVOURS ETC
Golden Plum	4.60	White Chocolate	6.64
Esterblend 12	5.00	Stimulin/Garlic	5.00
Squid/Octopus	9.09	Candy Sweetner	9.09
Fresh Fruit Powder	4.60	White Chocolate Powder	6.03
Candy Sweetener Powder	4.59		

RICHWORTH BASE MIX
50/50 Boilie Mix	1lb - 2.40, 5lb - 8.75

NUTRABAITS
Base Mixes all 3lb 2oz
Hi-Nu-Val	16.75	Fishfood Mix	10.36
Ener-Vite	9.16	Big Fish Mix	11.10
Ener-Vite Gold	9.16	Nutramix	5.55
The Biollix	13.50		

NUTRAFRUITS All 100ml
Strawberry - 5.30, Banana - 5.30, Blackberry - 5.30.
Greengage - 5.30, Cherry - 5.30, Peach - 7.05, Plum - 7.05.
Cranberry - 7.05, Guava - 7.05, Blackcurrant - 7.05.
Loganberry - 7.05, Tutti-Frutti - 7.05, Apricot - 7.05, Pineapple 7.05, Tropical 7.05

ADDITS 30gms for 10 x 1lb mixes
Addit Attract - 4.75, Addit Taste - 5.30, Adit Digest - 6.87

ESSENTIAL OILS
Juniper Berry - 5.20, Geranium Terpenes - 4.65.
Spearmint - 3.48, Ginger - 5.51, Garlic - 5.30.
Spanish Red Thyme - 5.51, Geranium - 4.65.
Leek on Almond - 7.84, Leek 12.33, Black Pepper - 7.84.
Ylang Ylang - 5.51, Parsley - 7.84, Bergamot - 4.65, Cassia Terpenes - 3.48, Clove Terpenes - 3.48

INTEREST FREE CREDIT | **INTEREST FREE CREDIT** | **INTEREST FREE CREDIT**

Terry Eustace

Gold Label Tackle

TERRY EUSTACE GOLD LABEL

Super "U" Rod Rest Head ... 1.70
Super "V" Road Rest Head ... 1.70

Carp Beads
4mm Olive - 1.55, 5mm Black - 1.65, 6mm Brown - 1.75
Peg Screw 2BA Thread - 1.80, Peg Screw M5 Thread - 1.80
Brolly Peg Screw ... 1.80
Slider Knot Beads ... 0.99 Polypops (Brilliant!) ... 1.45
Floater Float - Small ... 2.95 Floater Float - Large ... 3.25
Cobra Throw/Stick 1, 20mm ... 11.95
Cobra Throw/Stick 2, 23mm ... 13.95
Cobra Throw/Stick 3, 29mm ... 18.95
King Cobra 23mm ... 16.95
Marvic Boilie Punch/Foam - 2.40 ... Spare Foam - 0.9*
Buzz Bombs per 3 ... 2oz - 1.99, 2.5oz - 2.25, 3.5oz - 2.45
The Rig ... 1.95
Rod/Lead Bands ... 3.45 Multi Spool Case 5.45

DACRON AND BRAIDS

Kevin Nash
Gamastrand 10lb, 25lb, 50lb - 9.65
Gardner Dacron
1lb - 4.95, 6lb - 6.50, 8lb - 6.95, 10lb - 7.20, 12lb - 7.50
Rod Hutchinson
The Edge 6lb, 10lb, 15lb, 25lb ... 7.95

LINE

MAXIMA

	100M	600M	1000M
6lb	3.67	13.54	19.92
8lb	3.93	14.04	20.43
10lb	4.03	14.40	21.45
12lb	4.13	15.07	21.96
15lb	4.24	16.86	23.80

All other strains in stock

SYLCAST 1000M BULK SPOOLS

SORREL		SPECIMEN SUPER SOFT	
6lb	10.95	6lb	11.95
7lb	10.95	7lb	11.95
8lb	11.95	8lb	11.95
9lb	11.95	9lb	11.95
11lb	11.95	11lb	11.95
13lb	11.95	13lb	N/A
15lb	11.95	15lb	N/A

GARDNER MAINLINE 1000M

6lb	9.05	9lb	10.65
7lb	9.58	11lb	11.20
8lb	10.44	15lb	11.72

NEW! BERKLEY BIG GAME LINE
Excellent quality and fantastic Abrasion Resistance
10lb 1500yds ... 15.99 15lb 900yds ... 15.99
12lb 1175yds ... 15.99 20lb 700yds ... 15.99

AMNESIA
Memory free shooting shooting line, very tough, popular for shock/snag leaders
Black 20lb 200ft spools ... 2.45
Green 30lb 200ft spools ... 3.65

BITE ALARMS

NEW! Daiwa Sensitron
Highly endorsed by Kevin Nash ... 76.99

OPTONIC

OPTONICS

All inc. Battery
Super XL ... 77.00
Super Spec Hi or Lo ... 66.00
Special Hi or Lo ... 55.00
Compact Hi or Lo ... 39.95
Magnetonic Hi or Lo ... 49.95
Basic Comp Hi or Lo ... 32.95
Two Head Set/Box ... 85.00

Optonic Accessories
5m Special Leads ... 7.95
Sounder Box ... 27.95
Fixed V Extentions ... 1.65
V Extensions ... 1.65
Bank Stick Adaptor ... 0.80
Key ... 0.80
Spares Pack ... 3.35

BITECH VIPER ALARMS

Viper Alarm ... 49.95
Extension Box ... 34.50
Extension Leads ... 4.32
Spare Pack ... 2.58

KJB PRODUCTS

ROD STANDS
2 Rod Stand ... 61.25
3 Rod Stand ... 66.50
3 Rod Stand Special ... 71.50

BUZZER BAR SET
Include needle bar assembly ...
2 Rod Buzzer bars ... 16.30
3 Rod Buzzer Bars ... 19.40
3 Rod Special B/Bars ... 22.50

BAITMAKING
Professional Baitmate ... 30.25
Air Powered baitmate Excl. Compressor! ... 91.95

ACCESSORIES
Storm Rods 50" ... 21.41
Storm Rods 33" ... 19.36
P.V.A. 2lb ... 3.01
P.V.A. 4lb ... 3.52
P.V.A. 4lb Cord ... 4.04

FOX INTERNATIONAL

FOX INTERNATIONAL

Super De Luxe Bedchair ... 189.90
Standard De Luxe Bedchair ... 139.90
Super Adjusta Level Chair ... 74.90
Standard Adjusta Chair ... 49.90
Load Shift Trolley ... 97.90 Trolley Strap System ... 9.90

SUPABROLLY
guaranteed waterproof. Incorporates mini storm sides and complete with new storm pole bolts and full skirt for groundsheet ... 131.90
Infill Panel ... 54.90

SUPABIVVY
Dedicated all-in-one Bivvy System with storm pole bolts and groundsheet skirt included ... 154.90
Adjustable Rod Pod 34.50 Non Adjust Rod Pod ... 26.50

SWINGERS
Swinger Indicator ... 11.90
Swinger Heads, Red, Yellow or Green ... 3.90
Rod-Lok Rest Heads ... 6.40 Weigh Bar ... 5.35
Needle Bar System ... 9.90

ACCESSORIES

PVA String ... 1.99
PVA Bags ... 1.99
Ledger Booms ... 0.69
Ledger Stops Mini ... 0.51
Line Stops Large ... 1.01
Run Clips pair ... 0.97
Link Ledger Beads ... 0.51
5" Straight Forceps ... 2.29
8" Straight Forceps ... 3.32
12" Straight Forceps ... 5.61
Spool Clips per 3 ... 0.97
PVA Tape ... 1.99
Pop Up Polyballs ... 1.45
Ledger Stops Large ... 0.51
Line Clips pair ... 0.97
Cross Lok Links ... 0.66
5" Curved Forceps ... 2.29
8" Curved Forceps ... 3.32
12" Curved Forceps ... 5.61
Black Berkley Swivels
Size 10 per 10 ... 0.71 Size 10 per 50 ... 3.25
Starlit Red ... 0.86 Starlit Blue ... 0.86
Starlit Mini pair ... 0.86
Hook Hone ... 1.78 ABU De Luxe Hone ... 8.99
Thermometer ... 11.99
Stewart Large box, Grey or Yellow ... 6.99
Riva Float/Tackle Box ... 25.53
Black Dacron Hair Rigs, Size 6 or 8 ... 0.76

OPTIX

OPTIX CORMORANTS

HLT No1 Black Frames, Grey or Amber Lens ... 29.95
Flip Clips, Grey or Amber Lens ... 25.95
No3 Matt Black Frames, grey or Amber Lens ... 29.95
Carbon Frames, Grey or Amber Lens ... 36.95

SCALES

Avon Scales 40lb ... 37.99 Avon Carry Pouch ... 4.24
Super Samson 22lb ... 12.75 Super Samson 44lb ... 16.40
Super Samson 33lb ... 13.99
Kevin Nash 56lb ... 50.39 Kevin Nash 112lb ... 50.39

HOOKS

The business end of the tackle is so often neglected. Our range of hooks, some mass produced, some hand finished, cover every eventuality.

KAMASAN
B980 Chemically sharpened, needle point
SPECIMEN hooks. Forged, slightly reversed.
Eyed, bronzed, high carbon steel
Sizes 2-20 ... per 10 - 0.80, per 50 - 2.85

PARTRIDGE
Jack Hilton Carp Hooks Sizes 2 -10 ... per 25 - 3.10
Z11 Kevin Maddocks Hair Rig Hooks
Sizes 4 - 10 ... per 25 - 3.90
X1 Extra Strong Outbend Trebles Sizes 4 - 10 ... per 10 - 4.50
Z3 Semi-Barbless Trebles Sizes 4 -10 ... per 10 - 4.50

GARDNER
Black, forged, offset bend. Sizes 1 -10 ... per 25 - 3.15
Barbless Blues Sizes 4 - 10 ... per 25 - 3.40
Bent Hooks. Upturned Eye Sizes 4 - 10 ... per 10 - 1.25

DRENNAN
Super Specialist Sizes 2 - 20 ... per 10 - 0.75
Specimen Barbless Sizes 2 - 20 ... per 10 - 0.75
Boilie Hooks Sizes 2 - 10 ... per 10 - 1.10
Star Point Hooks Sizes 4 - 10 ... per 10 - 1.75
Star Point Barbless Sizes 4 - 10 ... per 10 - 1.75

KRYSTON PRODUCTS

All 20m Spools

Silkworm
10lb ... 6.99
12lb Standard ... 6.99
12lb Ultrasoft ... 6.99
15lb ... 6.99
25lb ... 7.99

Super Silk
14lb ... 7.99

Multistrand
15lb Twisted ... 7.99
15lb Untwisted ... 7.99

Merlin
10lb ... 6.75
12lb ... 6.75
15lb ... 6.75

Quicksilver Leader Braid
25m Spools
25lb ... 10.99
35lb ... 10.99
45lb ... 10.99

AMBIO
Biological Feeding Trigger ... 125ml - 3.99, 500ml - 11.75
No Tangle 1 for multi-Strands ... 3.49
No Tangle 2 for Braided Lines ... 3.49

SOLAR TACKLE

by Martin Locke
Brilliant range in top quality stainless

Buzzer Bars
2 Rod 6" ... 8.95
2 Rod 8" ... 8.95
2 Rod 10" ... 8.95
3 Rod 12" ... 10.95
3 Rod 15" ... 10.95
3 Rod Adjust Back ... 21.50
3 Rod Adjust Front ... 21.50

Lite-Flo Indicators
Brilliant new bodies that gives a soft coloured glow ... when a betalight is added. .. Red, Blue, Yellow or Green ..
Small 15mm 7gms ... 5.95
Med 20mm 15gms ... 5.95
Large 25mm 26gms ... 5.95
Adapt to fit all needles

Extending Banksticks
12" ... 12.95
16" ... 13.95
20" ... 14.95

Needle Systems
2 Rod ... 19.95
3 Rod ... 23.95
Adjustable Satellite ... 40.95
Guy Ropes ... 4.95
Bivvy Pegs x 8 ... 10.95
Stabiliser ... 5.50
Carp Sack Pegs ... 4.95

NEW ITEMS
Stainless Coin Slot
Opti Bolt ... 2.95
Stainless Back Rest ... 3.95

NEW! Stainless Rod Pod
Brilliant new fully collapsible design ... £89.95
Needle bars for above 2 rod std. ... £13.95
3 rod std. ... £18.95
3 rod adj. ... £29.95

NEW! Bow-Loc Carbon Landing Net
"One-Touch" fold design ... £125.00

CARP SACKS

Kevin Nash
Standard Sack ... 8.83
XL Sack ... 9.99
Big Sack ... 11.18
Zip Sack ... 10.12
XL Sack + Ext Cord ... 12.55
Zip Sack + Ext Cord ... 13.70

UMBRELLAS

Ready Converted Nu-Brolli
D64 45" ... 47.99 D65 50" ... 52.99
Tilt Wavelock
D19 45" ... 37.99 D20 50" ... 42.99
Kevin Nash
Hooker 50" ... 85.21
Oval Umbrella ... 97.28
Screw In Brolly Poles
29" ... 8.99
36" ... 10.50

Rod HUTCHINSON
FISHING DEVELOPMENTS LIMITED

ROD HUTCHINSON PRODUCTS

SUPREME BASE MIXES All 1kg Bags
Superfish ... 7.10
Super Savoury ... 6.75
Seafood Blend ... 6.75
Protein Mix ... 9.95
Boilie Mix ... 6.08
Pro Mix 50/50 ... 8.10
Monster mix ... 10.50
Red Seed Mix ... 7.10
Yellow Seed Mix ... 6.75
Essential Oil Mix ... 6.75
Ultra Spice ... 6.75
White Lightning ... 6.75
The Liver Mix ... 8.10
Super Fruit ... 6.75
Scopex ... 7.10

ROD HUTCHINSON INGREDIENTS 1 PINT BAGS
Lactalbumin ... 4.25
Acid Casein 80 ... 4.40
Rennet Casein 80 ... 4.40
Acid Casein 30 ... 4.40
Sodium Caseinate ... 3.05
Calcium Caseinate ... 3.15
Soya Isolate ... 2.35
Soya Flour ... 1.25
Nectarblend ... 2.25
Powder Fish Oil ... 2.05
Boilie Gel ... 3.95
Whitefish Meal ... 1.45
Anchovy Meal ... 1.50
Wheat Gluten ... 2.35
Sea Kelp Vitamin ... 2.12
Red Factor ... 2.15
PTX ... 2.15
Robin Red ... 3.50
Lactopro ... 2.35
Hydro Meat Meal ... 1.75

Colour/Sweeteners
Yellow, Orange, red, Brown or White ... 4.65
Powder Colours
Red, Yellow, Orange, Brown, White or Green ... 1.85

ROD HUTCHINSON FLAVOURS

Exclusive Flavours
Scopex, Maplecreme, Ultraspice, Malted Maple, Megaspice, Lugworm with Crab, Smelly Cheese, Fruit Frenzy, Malted Butter, Mixed Herbs, Coffee Creme, Nutty Buttermint, Mango/Pineapple, Mystere, Strawberry Cream ... Per 50ml - 3.25

Classic Flavours
Chocolate Malt, Monster Crab, Egg and Milk, Megamaple, Megamalt, Passion Fruit, Sweet Mango, The Big A, Rich Strawberry, Wild Cherry, Ylang Ylang, Fermented Krill, Blueberry, Crayfish, Freshwater Mussel, Full Cream, Banana, Lobster Thermidor, Blackcurrent Supreme, Blackberry Supreme ... Per 50ml - 3.15

100% Ethyl Supreme Flavours
Fresh Salmon, Dairy Butter, Coffee Bean, Cinnamon, Mega Tutti Frutti, Bramble Jelly, Super Cream, Mature Cheese, Strawberry Dream, Tomato Puree ... Per 50ml - 4.95
Special Vanilla Bean ... 100ml - 10.95

Essential Oils
RH1, RH2, RH3, RH4, Jamaican Special ... Per 20ml - 5.85

Scents of the Sea 300ml bottles
White Fish ... 5.25
Anchovy ... 5.25
Squid Oil ... 9.50
Red Fish ... 5.95
Salmon Feed ... 5.95
Induce Feed Oil ... 6.50

Appetite Stimulators
Fish, Savoury, Sweet, Fruit, Spice, Dairy ... 50 Mix Tube - 5.98

Sense Appeal Concentrates
Regular, Seedbait, Savoury, Fruit, Shellfish, Dairy, Spice ... per100ml - 5.99

Amino Acid Products
Amino Blend Supreme, The Liver, Vitamin/Flavour Enhancer ... Per 100ml - 6.25

Sweeteners
100ml - 3.95, 500ml - 16.00 Protaste 50ml - 3.85

INTEREST FREE CREDIT
UP TO NINE MONTHLY PAYMENTS AT NO EXTRA CHARGE

ORDERS UP TO £50
3 Monthly Payments
ORDERS UP TO £100
Choose 3 or 6 Monthly Payments
ORDERS OVER £100
Choose 3, 6 or 9 Monthly Payments

HOW TO ORDER: Send full cash price or divide cash total by number of payments chosen. Add carriage or express delivery charges (if any) to first cheque, together with any odd amounts. Other cheques at monthly intervals. Write cheque card number on back of first cheque and **SEND ALL CHEQUES IN WITH ORDER.** A daytime telephone number would be helpful. **PLEASE MAKE ALL CHEQUES PAYABLE TO PENGE ANGLING.**

CARRIAGE: All goods post free except BOOKS and BAIT Books - £1.00 for one or £1.50 total for several. Bait - not over 1kg £2.00, 2kg £2.52, 3kg £3.15, 4kg £3.40, 5kg £3.60, 6kg £4.00, 7kg £4.15, 8kg £4.30, 9kg £4.80, 10kg £5.00, 25kg £6.05

EXPRESS DELIVERY available at an extra £6.00.
We **RECOMMEND** you use express delivery for all Rods for safety. These terms only apply to U.K. Mainland, for N.I., Eire and Overseas please telephone.

TERMS: CUSTOMERS IN THE SHOP MUST BRING CHEQUE CARD AND PROOF OF ADDRESS.
We reserve the right to decline any order. All goods either in stock or on order at time of going to print.

ALL MAIL ORDER to:
PENGE ANGLING, 309 Beckenham Road, Beckenham, Kent BR3 4RL. Tel: 081 778 4652. Fax: 081 659 4770

BRANCHES AT:

Access VISA

PENGE ANGLING (RAYLEIGH)
Arterial Road, Rayleigh, Essex SS6 7TR
Tel: 0268 772331

PENGE ANGLING (ELTHAM)
5 Tudor Parade, Well Hall Road, London SE9 8SG
Tel: 081 859 2901

set up. I intended to use pop-ups on one rod and bottom baits on the other.

Of course, the one thing I didn't tell Mike about was the hair rig, which was still relatively unknown. I would think that, during opening week at Savay, besides Keith Gillings, Bob Davis and myself, there was no one else on it at all. I think this was something else that Mike Wilson also found a little strange, for he had revealed that Savay fish were peculiar feeders and he was strongly of the opinion that you very rarely got a run from the Savay carp at all. In fact, most of the fish that he had caught were from hitting twitches, even when the carp were preoccupied on his maize bait, so how on earth was I going to contend with hitting twitches at a 90 yard range?

Of course, I was fairly sure that I knew what the takes were going to be like! The combination of using the hair on a fairly short link with a two ounce lead and clipping up tight and I was sure that most of the takes were going to be as blistering as they were at Darenth. I had intended to use pop-ups just on the one rod but as it turned out, the takes were definitely more forthcoming on this particular set up so it did not take me long to use both rods on an almost identical rig. The only difference was that I was fishing about four inches off the bottom with one, and the other varied from anything from six inches to two feet – just to see what sort of reaction there was. Of course, the other factor that I'm sure contributed to the success, was that for most of the time I had a great deal of bait out there. Because the pop-ups stand out like a sore thumb over the top of these vast beds of bait, I'm sure that many times these are actually taken first. Probably I would have eventually got takes on the bottom baits, but I think it would have been at the stage when most of the free offerings had been cleared up, or certainly the vast majority of them.

With the pop-ups, the takes were just that much quicker. Something that worried me a lot was that I had seen these very large shoals of carp swimming around and I felt, even with a thousand boilies, they could drop down on a baited area and a thousand could be gone in a matter of minutes. If that was the case, I would not be able to hold them, so I really felt that I had to put a lot of bait out there if I was going to hold these fish in one area. I suppose it was really a case of putting all my eggs in one basket and I went for it in a very big way.

Mike left the swim and I spent the next two hours catapulting bait out. What Mike must have thought of all this, I hate to think, but when he came back for our final cup of tea before the start, he did comment on just how many baits I had put in! We had another cup of tea and chatted until around 10 o'clock, when Mike returned to his swim. He wished me well and said we would have another chat in the morning.

I could hear some of the other lads casting out and setting their indicators but I thought, no, I will hang on for a little bit longer and – guess what – have a cup of tea – but you know what it's like, it eventually gets to you and really, I couldn't wait any longer. It was 11 o'clock and I whacked them out. Although my expectations were really high, I did think with all that bait I had put out I would get a good kip until morning.

I had just started to make myself comfortable, getting the bedchair and sleeping bag arranged, when crack! – out of the clip and a real flyer. As I closed the bail-arm, there was certainly no need to strike as this fish was really flying. Over went the rod and even at 90 yards I had to give line immediately. After quite a scrap, the fish eventually rolled into the net. In the dim light of the torch I could see it was a magnificent looking leather and at 19lb 12oz I was over the moon. What a start – it wasn't even 12 o'clock and I had one on the bank.

There was no sacking at Savay and I for one wasn't going to take any chances. I was half hoping that Mike had heard the commotion and would come along, but I was not going to bother him at this moment, especially when the season hadn't really started. A quick photo on the floor and back she went. I thought that if anyone said anything I would just have to work out something a bit later.

I recast the rod and pulled the line back into the clip again. It started to rain again so I sat under the brolly on the bedchair for a while. I was just starting to think about getting into the bag when bang! – the other rod was away. By now it was just after midnight. This was absolutely ridiculous – this was meant to be a hard water. In an hour, two takes; another good scrap and yet another leather, this time 21lb. I remember thinking, 'sorry Mike, but I'm going to need to have a photograph of this one'. My first twenty from Savay, I couldn't let this one pass me by so I crept round and I think I frightened the life out of him! He was crouched low over his rods, twitcher hitting as you can

20-plus common taken early morning at Burton

106

ANOTHER NEW RELEASE FROM... BEEKAY

This long awaited carp book by Andy Little, one of the best known and most successful carp anglers of all time, will be of interest to every carp angler. In fascinating detail, Andy tells of his progression as a top carp angler, but particularly of the famous waters he has fished, the exact details of all his successful baits and rigs, and the well-known carp men who have accompanied him in his many thousands of hours of carp fishing.

Anglers who have fished the leading big carp waters of the last ten years, such as Savay Lake, Redmire Pool, Longfield and Darenth will find the accounts of Andy's extraordinary captures of huge numbers of twenties and thirties remarkable, whilst those who have never been able to fish the famous waters will come to know them well through his interesting accounts, which include his outstanding results in France and Bulgaria.

This hardback book is undoubtedly destined to become one of the most popular and best-selling of all the books on modern carp fishing.

Illustrations include 30 outstanding colour photographs, 48 black and white pictures and many line drawings.

PRICE: £16.95 available direct from **BEEKAY** post free or from all good tackle shops

NEW! 12 page catalogue listing more than 500 angling books and videos available free on request

BEEKAY PUBLISHERS · WITHY POOL · HENLOW CAMP · BEDS
CREDIT CARDS AND CATALOGUE ORDERS. TEL: 0462 816960

imagine.

I told him that I had a twenty and would he please come along to do the photographing for me. He said he would be pleased to do so. He reeled in and we both crept back to the swim. He seemed to be quite amazed that I had caught a fish so quickly; I didn't have the heart to tell him that I had caught a nineteen already. I thanked him for taking the photos and we both settled down again. It seemed as if I had only just closed my eyes when, around 3am my right hand rod was screaming at me again. Now this fish felt completely different from the first two – nowhere near as fast, but much more determined. It chugged away to my right, down towards *Alcatraz* and I had to give at least 50 yards of line on that initial run. I appeared to be making no impression. I now had at least 150 yards of line out and was really getting worried. I bent down hard and the fish started to kite in, to my right. I think it must have kited right into Mike's swim and I pumped and pumped and the fish just crashed into the margins some fifty yards down the bank to me. I leant over the water as far as I could, trying to increase the angle and eventually I did manage to get it away from the margins. It slowly circled round in front of me. By now it was pouring with rain and I was soaked to the skin. I'm glad to say it went into the net first time, but as I tried to lift the net I knew I had something quite special. I heaved it onto the bank, sorted out the scales and weigh bag and hoisted it aloft. 31lb 12oz. I was shaking like a leaf!

This was my sixth thirty. However, this was the first one I had taken at long range. Almost all my other thirties had been stalked and this, for me, was quite a mammoth fight, lasting at least 40 minutes, perhaps more. Bearing in mind, I hadn't seen the fish at all; as far as I was concerned, it could have been anything, I really didn't know. Most of my other carp I'd actually seen before I'd hooked them and very often the fight would be short lived, over in a matter of minutes; but this one was on relatively light tackle at long range and was probably one of the longest fights that I had experienced. My arms were aching, but I was obviously over the moon.

The twenties that I had caught at Darenth at long range were nothing like this. Slow, dogged, determined – call it what you like. If I hadn't felt its head every now and again I would have been mistaken into thinking it had been foulhooked. It was very, very exciting and I just had to go and get Mike again. I had no other choice.

I crept along to Mike, apologising beforehand, and I remember him saying,
"You haven't got another one have you? It's not another twenty pounder is it?"
"No", I said. "It's a thirty, Mike".
"Oh my God!" he exclaimed.

He obviously must have been quite impressed, because he brought his own two and a quarter square camera down and I was very grateful for this, because at the time I only had a little Mickey Mouse 110 compact camera and certainly, my photographs were nowhere near as good as his. We slipped the fish back and he patted me on the back and said that he had honestly thought that I would never catch anything – and now I had caught two. I thought I'd better tell him about the 19 pounder as well, just in case he had heard anything. I suppose there may have been a little bit of showing off as well – I think we're all a bit guilty of this from time to time.

By the morning I had caught two more – 20lb 10oz and 17½lb. Now what can I say? It was a hell of a start to the season, especially on the new water. If this was the standard of things to come, who knew what was going to happen? In fact, it just got better and better, for some of the catches were quite amazing. By the end of the first week alone, I had 14 fish.

It was quite amazing. I'd had a personal best of 34lb 4oz, which beat my old previous best of 33lb by a considerable margin. I'd also had a personal best common of 24lb. In fact, this was my first ever 20lb common and I shall never forget that fish.

A local guy, John Richards, who was on the other rota, had wandered round to see me. Obviously, the other lads had told him about my catches and seeing there was very little else coming out he was keen to find out just what he had got to do to catch fish. I'd never met John before, but by the end of the

WHAT A *Starmer Man* GETS FOR HIS *Money*

WHERE ELSE CAN £3.99 BUY YOU 400g OF SUPERIOR QUALITY CARP BOILIES

Plus FREE Boilie Booster Oil

● **QUALITY and PERFORMANCE**
Scientifically formulated for perfect amino and protein balance with continuous flavour leakage

● **PLUS** 7 protein packed mixes available
10 different booster oil additives in 125ml/250ml bottles

AVAILABLE NATIONWIDE ONLY FROM YOUR LOCAL FISHING TACKLE SHOP
or send SAE for nearest stockist to 9/11 RUTHERFORD CLOSE, LEIGH ON SEA, ESSEX, SS9 5LQ

Starmer 1992 Menu

MEGGA TUTTI
HEAVY FRUIT
STRAWBERRY MIVVI
CRAYFISH PASTE
FISHMEAL & NOD OIL
RED MARINE
HEMP MOLASSES
SPICED UP LIVER
CONDENSED MILK
CHOCOLATE MALT
PASSION FRUIT
HEAVY SCOPEX
BANANA SPLIT
CARIBBEAN COCKTAIL
NUTTY BIRDSEED
TIGER NUT
SWEETCORN FRUIT

BOILIE SIZES
10mm — 14mm — 18mm

PACK SIZES
Junior 150g
approx 75 boilies **£2.25**
Standard 400g
approx 200 boilies **£3.99**
Bulk 1000g
approx 500 boilies **£9.00**

season at Savay he turned out to be a very good friend.

It was change-over day and John asked if he could slot in next to me. I said, of course, no problem at all. There were obviously a lot of fish out there and they were taking a lot of baits. John had done a fair bit of long range fishing, but was certainly not on the hair.

We stood behind the swim, chatting to each other, when a good fish crashed out over my baits. It looked very much like it was a common and he agreed. There were one or two good fish in there that were commons, one of them known to be just under thirty. At that time I had not taken a common anywhere near that size.

As we stood there chatting I had another take – the indicator just zipped off, it was a blur. I had another hell of a struggle, this one being quite fast, dashing around all over the place. John helped me with the netting and, because of the surroundings in the swim, I was back up the bank while he was down at the water's edge, and I couldn't actually see the fish. Just as it went in the net, he said "You've got a 20lb common".

Well, that really was the icing on the cake and definitely a week I shall never forget.

The other lads unfortunately, really struggled. Mike Wilson did have a 28lb leather during the course of the opening week, but I honestly believe that I had so much bait out in front of me that I was holding the fish back and they were not going into Mike's swim. I think only one or two fish slipped through and this was probably one of the fish that he had caught.

The rest of the lake produced virtually nothing. Rod managed to get the carp going on the top before the off, but they had dwindled away and disappeared. He did manage to get a double, a 16 pounder I think, on maples, but during that first week the rest of the anglers certainly struggled. They obviously realised the potential and when some of them did get their act together, some of the catches were quite staggering. I learnt a lot during that first week.

I thought I could bait up quite well after the fishing at Darenth, but this was completely different. Although the range was roughly the same, Darenth being a smaller water and that much more sheltered, the baits were fairly unaffected by winds, but in my little *Reedy* swim the water out in front was quite open and the strong south westerlies would have the baits flying everywhere. It showed just how inadequate I was at putting bait out at long range. This was prior to the wrist-rocket days, so really all we had was the basic, standard type catapults with square elastics and a home made pouch. Latex was just not available at the time. The amount of catapult elastic I went through was just ridiculous. There were times when I had to beg, steal or borrow from the other members just to keep the bait going in. In fact, it was Rod who first introduced me to the Latex elastic. He had been given some to try on what was called a 'Whopper Dropper' catapult. I think this was meant for putting out large balls of groundbait and I remember him saying "You won't bust this one!" – but after a couple of thousand baits this too, broke, so he was none too pleased with me, as you can imagine.

I had to find something different that was going to last a little bit longer and it was in one of the gun shops that I found a hunting catapult, called a Marksman, which was an American made job. It was very strong and much more accurate, but I was still using four or five lengths of Latex per day. You hear people glibly saying that they have put a thousand baits out: well, I can assure you it takes a very long time to put that many baits out with a catapult, as I was doing on a daily basis.

After that first week was over I felt sad that I had to go away. I had arranged to meet Lennie on the Monday, and also my friend, Dave Reekie, down at Darenth. I packed up and I met Bob Davis in the car park. He obviously realised that I was keen to carry on and the response on the other rota had not been that great so he said that if I could find someone to swap rotas then I could carry on fishing, he didn't mind. This worked out very well and I took advantage of it.

One of John Richard's friends, Bob Harper, was on the other rota and for some reason or other, didn't actually end up fishing there at all. I managed to persuade him to let me have his ticket and obviously if he did want to fish there, I would

---

TACKLE UP
THE BEST EQUIPMENT · THE RIGHT CHOICE

THE VERY LATEST FROM SOLAR & DELKIM
DON'T MISS OUT – ORDER YOURS NOW
(available April–May)

BITE INDICATOR ACTUAL SIZE
AVAILABLE CLOSED SEASON

TACKLE UP, 151 Fleet Road, Fleet, Hants. Tel: 0252 614066

give it back at any time. This he kindly agreed to do, so I was able to fish all the time from there on. It's a much harder water than most people realise. When it's on song it is like a lot of waters, it can look very easy, but it wasn't easy all the time. You've only got to look at some of the other guy's catches for proof of that. There were some very proficient anglers there who really struggled to catch fish and because the carp at Savay generally proved to be shoal fish, one, maybe two people, could get on fish but there was no way that 25 were going to.

holidays were exhausted, I would leave for work around 7am - it was between 40 and 50 miles drive from Savay to work, depending on which way I went. Once I arrived at work I would have a shower, eat breakfast and make a few baits. Lunchtime too was bait making time too, but at least I was able to have a good meal virtually every day. I would arrive back at Savay between 6–6.30pm, depending on the traffic. I was very fortunate that there were many times when I was able to leave my tackle at the back of the swim. I obviously wouldn't occupy it, but when Lennie or Rod were about they would just keep an eye on it for me. If I was on fish, I would naturally return to the place I had left in the morning, but if not, I would spend much of the evening looking for visual sightings. Also, the other lads who were present would fill me in with all the info by the time I got back because as the season wore on, both Rod and Lennie were spending a great deal of time there. It was a friendly atmo-

sphere and if you had a particular swim going no one would jump in it the moment you vacated it. They would leave it alone – which something you just don't get these days. I must admit, I did feel quite guilty at times, when I was really on the fish and they would leave it vacant all day until I got back in the evening. There is something to be said for this type of friendship.

A lot of the time would be spent baiting up, just to ensure that there was a constant food supply for the carp to drop in on any time. I could never make enough bait up at work to see me through the day, so there was still bait making to be done on the bank, virtually every day.

Because I was working every weekday I would try to get my head down by 11 o'clock at night at the latest, as I had to be up early to be at work.

There were many nights when the carp did not respond at all. In fact, what would generally happen was that there would be long periods of

Lennie Middleton and Andy with a magnificent quartet

In the end there was probably less than half the rota who fished seriously, so at least this did allow the guys who wanted to fish full time to do so, as they were able to swap with those who didn't fish.

I naturally wanted to stay on at Savay, especially as it was going so well, but I had arranged to go to Darenth, so off I went. Once the Savay season was in full swing, what usually happened was that once all my

inactivity followed by short, hectic spells of feeding. Several fish would come in the same night. If these feeding times coincided with weekdays, there were moments, believe it or not, when I dreaded them! It was often the case that they would feed all night: I would get no sleep at all and often be late for work – inevitably getting a telling off in the process. At times it was hard work and I just felt like going home, going to bed and getting away from it all. However, this was going to be a one off and I had to put myself out if I was going to do well, for there was a chance I would never fish Savay again. I was determined to make the best of it. As the season progressed, I was beginning to have pressures exerted on me that I didn't particularly want. Because I was doing so well, and through the friendship that I had with the others on the bank, they were all spurring me on to catch even more fish. Somehow or other I seemed to have got wound up in this numbers syndrome. I'm not quite sure how it happened and I was surprised that I was actually getting myself involved in it. Kevin Maddocks had had a great season the year before and was the first person I knew of to catch 20 twenties in a season. This appeared to be some sort of target that he set; quite silly in hindsight, because it's all relative; hours, water, ability etc., but I was egged on to catch more fish. I had gone through the 20 twenties barrier fairly early in the season. It was then 25 twenties, 30 twenties and, quite honestly, it was just getting ridiculous. It was pressure that I felt I didn't really need; I just wanted to enjoy myself and not thrash the water to death. It turned out to be a ridiculous season and I'm the sort of person who tries hard anyway, regardless of whether the fish are feeding or not. Anyway, back to the beginning of the season. After the first week I went to Darenth and told Lennie of my success: I was all fired up with the enthusiasm there and now Lennie was all raring to go. The next trip, when we were there together, I was in my little *Reedy* swim and Lennie went out onto the area at the end of *Alcatraz* so that we could fish on virtually the same hotspot but from different positions in the lake. It was a much longer cast from the end of *Alcatraz* than it was from the *Reedy* swim, and although he did catch from there, the *Reedy* swim was a much better vantage point and Lennie never quite had as many fish.

It was really funny, because after that session the carp avoided that area for quite some time. I remember Lennie staying put there for something like a week, even though I do believe the fish had moved off. I went round to the Cottage Bay where there were some more carp showing. John also joined me around this area. This is a part of the lake that you can't actually fish these days, which is a shame because it's a lovely little area. We fished round outside the cottage itself; there were a lot of fish moving into the Cottage Bay, I think they had slipped through the channel and had congregated in large numbers just off the islands at the entrance to Cottage Bay.

By now I had got quite friendly with John and I asked him if he fancied coming in on the bait with me. This was for two reasons; one, I obviously wanted John to catch fish and secondly, at least someone else could help with making this ruddy bait! I was in something of a dilemma however. Although I was quite happy to tell him about the bait I was using, I was still sworn to secrecy on the hair and I stuck to it, even though I felt bad about it at times. I'm sure John realised something strange was going on but he accepted it and did not ask too many questions.

The first session round in Cottage Bay we put a stack of baits out – round about seven thousand between us. I think it was the next day when the fish actually moved onto the bait. John was at the head of the swim and he was first in, using fairly standard rigs. I remember thinking at the time, 'I wonder what is going to happen when they finish up at my end of the swim with the hair rig and all'. This was John's first Savay fish he was hooked into and, as usual, it was a really good scrap and it turned out to be a thirty pound-plus. I remember kidding him that it was only a double and he should stop messing about and get it in. Rod had come round and was looking over our shoulder and even when the fish was four feet down in the water he said, "Blimey, it's another thirty!"

Then it really started to happen. The next day I had a brace of thirties in consecutive casts; it just went on and we held the fish there for quite some time.

A brace of thirty pounders had to be special at any time, it really was quite something – this is probably going to sound awful – but it was all starting to get a bit too easy and I was almost becoming blasé about it. I'd never had it so good, never had so many big fish in front of me and never put so many on the bank. I remember catching fish in the 25 pounds bracket and thinking, 'that's a nice fish, but I wonder if the next one will be an upper twenty or thirty'. This area round the Cottage Bay seemed to be almost better than out in front of the *Reedy* swim and I recall we really built up the swim. Late one particular night I had five fish over 20 pounds, most of them being upper twenties, in very short succession.

At first you could almost predict where the carp were going to be, according to the weather. You could hold them with baits for quite a while, but eventually a big wind pushing down would move them. In fact, this weather syndrome started up quite a bit of a lark. There would be one or two of us who would go to the phone box every day and ring up the Met. Office and try to predict exactly what the weather was going to be; in some respects it was a bit like the Secret Society. A little bit of friendly competition was now coming into play; there was a lot of secret phoning up the Met. Office and a lot of moving around in the middle of the night, trying to get to a certain area before the carp arrived.

Very often weather conditions would change during the course of the day and if a lot of bait had been eaten during the night and I had to go to work in the morning, I could get back and all the carp had moved from one end of the lake to another. There were odd occasions when the weather conditions were just right, when the major three shoals that seemed to be resident in Savay all got together in one area or another. This was quite a phenomenal sight I can tell you. It's very difficult to be precise about numbers, but I would have thought at least 70 very good carp could be present at any one time. There were two main strains of carp in Savay. There was the original Leney stocking and these were very long, streamlined fish and were very hard fighting. The best of these that season was a 34lb 4oz fish, that I managed to catch twice. In fact, it was one that Lennie caught a bit later in the season, although he didn't actually count it – but that's another story...

Then there was the Italian strain of fish – these were much shorter and fatter and I wasn't that keen on them at all. The best of these were around 28lb and included a very famous fish that ended up being called *Popeye*. I don't think any of the Italians went over 30 pounds during that first season and I'm fairly sure *Popeye* was the biggest of them all.

There were a few commons in the 20 pound bracket as well, the largest of which was the one called *Sally*. This was a fish that you could recognise instantly as there was a half moon shaped lump missing from the tail. This was a fish that Mike Wilson had caught at just under 30lb the previous season, but during the course of our year it was down slightly in weight and Paul Bray caught it at about 27lb. When you think that fish today (1990) is nearly 40lb., it is quite remarkable. Sadly, I never caught Sally myself; I think it was the only one of the big fish that I didn't catch. I captured two other 20lb commons there; a 24lb and a 26lb but it would have been really great if I had caught Sally as well. However, it was not to be and I suppose, at the end of the day, I caught so many fish did it really matter?

As the season progressed, inevitably the hair rig started to get out. In actual fact, I was caught using it by Sam Gates. He saw me striking into a fish and came round to help. This was during one of my bumper sessions when everything started to click together and I was absolutely stacking them up. I'd only just caught another carp a few minutes beforehand; I had baited up my rig and was about to cast out when I had a take on the other rod, so there it was, lying against the bedchair for the world to see and of course, as Sam came round the corner there it was, staring him in the eyes. The thoughts of netting my fish went completely out of the window – all he was interested in was looking at this peculiar set up!

Having been caught red-handed with it, there was no way I was going to lie, so I came clean. I told him it was not mine, but Lennie and Kevin's idea and said that he really must keep it to himself. Of course, like all good things, inevitably they do get out and I thought we had done quite well in keeping it quiet for so long!

I was still fishing every evening – that continued right through until November. I did have the odd couple of days off the water, but not that many. It was certainly a very expensive season; I could not have done it if I had been unemployed. The cost of petrol, bait, food and everything else was taking its toll. I even changed the bait to a much cheaper and simpler mix of just semolina and gluten to try to save a bit of money. I still carried on with the Maple flavour and the sweetener but nothing else – quite amazing really.

I was on size eight Au Lion d'Or hooks, which were quite small compared to the size of the baits, which were roughly three-quarters of an inch in diameter.

Although I was paying my rent regularly at the flat, I think my landlord wondered where on earth I had got to: I would only rarely go home and only then to get a change of clothing or to pay a few bills. I've got absolutely hundreds of memories of Savay, some funny, some sad and some just ridiculous. There is one situation I shall never forget. Lennie and I had doubled up in the *Bonfire* swim at the start of what was to be a fantastic season. We were on fish immediately and the first night I think I had four takes within a very short space of time – three of which I landed, the other unfortunately came off. I believe that there was at least one thirty, if not two and an upper twenty nine amongst these fish. Lennie too, managed to put an upper twenty on the bank, so this was a really great start to the session. Up until this point, Lennie had never caught a thirty pound plus carp; plenty of 29s but no thirties, so obviously Savay was a real opportunity for him. Lennie, never being one to sit on his laurels, started experimenting once again, even though we were in the middle of catching fish. In all fairness, I don't think Lennie ever stopped experimenting and it was on a new rig that he got his next take.

This was on his right hand rod which was fished to the far right of the *Bonfire* swim. Now this was obviously a very good fish that he had just hooked into. It kited way round to the left over Lennie's other rod, plus mine, and it was some 150 yards down the lake when it crashed into the margins. No matter how hard Lennie pulled into the fish, he was just not making any impression on it. The hooked carp just kept powering away from him; it was now right down by the *Gate* swim, still in the margins, but Lennie's line was through loads of sunken branches so he had very little chance of getting the fish back to him. After a bit of quick thinking and I grabbed my spare rod and cast out between the gaps in the branches to hook his line up. I would retrieve it onto the bank where we would break it and retie. I don't know how many times this was repeated, but I do know that it was getting on for an hour later when we eventually landed the fish.

We could see immediately just what the problem was – it was foul hooked in the pectoral fin! I recognised the fish as one I had caught earlier at 34lb 4oz. I just couldn't believe it; Lennie's first thirty and the ruddy thing was foul hooked. There was a scratch and a mark in the carp's mouth, but Lennie was not happy about it and refused to count it. That just goes to show the calibre of angler that he is: I wonder how many people would have counted that fish, given the circumstances. Anyway, one thing was for sure, I was going to have a photograph of him and this fabulous fish, no matter what he said. I was very impressed by Lennie as an angler. We were very lucky really, a nicer bunch of guys would be hard to find, but, as with any group, one or two stand out above the rest for various reasons.

As well as Lennie, there were people like Rod Hutchinson. What can you say about Rod? Rod is just Rod, quite a character and a very likeable chap and probably the most instinctive angler I have ever known. Also Kevin Maddocks whose sheer technical ability and the methodical way he approaches his fishing has to be commended. I have always thought that if you could get Lennie's forward thinking and rig craft, Rod's originality and watercraft, and Kevin Maddocks' accuracy and drive, there would be an angler in the country that no one else could possibly touch. Cor, wouldn't it be horrible?!

Good catches kept coming periodically right up until the beginning of November, then I think the sheer pressure that we were exerting upon the carp completely pushed them out of the area that we could fish. As the autumn progressed, the carp seemed to get further and further down the Canal bank towards the *Sluices* and by the beginning of November the fish that were being caught were either coming from the *Birches* or the *Gate* swim. These were just about the last two fishable swims along the canal bank.

Eventually they moved down to the *Sluices* and round the other side of the Ruislip island. Now this was awfully frustrating, as we could see the carp through the trees, on the far side of the island but could not put a bait to them. The catches completely dropped off and in actual fact, the last carp that I was to catch from Savay was on November 10th.

Although I went back several times throughout the winter, I neither caught, or could find, any more carp. So really that was the end of a truly phenomenal season at Savay and from June 16th until November 10th, I put 43 twenties on the bank, 13 of these being over thirty pounds. I had never had a season like it and, to be honest, I really can't see me repeating this on any other U.K. water in the future.

It really was a case of everything coming together at the right time – the access onto one of the most prolific big fish waters in the country, virtually being the first in with the hair rig and using boilies at long range. The ironic thing is that we truly believed that this was going to be a one off and, I for one, fished my socks off. Then at the end of the season, we heard that the syndicate was to carry on and I was duly offered the chance to renew my place.

I thought about this long and hard and, in the end, decided against it. There was no way I was going to repeat the success and just how many more carp did I want to catch from Savay? I suppose there was always *Sally* to go back for, but then again, I never seemed to have a lot of luck with the commons and may have fished the water for the rest of my life without bumping in to her. So in the end I declined, at least knowing that someone else would have the opportunity of fishing this marvellous water. With hindsight, I now believe that this was the right decision, for things at Savay were, inevitably, never to be the same again. I have wonderful memories of that year, with the fish I caught, the friends I made, and becoming almost a part of the bankside. I don't think I could ever have repeated such a magical time. I started to take things a bit easier after November, but still spent the weekends at Darenth, adding a few more twenties during the course of the winter and the back end. I finally ended up with a phenomenal tally of fish with 206 over ten pounds, 50 of them being over twenty, including 13 over the magical thirty. It was certainly an exhausting season, fishing a ridiculous number of hours, but I enjoyed every minute of it. I don't think I will ever put that much effort into my carp angling again. I have a much better perspective on life these days but I don't think I would have missed the experience for the world.

IMPORTANT NOTE
Please only telephone our Customer Enquiries Number (021) 373 4523) if you require product information or cannot obtain a catalogue from your dealer

Terry Eustace Gold Label Tackle

A Dealer List appears at the bottom of these 3 pages — Contact these stockists for your GOLD LABEL products

TRILENE

Independent tests conducted at NASA conference 4th April 1992

	MAXIMA	TRILENE XL	TRILENE XT	BIG GAME
STATED B/S	2lb	2lb	2lb	not available
MEASURED B/S	3¾lb	3¾lb	5¼lb	n/a
MEASURED DIA.	.0055"	.0045"	.006"	n/a
STATED B/S	6lb	6lb	6lb	not available
MEASURED B/S	8lb	8½lb	9¼lb	n/a
MEASURED DIA.	.009"	.0075"	.0085"	n/a
STATED B/S	10lb	10lb	10lb	10lb
MEASURED B/S	10¾lb	13¼lb	17lb	13lb
MEASURED DIA.	.011"	.0105"	.0125"	.0105"
STATED B/S	12lb	not available	not available	12lb
MEASURED B/S	13½lb	n/a	n/a	17¼lb
MEASURED DIA.	.012"	n/a	n/a	.013"
STATED B/S	15lb	not available	14lb	15lb
MEASURED B/S	16¼lb	n/a	22¼lb	21¾lb
MEASURED DIA.	.015"	n/a	.014"	.0145"

more than just another line

WHAT THE EXPERTS SAY

Its abrasion-resistant qualities are really quite remarkable for a mono line, I use it with total confidence — **JIM GIBBINSON**

When it comes to fishing amongst weed or any form of snags, there is no line I know in comparable breaking strains to compare with Terry Eustace Big Game Line — **ROD HUTCHINSON**

Too good to be true, the most impressive line I've ever seen — **LEE JACKSON**

Incredible abrasion resistance yet still very soft, available in 12lb but to be honest it casts as smoothly as many 8lb lines — **SHAUN HARRISON**

It's a fact... the best lines are not made in Europe any more — **CHRIS BALL**

BIG GAME
The ultimate line for the big fish angler. Superb line lay, casting performance, high shock and abrasion resistance, incredibly strong for diameter and almost invisible in water. Do you really need any other line? Used by many of Britain's leading carp and pike anglers.

CLEAR - £15.99
Ref
225 - 10lb x 1500 yards
195 - 12lb x 1175 yards
196 - 15lb x 900 yards
197 - 20lb x 700 yards
198 - 25lb x 595 yards
199 - 30lb x 440 yards

200 - 40lb x 370 yards
201 - 50lb x 275 yards
GREEN - £15.99
Ref
260 - 10lb x 1500 yards
261 - 12lb x 1175 yards
262 - 15lb x 900 yards
263 - 20lb x 700 yards

TRILENE XT
Trilene XT (Extra Tough) will stand a tremendous amount of knocking about. Its superior abrasion resistance is due to an extra tough layer of protection that resists nicks, cuts and scrapes. For all those anglers who want Big Game performance in lower strains this is the answer.

CLEAR - 110 yards
Ref
300 - 2lb - £4.85
301 - 4lb - £4.85
302 - 6lb - £4.85
303 - 8lb - £4.85
304 - 10lb - £5.95

CLEAR - 330 yards
Ref
301 - 4lb - £12.75
311 - 6lb - £12.75
312 - 8lb - £12.75
313 - 10lb - £14.95
314 - 14lb - £14.95
315 - 20lb - £18.95
316 - 25lb - £18.95
317 - 30lb - £18.95

TRILENE XL
Trilene XL (Extra Limp) has a unique nylon alloy formulation which gives incredible strength whilst its extra limpness and low memory provide exceptional handling, casting characteristics and outstanding knot strength. A brilliant floating line for the angler who wants supreme control.

GREEN - 110 yards
Ref
320 - 2lb - £4.85
321 - 4lb - £4.85
322 - 6lb - £4.85
323 - 8lb - £4.85
324 - 10lb - £5.95
WHITE/FLUORESCENT BLUE now available

GREEN - 330 yards
Ref
331 - 4lb - £12.75
332 - 6lb - £12.75
333 - 8lb - £12.75
334 - 10lb - £14.95

YOU HAVE THE LATEST TECHNOLOGY TRILENE ONLY IF THE BOX CARRIES A GOLD LABEL STICKER

GOLD LABEL STOCKISTS GOLD LABEL STOCKISTS GOLD LABEL STOCKISTS GOLD LABEL STOCKISTS

AVON
Bristol Angling Centre
12-16 Doncaster Road
Southmead, Bristol
0272 500201

Veals Fishing Tackle
61 Old Market Street
Bristol
0272 291788

BEDFORDSHIRE
Dixon Brothers
95 Tavistock Street
Bedford
0234 267145

Leslie's of Luton
89/91/93 Park Street
0582 453542

BERKSHIRE
Thatcham Angling Centre
Shop 4, 156-158 Sagecroft Rd
0635 871450

The Bracknell Angling Centre
2 Fowlers Lane
Bracknell
0344 425130

The Reading Angling Centre
69 Northumberland Avenue
Reading
0734 872216

BUCKINGHAMSHIRE
Marsh Tackle
4 Cross Court
Plomer Green Road
Downley, High Wycombe
0494 437035

CAMBRIDGESHIRE
Ouse Valley (Specialist) Angling
Unit 4, 25/31 Huntingdon St
St Neots
0480 476088

CHESHIRE
Barlows of Bond Street
47 Bond Street
Macclesfield
0625 619935

Dave's of Middlewich
'Angling Centre of Cheshire'
67 Wheelock Street
Middlewich
0606 843853

Scott's of Northwich
185/187 Witton Street
Northwich
0606 46543

Trev's Wilmslow
16 Altrincham Road, Wilmslow
0625 528831

CUMBRIA
Ambleside Angling
3 Old Post Office Blds
Millars Park Road, Ambleside
05394 31242

DERBYSHIRE
Angling Centre Derby
29-33 Nightingale Road
Derby
0332 380605

The Bridge Shop
39 High Street
Measham, Swadlincote
0530 272864

DORSET
Bournemouth Fishing Lodge
904 Wimborne Road
Moordown, Bournemouth
0202 514345

Davis Fishing Tackle
75 Bargates
Christchurch
0202 485169

DEVON
Exeter Angling Centre
Smythen Street, Off Market St
Exeter
0392 436404

ESSEX
Basildon Angling Centre
402 Whitmore Way, Basildon
0268 520144 and at
Hornchurch 04024 77834

Bowlers Angling
2-3 Cinema Parade
Dagenham
081 592 3273

Bromages Fishing Tackle
666 Green Lane
Goodhayes, Ilford
081 590 3521

Edwards Fishing Tackle
16 Broomfield Road
Chelmsford
0245 357689

Southend Angling Centre
5-6 Pier Approach
Southend
0702 611066

Specialist Tackle
223 Petits Lane North
Rise Park, Essex
0708 730513

Trev's of Loughton
70 The Broadway
Debden IG10 3SY
081 502 3011

Trev's of Romford
209-211 North Street
Romford
0708 763370

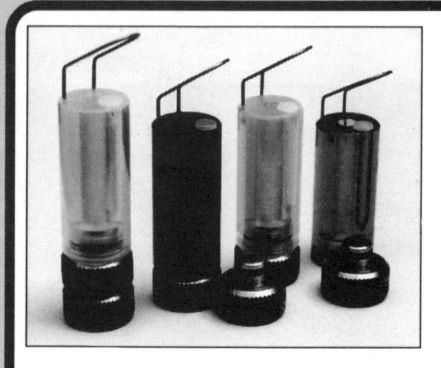

Terry Eustace Gold Label Tackle

THE PENDULATOR

In a range of high visibility Yellow, Green, Blue and Red bodies, these indicators are available with standard nine inch, or long fifteen inch arms. The clear arm is attached to a hinge and clip which fits securely onto standard buzzer bars or banksticks. The body is detachable from the arm, and isotopes, when inserted, are retained when the arm is fitted back into the body.

Two weights are supplied with the indicator, and these fit precisely both the indicator body, and themselves, allowing the indicator to be used either with or without weights attached. The two weights supplied total 2oz. Extra weights are also available. The clips used in this indicator have the same ends as the Super-Clip, and can be tensioned to give minimal pressure against line release, or to support several ounces. The hinge which fits the buzzer bar remains stable, even on the long arm indicator when it drops in "free fall" with a six ounce load. Weights can be simply added or removed, with the Pendulator in place.

Yellow Pendulator Ref 293 - £10.75
Red Pendulator Ref 294 - £10.75
Green Pendulator Ref 295 - £10.75
Blue Pendulator Ref 296 - £10.75
Long Arm Yellow Pendulator Ref 289 - £10.95
Long Arm Red Pendulator Ref 359 - £10.95
Long Arm Green Pendulator Ref 291 - £10.95
Long Arm Blue Pendulator Ref 292 - £10.95

Spare Standard Arm Only Ref 297 - £2.75
Spare Long Arm Only Ref 298 - £2.95
Extra Bobbin/Pendulator Weights
Ref 357 - £1.95 per pair

Standard *(top)* Long Arm *(below)*

FLUO-BOBBINS

High Visibility bobbins, with our favourite colours being Yellow and Green, which show up extremely well in daylight and are also, as with the Blue, extremely visible after dark with an isotope fitted. The red is not good in darkness. Unlike some coloured bobbins, which have to be released by hand before you strike, these drop smoothly off the tangle free stainless loops. As with the Pendulators shown below, two weights are supplied and these can be interchanged with the Pendulator weights.

Yellow Fluo-Bobbin Ref 285 - £7.95
Red Fluo-Bobbin Ref 358 - £7.95
Green Fluo-Bobbin Ref 287 - £7.95
Blue Fluo-Bobbin Ref 288 - £7.95

SUPER CLIPS

These ball end line clips with rubber tension adjuster, have an extended shank 33mm long and have many different applications
Ref 299 - £1.95 per pair

STAINLESS STEEL SQUARE SECTION BUZZER BARS

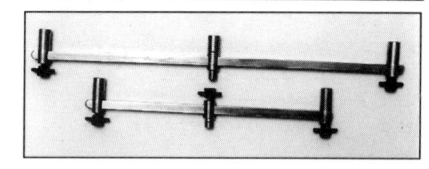

The obvious solution for perfect alignment. 100% stability, the ultimate buzzer bar.
2-Rod 10" Ref 218 - £12.95
3-Rod 15" Ref 219 - £13.95

STAINLESS STEEL BANKSTICKS

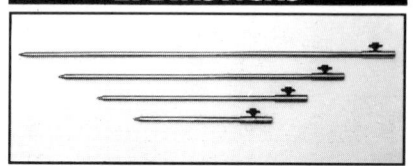

No roll pins or pegs to hold together parts which fit like a banana in a shirt sleeve. All machining is to precise interference tolerances so that assembly requires a press. The Peg Screws allow precise adjustment and positive locking. Slim, light and stronger than some models of comparable dimensions they look good and function perfectly.
10" Ref 242 - £7.95   15" Ref 243 - £8.95
20" Ref 244 - £9.95   25" Ref 234 - £10.95

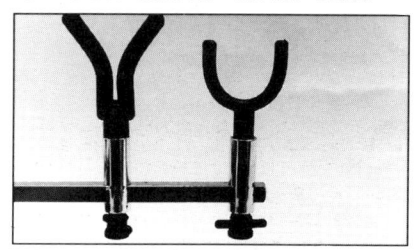

SUPER 'U' & SUPER 'V' ROD REST HEADS

Neat and practical fittings which have proved immensely popular.
Super 'U' Ref 043 - £1.69
Super 'V' Ref 044 - £1.69

STAINLESS STEEL NEEDLES

Robust, 3/16" dia stainless, capped at one end with a brass tear drop-shaped stop.
12" Ref 235 - £2.95   18" Ref 236 - £3.35
24" Ref 237 - £3.75

GOLD LABEL STOCKISTS

GLOUCESTERSHIRE
Bateman's (Sports) Ltd
Kendrick Street
Stroud
0453 764320

HAMPSHIRE
Raison Brothers
2 Park Road
Farnborough
0252 543470

Tackle Up
151 Fleet Road, Fleet
0252 614066

HERTFORDSHIRE
North Herts Angling Centre
25 London Road
Baldock
0462 896336

Simpsons of Turnford
Nunsbury Drive
Turnford, Broxbourne
0992 468799

KENT
Bob Morris
1 Lincolnshire Terrace
Lane End, Darenth, Dartford
0322 278519

Country Way Gun Shop
86 High Street
West Malling
0732 870023

Maidstone Angling Centre
15 Perryfield Street
Maidstone
0622 677326

KENT
Penge Angling
309 Beckenham Road
Beckenham
081 778 4652
(Also at Eltham & Rayleigh)

Romney Tackle
19 Littlestone Road
Littlestone, New Romney
0679 63990

Sandwich Bait & Tackle
13 The Chain, Sandwich
0304 613752

The Tackle Box
198 Main Road
Sutton at Hone, Farningham
0322 865371

LANCASHIRE
Chorley Anglers
12 Gillibrand Street
Chorley
0257 263513

North West Angling Centre
16c Market Street
Hindley, Wigan
0942 55993

LEICESTERSHIRE
Arbon & Watts
39 Sherrard Street
Melton 0664 62876
and at Grantham 0476 63419

LINCOLNSHIRE
Wheater Fieldsports
3-9 Tentercroft Street
Lincoln
0522 521219

LONDON
Ashpoles of Ilsington
15 Green Lanes, Islington
071 226 6575

Browns Fishing Tackle Ltd
682 Romford Road
Manor Park
081 478 0389

Frames Fishing Tackle
202 West Hendon Broadway
Hendon
081 202 0264

Southwark Angling Centre
346 East Street
London SE17
071 708 5903

T.D. Tackle & Bait
8 Camberwell Road
London SE5
071 708 3882

Trev's of Leyton
512 Leabridge Road
London
081 558 5718

Trev's of Walthamstow
123 Fulbourne Road
London E17 4HA
081 527 1135

MANCHESTER
Trafford Angling Supplies
34 Moss Road
Stretford
061 864 1211

MERSEYSIDE
Johnson's Angling Centre
469 Rice Lane
Liverpool
051 525 5574

Star Angling
101 Duke Street
St. Helens
0744 38605

MIDDLESEX
Davies Angling
47/49 Church Street
Staines
0784 461831

Harefield Tackle
9 Park Lane
Harefield
0895 822900

Hounslow Angling Centre
265/267 Bath Road
Hounslow
081 570 6156

Judd's of Hillingdon
3 Westbourne Parade
Uxbridge Road, Hillingdon
081 573 0196

Terry Eustace Gold Label Tackle

ROD/LEAD STRAPS
I know how extremely useful these are, but I still cannot believe the amount we have sold. After folding the rod, go once around both joints with the strap, then drop the lead along the material, then continue around, until the velcro holds securely. The other strap holds the butt-end together. One of the most useful items we have ever sold.
Ref 174 - £3.45 per pair

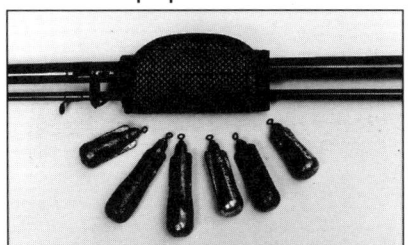

BUZZ BOMBS
Until the introduction of the Buzz Bomb, you couldn't get an aerodynamic lead which lifted clear of weeds, bars and snags on the retrieve. The problem with fluted bombs, was that they either spun and twisted on the retrieve, and often cast so badly, that where they were going to land was pure guesswork. Not only does the Buzz Bomb cast well but, the positioning of the fins seems to make them even more stable in cross winds than a standard bomb. Swivels used are Berkley 100lb. Three leads per pack.
2oz Buzz Bombs Ref 204 - £1.99
2½oz Buzz Bombs Ref 205 - £2.25
3oz Buzz Bombs Ref 206 - £2.45

'THE' RIG
Still the most successful anti-tangle rig that I have used, and the many thousands sold last year confirm its efficiency. One point well worth considering is that last season, many dealers informed me of anglers complaining about all brands of line breaking cleanly "for no reason at all". When asked if they used anti-tangle rigs, the answer was invariably yes, but not "The" Rig. When you use a helicopter type rig, you should hold the main line in one hand, take the hook and do what the fish does — pull! You will see that if you don't use tubing, the swivel, even some of those designed for this type of rig, pulls across the bottom bead at right angles, with a guillotine effect. With "The" Rig, the tubing and the soft rubber buffer-stop, cushions this effect.
Ref 172 - £1.95 per packet of three

FLOATER FLOATS
I was using these floats ten years before I had the first models produced for sale a couple of years ago, and there simply isn't anything available anywhere near as good. It is not possible to see the top of floats which sit virtually level with the surface, if you have cast to any distance.
With The Floater Floats, as soon as the hookbait is taken, the float will tilt and sink at the same time.
To set up, simply put the float on the line (no stops above the float) pop on a black or brown carp bead and then tie on a swivel. Tie a length of nylon to the swivel and allow three to six feet between the swivel and the hook. The Small Floater will cast forty yards with 8lb line and the Standard Floater out of sight.
Floater Float Small Ref 071 - £2.95
Floater Float Standard Ref 072 - £3.25

CARP BEADS
Shatterproof beads with smooth bores to eliminate problems of line wear. The 5mm dia. and 6mm dia. sizes have bores which allow the bead to sit over the swivel knot to avoid damage in this area when casting or playing fish. The 4mm size is suitable to use above the swivel or bomb swivel and also, being small and light, is ideal in floating line situations.
4mm Olive colour Ref 073 - £1.55
5mm Black colour Ref 074 - £1.65
6mm Brown colour Ref 075 - £1.75

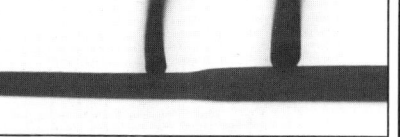

SUPER RIG SHRINK
Available in two sizes. Ideal for firmly positioning hairs, joining different diameter rig or silicone tubes, and a number of other uses. Super Rig Shrink 1 has a bore of approx 1mm, Shrink 2 approx 2mm. Super-Shrink contracts drastically, merely with the application of hot water.
Super Rig Shrink 1 (1mm Bore) Ref 353 - 95p
Super Rig Shrink 2 (2mm Bore) Ref 354 - 99p

BLACK ALLOY NET SPREADER
To replace that broken plastic one or why not replace it before it breaks, and costs you a Whacker?
Ref 038 - £8.95

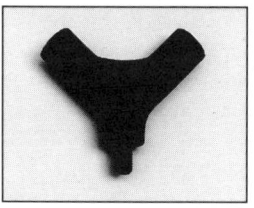

P.V.A. THREAD
Faster dissolving than strings.
240" Ref 089 - £1.80   1,000" Plus Ref 090 - £4.25

POLYPOPS
Of a sensible size for popping up boilies.
Ref 091 - £1.45

BOILY NEEDLES
Standard Size Ref 239 - £1.05
Long Size Ref 240 - £1.35

NUT DRILL
If your nuts haven't got holes in, this is the tool!
Ref 271 - £1.55

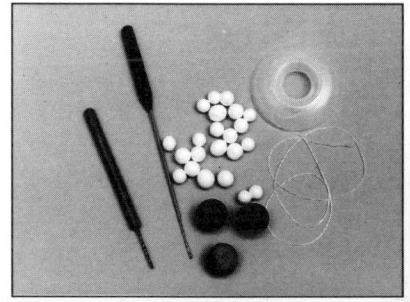

GOLD LABEL STOCKISTS

MIDDLESEX
Angling Centre
1288 Greenford Road
Greenford
081 422 8311

Tackle Up
363 Staines Road West
Ashford Common, Ashford
0784 240013

NORFOLK
Tom Boulton Fishing Tackle
173 Drayton Road
Norwich 0603 426834
and at 6 St. Johns Close
0603 626770

NORTHANTS
The Angling Centre
85 St. Leonards Road
Far Cotton NN4 9DA
0604 764847

The Sportsman Lodge
44 Kingsthorpe Road
Kingsthorpe Hollow
0604 713399

NOTTINGHAMSHIRE
Mansfield Angling
20 Byron Street
Mansfield
0623 633790

Walkers of Trowell
9-15 Nottingham Road
Trowell
0602 301816/307798

OXFORDSHIRE
Catch 1 Tackle
14 The Parade
Kidlington
08675 2066

J & K Tropicals & Pets
8-10 Wesley Precinct
Bicester
0869 242589

SHROPSHIRE
Kingfisher Angling Centre
8 New Street
Frankwell, Shrewsbury
0743 240602

SOMERSET
Avalon Angling Company
191 High Street, Street
0458 841761

STAFFORDSHIRE
Pickerings of Burslem
4-8 William Clowes Street
Burslem, Stoke on Trent
0782 814941

Alan's of Kingsbury
1 Jubilee Court
Kingsbury
Tamworth
0827 872451

SUFFOLK
Tackle Up
49A St John's Street
Bury St Edmunds
0284 755022

SURREY
Apollo Sales & Service
2b Woodham Lane
New Haw, Weybridge
0932 848354

Davies Angling
3a Brook Road
Redhill
0737 771888

Esher Angling Centre
Weston Green
Thames Ditton
081 398 2405

SUSSEX
Lagoon Bait and Tackle
327 Kingsway
Hove
0273 415879

Tropicano
5-6 Pier Road
Littlehampton
0903 715190

WALES
Garry Evans
105 Whitchurch Road
Cardiff
0222 619828

Garry Evans (Newport) Ltd
29 Redland Street
Newport, Gwent
0633 855086

WILTSHIRE
Cotswold Angling
Kennedy's Garden Centre
Hyde Road, Kingsdown,
Swindon 0793 721173

The House of Angling
59/60 Commercial Road
Swindon
0793 693460

YORKSHIRE
Catterick Angling Centre
17 Hilyard Row
Catterick Garrison, N.Yorks
0748 833133

C. J. Fishing Tackle
182 Kings Road
Harrogate HG1 5JG
0423 525000

Eric's Angling Centre
401 Selby Road
Whitkirk, Leeds
0532 646883

Westgate Anglers
63 Westgate
Bradford
0274 729570

CHILLIN IN FRANCE

ALAN TAYLOR

Editors Note:
The catch of the year? Or of all time?
It's hard to say.
However here it is the exclusive on Alan and Joe's French session exclusive to Big Carp *and told in Alan's unique style.*

There we were, standing having a quiet pint, taking the piss out of J.J. and his latest northern designer fashions, black velvet jacket and flappy flares, (this man is to fashion what Kylie Minogue is to singing).

"Had a good trip to France then? Any chance of doing us an article?" said Mr Mayhem. "Yeah sure Rob", the things you say when you have had a few 'sherberts' (and regret later).

Well here I am a few months later still trying, where do you start? Well, as they say – start at the beginning: That was in Joe's shop, we were discussing Merv's 'Nuremburg trials', when the conversation got round to our forthcoming trip to France.

We were planning to go down south but were having a few hitches. We had been lucky to squeeze in a couple of trips earlier in the year – luckily I say, as it's very difficult to get Joe to leave the shop, and with me being very reluctant to tear myself away from my *really interesting job in the factory* it's quite surprising we ever get away.

Anyhow, the last trip had been quite successful as we managed to catch a few fish between us up to mid-thirty: a result from a very large water. Due to the extra days we would have needed for travelling south we opted to return to the Big Lake.

Time soon flew by at work... weeks seemed like months and days like years, as usual there was loads to do before the off, I had to um... um... sort out my tackle and tie a few rigs, Joe did his usual bit, got the van serviced, booked and paid for the ferry, got the insurance, got the green card, ordered the bait, cooked the particles, got the francs, bought the food etc.

The day soon arrived and the four of us met at Joe's shop the infamous J & K of Bicester, myself, Phil 'NASA big bream Smudger' Smith, Sean, 'I don't know how to boil a kettle' Walker and of course Joe. What's a nice bloke like Sean was doing with us three I don't know, he is the sort that gets out of the bath for a pee! After a bit of friendly banter from Merv, the tackle and bait were loaded into the trusty Transit. We managed to get everything in like you do, except for Smudger's clothes bag, but we managed to find room in the glove compartment (what a smart dresser that Smudger is).

With the van loaded we switched to auto-pilot, stuffed him with sweets and put on the Foster and Allen tapes, what a pair of DEF Geezers that Foster and Allen, kinda spooky. We soon arrived at Dover and got loaded onto the Sea Cat, that was as much fun as usual, middle of the night, middle of the channel, big bang... lights go out... pitch black, ferries everywhere... engine stops. F. A. bit like the last trip when something came loose and it had to stop mid-channel, while a bloke went on the roof with a big hammer and 'adjusted' something, anyway lights came back on, went off, came on, went off eventually we were moving, and arrived in Calais. Calais by night... this must be the time to see it, (picturesque France – you must be joking) what a dump! The drive seems to take no time at all, (probably 'cos I slept all the way).

Anyway into the local bar for permits, that was good for a laugh after nearly buying permits for pole fishing, pike fishing from a boat, spinning we think we have the right permits so off to the lake. By the time the three of us have clambered out of the van to start unloading we could just make out the auto pilot disappearing round the corner with his armoury of rods. By the time we had finished unloading the van Joe had got his first five rods out and was busy setting up his others. The next two days were forgettable, but we managed to catch a couple of nice fish between us and were moved on by the Gendarmes, they were keen for us to spend the nights on a near-by camp site about 100 kms away, (probably owned by one of their brothers). We declined their kind offer. As they had made it quite clear about the night fishing or lack of it and how strict they were going to be about enforcing it a little despondently we parlayed and finally decided to move to another big water further south. Optimistic as ever we hoped for big fish and better weather (some hope). After much driving and map reading we arrived at the lake totally 'exhausted' about four in the afternoon we had been up all night, then as we stepped from the van the heavens opened. Oh! this is nice, we commented jovially totally ...... off (or words to that effect). I think *a good nights kip* was on all our minds, as much as anything. Anyway the boat was unloaded the sounder was connected and we soon had an idea what was in front of us, apart from not being able to see the lake which was disappearing into the horizon. The lake bed gradually shelved off to 15 feet at a good chuck, not too many snags. Out with the markers (Gino Ginelle ultimate markers exclusive to J & K Bicester), at a very reasonable price. A bucket of maize around each marker, a scattering of boilies, then Bosh! Three rods out to the mark length (because it's the most reliable) Owner hooks, short hair, three boilies, anti-tangle tube, round leads. Up with the umbrella as it was still chucking it down. We had a bite to eat and parlayed – we decided this would do for tonight, a good kip, then we would have a good look around and try and find some fish in the morning.

I was so glad to get into the warmth of the sleeping bag, with the rain, tiredness and the disappointment of having to leave the other lake. I had just got warm and was drifting off when beep... beep... scream from the Baitrunner, out into the rain and the cold into the wet boots, pull into the fish, beep... beep... scream one of the other rods was away, give the first one a bit of the Captain Pugwash and heave him into the net, call Joe for another net only to see him and Phil playing a fish ah! Well two in the same net then, weigh 'em up put 'em into sacks, and then recast back to bed. NO hope, before I could get both rods out I'd had another two fish, anyway the fish were going in and out of the sacks, as they got bigger by the morning we had filled every sack we had. In 12 hours I had managed six 30's, eight 20's and two doubles to 39 pounds.

We parlayed over a cup of coffee in the morning and decided we would give the swim a few more hours to see if anything else would happen. We weren't disappointed. The weather was atrociously cold and wet, and at times very windy You can't keep dry when you are catching – especially under just a brolly. I soon ran out of dry clothes so gave up trying to keep dry and made do with a pair of shorts, boots and whatever was handy. Netting some of the fish was 'good fun'. If you can imagine paddling in the sea in two foot waves as the tide i going out, you are just going for the final heave into the net when the water flies over the top of your boots as a wave breaks on the bank, or the opposite happens and as the wave retreats, leaving you with a big carp floundering in the mud. The action was thick and fast for the next three days which obviously meant very little sleep by the fourth night I'd 'had it' and felt really rough. I remember casting out in the dark, and when I woke it was well light. I had slept for ten hours solid, so solidly in fact, my umbrella was turned inside out and lay in a big heap beside me, I'd managed to sleep through an atrocious storm and Joe catching a 51lb mirror. Anyway seeing the big one cheered me up no end even when I discovered I had cast out the night before without tying any baits on.

I am not good enough at this writing game to explain, or put into words adequately the couple of days fishing we had but with me catching in total three 40's, 30 thirties, 36 twenties, 13 doubles and lost two (what a bitch), and altogether the four of us had one 50, six 40's, 72 thirties and 82 twenties between us, you can imagine there wasn't much else going on other than cooking particles, baiting up, weighing and photographing fish. There were several times when we had a couple of fish together and had them on the bank for photos at the same time which was nice. Twice I had two together and both times they were over 30lb. Smudger was keeping a 'Top 20' of the biggest fish as well as being official record keeper and tallying all the weights – one ton of fish in ... hours etc. The top ten was fun, causing comments like "I've just had a 36 that's you out the top ten – ......". On the middle of the fifth afternoon we were visited by the local Gendarmes, we had not put up bivvys, or anything other than umbrellas and had parked the van well away from the water's edge, keeping as low a profile as possible.

I was up to my waist in water playing a big fish that had been on for 20 minutes or so when they arrived, a further 20 minutes later I landed the fish – a 43lb leather, they watched as we photographed and weighed it and slid it back. I could hear them chattering away to Joe, and I knew it would be bad news. They had made it quite clear that night fishing was strictly forbidden and that we were not to sleep at or near the lake, rough camping not allowed, and told us we must sleep at a camp site. Reluctantly we decided it would be best to pack up every evening on time, drive away from the lake, kip by the van and then return in the morning. This we did for the rest of the week which obviously cost us fish. The weather continued to be terrible, wind and relentless rain which made getting to and from the lake very difficult. We were getting stuck two or three times each trip as the tracks became worse with the heavy rain, but the carp kept obliging. Every night as we pulled off we piled maize into the swims in the hope of holding the fish and sure enough first chuck in the mornings we had a few. We had run out of boilies and film for the cameras, along with food and water. So me and Joe went for a ride round to do some shopping. We stopped to chat to another carp angler who turned out to be a Belgian. He spoke a little English, but it didn't really matter as Joe can speak any language fluently.

"Any carp you catch?" he say.
"Yes, we have had a few" (understatement of the year).
"You have problems with trouble makers?" he say. "Non, have vous?" said Joe in a strong Belgian/Oxfordshire accent.
"No, I have weapon, you have weapon?" said Belgian Bertie.

Dodgy I thought, what does he mean, he must have noticed our quizzical expressions. "You know, gun", said Bertie.
"Oh! Ah! Yeah" (I thought he was after a look at me 'tackle') I said. I didn't really want him to know we only had a catapult between us. "This place very dangerous", with which he produced a nine millimetre automatic pistol.
"Ah! shotgun" I said aiming into the sky shouting "Boom, Boom" thinking that would impress him.
"It is very big", said Bert.
I thought he must have been talking about me "tackle" after all, I don't remember him at Merv's stag night.
"No", I said "We saw off the barrels". Well the look on his face – no problem there Joe, I thought and we went off in search of provisions.

We found a nice shop selling our favorite chocolat du pains and fresh bagettes. Joe purchased a couple of the most expensive cakes in the shop with Smudger's money (as we know he loves to treat us) –tight b'stard. As we left the shop a young lady in fishnet stockings and no knickers greeted us with a vertical smile, Joe had a quick chat in his best French, "What did she say Joe?" he said he wasn't quite sure but he thought she asked if we could go back to her place and help her unblock some pipes. "Yeah, what did you say". "I told her we weren't plumbers", he said.

It rained all day and when we came to leave we found we could not shift the van. As we only had two nights left we decided to stay put by the lake for the night and chance it. We were a bit concerned that the Gendarmes would return so we talked over a plan of action. "Shall we top 'em and dump the bodies in the lake! By the time they find them we would be home in England . No not a good idea, we put this to one side because we could not find any really round stones for the catapults, which would have given them an advantage with their guns. If they were going to throw us off at least we could have a bit of a crack so we went to bed wearing our masks.

We still had the masks on the next morning when three French geezers walked down the track towards us, one saw Joe and stopped about 50 yards away and would not come any further, the other two walked past very slowly with a strange look in their eyes, then they saw the English van mumbled something to each other and gave a knowing look.

Anyway, back to the fishing: the last day arrived and things had slowed slightly. We were due to leave at around 12.30 and I was hoping to catch one more over 30lb to give me 30 thirties for the week. At about 11 o'clock it was thundering and lightening and pissing down beep! beep! szzzz as the Bait-runner screamed. There I was bent into another one, shorts, tee shirt, absolutely soaked, freezing cold, covered in mud. Encouragement was coming from under Phil and Joe's brolly.
"It's only a little 'un".
"Hope it falls off".

Into the net and onto the scales! "30lb 8oz Ye! Ha!" Cold, wet, shivering, knackered I couldn't care less. Absolutely brilliant, great fishing, great company, great trip, here's to the next one. And in the words of that famous song.

Come on baby let's take a chance,
Put your hands down my under pants,
and let's dance.

Foster and Allen

The following pages of photographs show just some of the fish from Alan's awesome catch.

CYPROQUEST DEVELOPMENTS
TEL: 0303 220928

FEATURES – RADIO CONTROL UNIT
One year's parts and labour guarantee. Full back up service. Fail-safe receiver. Direct to mainline battery. Radio handset and aerial. Two spare navigation six volt bulbs, white with red and green waterproof sealant for decking. Two tube system with hookbait holders. Sensible low drag prop guard.

THE EDGE
The edge 'silent running' feature. Delivery of particles, seeds, floaters, floating seeds and last but not least the old and well known circular food source at ranges inaccessible by catapult or throwing stick etc, with on top accurate delivery to marker or known spots of a low visibility rig, to five ounce capability and two ounce drop back-lead at the distance you choose from the loose baits, and with the hookbait on top creating a fish catching situation I call proximity baiting. Normally only obtainable in the margins and with swim width restrictions and bank noise there are unknown limitations.

Boat Capability on continuous open throttle drawn down produced over 2000 yards with enough battery life to return to swim at over 100 yards. On this basis we estimate a single angler to deliver six hookbaits around the 150–160 yard mark for a full five days (night and day) using two rods, with no crack-offs, no ballistic deaths of man, fish or bird, no anti-tangle tube or tangles and delivery of anchored floater controllers and floating hookbaits. All units twin water sealed. Also designed for people who would like to use full or 95% of their spool capacity, without having to find £160.00 per rod. Making a saving on lost leads, expensive hooklengths and carefully prepared hook arrangements which consume a lot of time, reduces ring-wear, rod deterioration and various degrees of arm-ache on volumes of boilies. Projected individually at range depending on conditions, bait gravity etc. The partially/disabled anglers can fish at ease, at the same range as the able-bodied. There is a little extra included in the form of a boat placement pole which allows the boat to be placed into the water at bank height four feet sheer above water, or over weed without the danger of slipping on casting etc close fences and bushes prohibiting casting or places where you can't overhead or side-cast – this widens your scope for available swims on the lake. We hope there will be some debate promoting the full advantages mentioned. The price is accessible, with interest free credit or it can be split between a group of say four anglers, it would be £51.25. No VAT and they have **the edge**.

ACCESSORIES
LED long range marker float system. Marker placement and retrieval system (no lines in the water). Spare 12 volt 6 amps power lead acid batteries. Two to three year cyclic charge life, minimum spare floater tube, extra lengths. Larger volume tubes supplied with universal tubes. HP7 batteries and charger, 12 volts, 6amp hour trickle and fast charge, or apply your own household or car charger. Enquire for matching charge ratios.

PAYMENT FACILITIES
Price exclusive of postage and packing or direct collection £205.50 (No VAT applicable). Available by direct collection or security delivery. A £115 deposit, the remaining £90 paid by four monthly instalments of £20, the £15 arrangement fee and administration payments interest free. Subject to application. All the usual rights reserved.

We also offer a personalised, framed, aerial photograph of your favourite fishing retreat. Full quality prints. Please enquire. Keep an eye on *Big Carp* for further developments or contact us on the number above for further details anytime.

TREV'S ANGLING GROUP
INCORPORATING ROMFORD ANGLING CENTRE
Walthamstow • Leyton • Loughton • Romford
MAIN STOCKISTS FOR ALL YOUR CARP REQUIREMENTS

SPECIALIST BAITS
☐ Nutrabaits ☐ S.B.S. ☐ Rod Hutchinson ☐ Kevin Maddocks ☐ Richworth

PREMIER STOCKISTS

Kevin Nash	Fox	Daiwa
Gardner	Terry Eustace	Optonics
Kryston	Bitech Viper	Solar Tackle
KJB	Kingfisher	Mainstream
Barbour	Wychwood	

and all other leading manufacturers

CALL IN AT ANY OF OUR BRANCHES FOR FRIENDLY SERVICE AND ADVICE

Mail order available.

TREV'S OF WALTHAMSTOW	**TREV'S OF LEYTON**	**TREV'S OF LOUGHTON**	**ROMFORD ANGLING CENTRE**
123 Fulbourne Road	512 Leybridge Road	70 The Broadway	209-211 North Street
Walthamstow	Leyton	Loughton	Romford
London E17 4HA	London E10 7DT	Essex IG10 3SY	Essex RM1 4QA
TEL: 081-527 1135	TEL: 081-558 5718	TEL: 081-502 3011	TEL: 0708 763370
FAX: 081-531 0569			

30-plus 32lb 32lb

32lb 32lb/31lb 31lb

30-plus 32lb

30-plus

30-plus

33lb

33lb

33lb

32lb/34lb

31lb

32lb 8oz

120

30lb 8oz

30-plus

30-plus

33lb

37lb

35lb

30lb 8oz

41lb

● **NEW FOR '92** ● **NEW FOR '92** ● **NEW FOR '92** ● **NEW FOR '92** ●

FROM KRYSTON – PRODUCTS AHEAD OF THEIR TIME

HEAVY METAL

SIMPLY THE FINEST LEAD SUBSTITUTE EVER DEVELOPED!!
MAXIMUM DENSITY/IMPROVED LOW PROFILE

To call HEAVY METAL a lead substitute is only half the story, not only is this compound light years ahead of any other putty on the market, it is, without question, better than lead itself. HEAVY METAL's sheer physical size, or lack of it, for its given weight is its first most striking feature, weighing in at least twice and in some cases three times the weight of any other putty on the market, this hi-tech compound will allow you to counterbalance your rigs with pin-point accuracy by using the minimum amount of material. HEAVY METAL is without doubt a brilliant technological achievement. By using the highest quality tungsten available, plus rare materials, maximum density has been achieved, meaning that the days of using pieces of putty the size of your bait are now well and truly over!

MOULDING AND SELF CURING

Ease of moulding makes HEAVY METAL a joy to use, its built-in uncanny ability to cure and harden in water (MICRO CRYSTALLIZATION) guarantees the product will literally cling and stay put on any item of tackle you have chosen. Now you can see why this product is that little bit 'special'.

HEAVY METAL will come as a godsend to anglers wishing to critically balance their baits without sacrificing the presentational profile of the hook-bait, the merest sliver along the shank will be enough to balance most baits. New dimensions in fishing buoyant baits can also be reached, a micro fine skin of the product can be easily applied along the hook-length to form a purpose-built HEAVY LINK which will counterbalance a pop-up whilst still retaining its flexibility, as opposed to the weight being concentrated in one heavy spot.

HEAVY METAL's adhesion qualities on all known lines, modern braids, Multi-strands and Monos is unrivalled. As a medium for backleads 'HEAVY METAL' is in a league of its own, a micro streamlined sausage shape which will not hinder casting can be moulded in seconds on to those vital first few feet behind the lead, the product's tremendous weight plus adhesion will ensure that the backlead will stay put cast after cast — what more could you ask for? Simply brilliant.

In use HEAVY METAL is child's play: simply snap a piece off, manipulate and stretch the product to achieve full pliability (friction generated from stretching, plus the heat from your fingers, makes it pliable in seconds). Mould to your desired shape and immerse in water for approx 60 seconds to cure.

At the end of your session remove the material from your rig and return it to the original block where it can be used over and over again.

Because of its weight, a single tub of HEAVY METAL will last the average angler a long time. Its retail price is reflected by its content of tungsten and rare materials. If it was cheaper it would not work, it's as simple as that . . . as it is **IT'S SIMPLY THE BEST!**

KRYSTON HEAVY METAL £4.35 per tub with full instructions

KLIN-IK

CARP CARE ANTISEPTIC — *CARE FOR YOUR FUTURE*

KRYSTON PRODUCTS are proud to present KLIN-IK

Due to the popularity of the sport, many of today's specialist anglers are now, quite rightly, aware and concerned about the welfare of their favourite species. Major developments in areas such as fish retention means that today the catching and returning of a specimen is a much easier and safer affair than that of yesteryear. This has resulted in a marked improvement in the condition of the fish, even on the most pressurised waters.

Sadly, however, there is one important exception. Fish treatment! In an effort to aid the fish many well meaning anglers are completely unaware that they are treating fish with substances which can actually cause physical harm to fish and angler alike!

The practice of treating fish using neat aniline dyes in an effort to speed up the healing process should be avoided at all cost. In unskilled hands they are without doubt highly toxic to skin tissues to both angler and fish and are also thought by some to be carcinogenic!

KLIN-IK is a totally safe approved laboratory formulated antiseptic for carp and all coarse fish. A one shot treatment of KLIN-IK following hook removal will sterilize the hook-hold to prevent secondary infection setting in and also assist in speeding up the natural healing process.

KLIN-IK contains active bactericides specifically for the immediate treatment to hook-holds, mouth damage, or fresh body lesions caused whilst landing the fish.

Safe KLIN-IK will not dye you or the fish green or violet, and is very easy to use. Following hook removal, simply apply 2/3 drops to the treatment area, allow 5 to 10 seconds for skin penetration and return fish.

Each bottle of KLIN-IK contains well over 1000 drops which is enough to last the average angler a full season. It is supplied with a special elongated nozzle for ease of application to difficult area (pike!).

KLIN-IK is an essential product for today's caring angler and will help you help your fish in a safe manner. Instead of returning fish that would look more at home in a disco, play safe. This is your opportunity to put something back into the sport that gives you so much pleasure.

Please note KLIN-IK's ingredients/materials and formula have not been developed as a cure-all for controlling established parasitical, fungal or viral infections, or fin rot which in the main always require specialised quarantine treatment.

KLIN-IK — FROM KRYSTON . . . WHO ELSE   Available in 30ml bottles £3.25

If your local tackle shop doesn't stock HEAVY METAL or KLIN-IK ask them to order it or go to a proper dealer!
All trade enquiries to: Kryston Advanced Angling Products, Bolton Enterprise Centre, Washington Street, Bolton, BL3 5EY. Tel: (0204) 24262 Fax: (0204) 364283

IS THIS YOUR FORTÉ

40+   40+   40+
40+   40+   40+
40+   40+   40+

HOOKLENGTHS ARE OURS!!

KRYSTON® ADVANCED HOOKLENGTHS – ONCE AGAIN THE NATION'S No. 1 CHOICE

Water records throughout the country have once again tumbled to the leading and thinking anglers who place their faith in our advanced lines and hooklengths. Kryston has once more swept the honours field with its unrivalled and unparalleld success. By producing the largest and greatest range of specialist braided hooklengths in the World our fingers are well and truly on the pulse of the carp world. Whatever the type of presentational techniques you may wish to pursue we can offer you a specialised line to meet those exact requirements. Having pioneered and led the field we have single handedly changed the face of specialist braided lines as we knew them. Kryston have brought them out of the dark ages by utilising ultra modern materials coupled with the use of high technology.

♪ SOMETHING IN THE WAY IT MOVES – 'da de da da da de da da' ♪
(With apologies to Shirley Bassey)

SHOULD YOU REQUIRE...

Something that will truly present your bait in a totally realistic and natural manner. Something with such a low diameter that it makes a mockery of conventional breaking strains. Something that would give you choices of buoyancy: neutral, below neutral, or above neutral. Something that will give you incredible softness and suppleness. Something who's many users would read like the 'Who's Who,' and the Hall of Fame of Carp Fishing. Something with an unequalled track record second to non... And finally and most importantly! Something which will not immediately sink like a stone and without any doubt whatsoever will not control, tether, or restrict the freedom of your carefully critically balanced preparation...

...THEN WE HAVE THAT SOMETHING... SOMETHING SPECIAL
IT'S CALLED KRYSTON AND IT'S SIMPLY THE BEST!

SILK-WORM   MULTI-STRAND   MERLIN   SUPER-SILK   QUICK-SILVER

PROVEN BY RESULTS ~ TRIED ~ TESTED ~ TRUSTED

KRYSTON® ADVANCED ANGLING PRODUCTS
Bolton Enterprise Centre, Washington Street, Bolton BL5 5EA
Telephone (0204) 24262   Tel/Fax: (0204) 364283

45lb

38lb 12oz

35lb

39lb

35lb

34lb

34lb

36lb

125

34lb

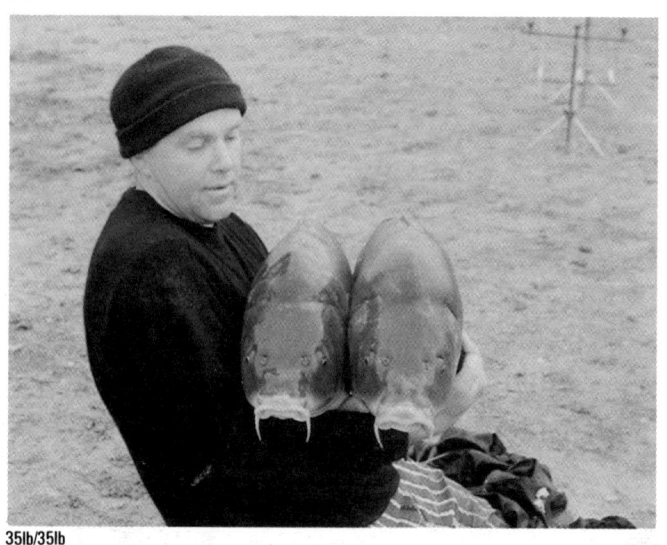

43lb 8oz

35lb/35lb

33lb

HINDERS SWINDON

Bird Seed Manufacturing Specialists

Importers Specialists Particles

ANIMATED PURSUITS

HINDERS SPECIALIST BAIT CENTRE, ERMIN STREET, STRATTON ST. MARGARET, SWINDON SN3 4NJ
☎ 0793 828961 or 822145

Europe's Largest Supplier of Specialist Particles

PARTICLES	2 kilo	5 kilo	12½ kilo	25 kilo
IGER NUTS	5.75	11.50	26.00	44.00
MALL PEANUT KERNELS	2.25	5.00	11.50	21.00
0K ORIGINAL	£37.00			
EDIUM PEANUT KERNELS	2.30	5.25	12.00	22.00
0K ORIGINAL SACKS	£35.00			
ARGE PEANUT KERNELS	2.55	5.75	13.00	23.00
0k ORIGINAL	£36.00			
INENUTS	AVAILABLE SOON			
HOLE BRAZIL NUTS	8.75	19.30	45.00	78.75
ROKEN BRAZILS	5.90	13.20	30.50	54.00
LMONDS	12.00	27.80	63.00	118.00
AZEL NUTS	9.15	20.00	47.59	83.00
ASHEWS	19.20	43.00	100.00	175.00
ISTACHIOS	19.20	43.00	100.00	175.00
EMP(STANDARD)	1.90	4.00	8.80	13.50
EMP (3½ mm)	2.70	5.70	14.00	24.50
ARES (CHINESE)	1.50	3.10	6.50	10.75
ARES (POLISH)	1.70	3.60	6.90	12.65
ED DARI	1.40	2.95	5.50	10.85
HITE DARI	1.80	4.10	9.70	18.50
UCKWHEAT	1.70	3.60	6.90	12.60
OATS	1.70	3.60	7.00	12.10
INHEAD OATMEAL	1.70	3.60	7.00	12.10
D RAPE	1.55	3.15	6.50	11.45
ACK RAPE	1.55	3.15	6.50	11.45
RTI BLEND	2.25	5.20	12.35	23.00
TH BEANS	3.35	7.75	18.50	35.00
NICUM MILLET	2.00	4.20	10.00	15.70
PANESE MILLET	2.00	4.20	10.00	15.70
D MILLET	2.00	4.20	10.00	15.70
HITE MILLET	2.00	4.20	10.00	15.70
SEED	1.50	3.10	6.50	10.75
DDY RICE	1.80	3.70	8.80	16.65
OLE OATS	99p	2.15	3.99	7.00
EAT	99p	2.15	3.99	7.00
RLEY	99p	2.15	3.99	7.00
AKED MAIZE	1.30	2.80	5.50	9.80
YERS MASH	1.10	2.25	4.75	7.90
AN	1.10	2.25	5.50	7.99
ICK PEAS	1.85	4.10	9.70	18.50
ENCH MAIZE(DEEP YELLOW)	1.45	3.00	6.30	10.50
ACK EYED BEANS	2.25	5.20	12.35	23.00
ZUKI BEANS	2.75	6.30	15.00	28.35
D KIDNEY BEANS	2.25	5.20	12.35	2300
EET LUPINS	2.25	5.20	12.35	23.00
PLE PEAS	1.55	3.40	7.30	12.20
I MAPLES	1.60	3.50	7.50	13.25
N PEAS	1.60	3.75	9.00	16.90
BEANS	1.35	2.70	4.95	N/A
NG BEANS	1.60	3.75	9.00	16.90
VA BEANS	1.60	3.75	9.00	16.90
A BEANS	3.10	7.20	17.00	32.00
ICOT BEANS	2.10	4.70	11.20	21.15
TO BEANS	2.10	4.70	11.20	21.15
E PEAS	1.60	3.75	9.00	16.90
UT PELLETS NO 4 (SMALL)	2.10	4.50	10.95	19.50
UT PELLETS NO 6 (LARGE)	2.30	5.20	11.90	21.65
W SINKING TROUT PELLETS	2.30	5.20	11.90	21.65
MON FRY CRUMB	4.45	10.00	18.60	33.75

TICLE BAIT' SWEATSHIRTS AVAILABLE IN NAVY, BLACK OR BOTTLE GREEN £12.50 EACH
TICLE BAIT' POLOSHIRTS AVAILABLE IN EMERALD, NAVY, or WHITE £12.50 EACH

ATERS

M MIXER	9KILO BAG ONLY	£7.85
NO 2	2K £2.00	5K £3.90
MIX	2K £3.75	5K £8.75
RTED FLOATERS-SPECIAL OFFER	3KILO BAG ONLY	£2.50
PED SUNFLOWER	2K £1.95	5K £4.20
LOWER	2K £1.95	5K £4.20

MIX INGREDIENTS	1KILO	5KILO
VIMI FISH MEAL	£2.00	£9.00
LIN MEAL	£2.00	£9.00
OVY MEAL	£2.10	£9.10
FISH MEAL	£2.10	£9.10
MEAL	£3.50	£16.00
ALBUMIN	£7.25	£35.00
WHEY POWDER	£7.50	£36.00
ESH RENNET CASEIN	£7.25	£35.00
ESH LACTIC CASEIN	£7.25	£35.00
IUM CASEINATE	£7.25	£35.00
ALBUMEN	£12.50	1lb £6.50
LE EGG REPLACER	£6.50	£30.00
FAT SOYA FLOUR	£2.00	£7.50
PICAL' HIGH FAT BINDER	£1.70	£7.00
N EXTRACT	6oz £11.50	
EXTRACT	6oz £8.50	
GRUESO RRR PAPRIKA	£6.50	10K £55.00
HED HEMP 1½ KILO BUCKET	£3.00	
FLOUR 16K BAG ONLY	£7.90	
NDBAIT - FINE OR COARSE		
N OR WHITE	42lb BAG FOR £10.00	

BIRD FOOD INGREDIENTS

SUPER SEGGO takes bird food ingredients one step further - this excellent ready-ground product will make the bird food bait of your dreams. The make-up and consistency is perfect for holding large amounts of liquid additives and should be used for up to 70% of your base mix. **SUPER SEGGO** Analysis is as follows:

ADDED PER KG

Vitamin A-19,500 I. U.	Vitamin D3-2,00 I. U.	Vitamin E-30mg	Vitamin K3-2.2mg
Vitamin B1-12mg	Vitamin B2-38mg	Pantothenic Acid-55mg	Choline Chloried-475mg
Niacin-10mg	Vitamin B6-1.75mg	Vitamin B12-0.075mg	Folic Acid-6.8mg
Biotin-0.36mg	Vitamin C-4mg	Calcium-0.9mg	Phosphorous-0.4%
Sodium-0.05%	Magnesium-125mg	Magnese-80mg	Zinc-58mg
Iron-29mg	Cobalt-18mg	Copper-5mg	Iodene-1.2mg
DL Methionine-500mg	L-Lynsine 1,150mg	Selenium-0.1mg	

SUPER SEGGO	1KILO £2.99	5KILO £11.99	20KILO £39.99		
SUPER REDOSEG	1KILO £3.40	5KILO £13.30	20KILO £49.50		

ROGER RED
Highly concentrated bird food colouring containing many different peppers/colours etc. Bright red a very popular ingredient for many years now.

1KILO £6.00   5KILO £25.00

B.L.O
Excellent binder or bulk ingredient high in oils and has been a very popular bird food for many years now.

1KILO £1.75   5KILO £7.50

HONEY BLEND
Mixture of egg biscuit honey small seed vitamins and minerals has been a very popular bird food ingredient for many years now.

1KILO £2.95   5KILO £12.50

OPTIMA   HIGHLY CONCENTRATED VITAMIN, MINERAL & AMINO ACID SUPPLIMENT
£4.99 100g   £21.99 lb

AMBIO FEEDING TRIGGER   125ml £3.53   500ml £11.20

'MYSTIC' As its name suggests is no ordinary base mix. It is a well balanced, high carbohydrate bait containing a vast array of vitamins, minerals, amino acids and finest quality milk proteins. You will find it a dream to roll and it will fly through any roller process. We have added the best egg albumen to ensure the quality is not affected by excessive boiling. The bait has been designed to be free fed at long range and has had excellent results both home and abroad.

MYSTIC ORIGINAL	1 KILO £6.50	5KILO £29.00	20KILO £95.00
MYSTIC FISH	1 KILO £6.50	5KILO £29.00	20KILO £95.00
MYSTIC SURPRISE	1 KILO £6.50	5KILO £29.00	20KILO £95.00

"MYSTIC" HOODED SWEATSHIRTS (BLACK)   £16.75 EACH
"MYSTIC" BASEBALL CAPS (BLACK)   £3.75 EACH
"MYSTIC" T. SHIRTS (BLACK)   LARGE £6.75   XL £6.95

ESSENTIAL OILS   20ml DROPPER BOTTLES

CINNAMON	£4.70	EUCALYPTUS	£4.70
GARLIC	£9.75	GERANIUM	£4.70
ASOFOETIDA	£13.80	SAVAGESPICE	£7.15
PEPPERMINT	£4.70	ANISEED (10ML)	£2.00

BULK OILS   500ml BOTTLES

SCREAMER FISH OIL	£4.50
SCOFF FISH FEED INDUCING OIL	£4.50
SNARE CAPELIN OIL	£4.50
SERPENT COD LIVER OIL	£4.50
SHADOW PURE SALMON OIL	£10.00
SAPPHIRE DOG FISH OIL	£4.50
SHIVER WINTERISED PURE SALMON OIL	£10.00

CIPRO
These **ETHYL ALCOHOL FLAVOURS** are not only the best acceptable solvent for carp. They do more. For instance they will give you a smell for at least 12 hours in summer and winter.

BANANA ROYAL	pH. 5.3	PISTACHE	pH. 5.4	REAL CHOCOLATE	pH. 5.5
CREAM	pH. 5.5	RASPBERRY	pH. 3.7	PEANUT	pH. 4.4
PINEAPPLE	pH. 5.6	WATERMELON	pH. 5.2	SPICE MIX	pH. 5.1
BUTTER-CARAMEL	pH. 5.1	APRICOT	pH. 6.1	NOUGAT	pH. 4.2
STRAWBERRY FORT	pH. 2.8				

50ml £4.99   250ml £16.99

CONCENTRATED LIQUID SWEETENER	CONCENTRATED POWDER COLOURS	SWEET FLAVOUR ENHANCER pH. 4.2
50ml £2.74 250ml £10.90	RED, YELLOW, ORANGE and PINK 50gr £3.35	50gr £5.75

Videos   £19.99

La Carping
Complete guide to carp fishing in **France** with Andy Little. Loads of action carp to 40lb.

Carping on Particles
The much acclaimed video starring **Andy Little** with information on preparation rigs etc. Superb action as well as being a complete guide to particle fishing.

Gravel Pit Carping
How to approach large gravel pits with **Andy Little** and Arsenal & England Goalkeeper David Seaman. Rigs/bait etc, etc, + footage of three 20's.

Winter Carping
The complete guide to winter carping with **Andy Little**. Loads of information. Location, rigs, baits, etc, etc. With Footage of Andy's first English

+ Other titles coming **Soon**

W TO ORDER   **BY POST** SEND CHEQUE OR P.O INCLUDING P+P. PAYABLE TO HINDERS OF SWINDON TO THE ADDRESS ABOVE   **BY TELEPHONE** QUOTING YOUR ACCESS OR VISA CARD NUMBER DURING OPENING HOURS.   **PERSONAL CALLERS** BAIT CENTRE OPEN MONDAY-SATURDAY 8.30AM-5.30PM. WE ARE ONLY 10 MILES FROM HORSE SHOE LAKE!

MARSH TACKLE

LATE NIGHT TILL 7PM FRIDAY

4 Cross Court · Plomergreen Avenue · Downley · High Wycombe · Bucks · Tel: (0494) 437035

Free car parking outside shop

FOX INTERNATIONAL

BEDCHAIRS AND CHAIRS
Ultra Deluxe **NEW** Available May	£219.90
Super Deluxe	£189.90
Std Deluxe	£139.90
Super Adjusta Level Chair	£74.90
Standard Adjusta Level Chair	£49.90

BIVVIES AND BROLLIES
Super Bivvy	£154.90
Super Brolly	£134.90
Super Brolly In-fill	£54.90
Specimen Brolly	£74.90

ACCESSORIES
Fox Pod 48"	£34.50
Fox Pod 30"	£26.50
Super Pod **NEW** Available April	£47.50
−10°C Sleeping Bag **NEW** Available April	£49.90
Bechair Frame Support Tube	£7.50
NEW Swinger	£11.90
Swinger Heads – red, green, yellow	£3.90

REELS — SHIMANO
Aero GT 3500 (2 spools)	£89.90
Aero GT 4000 (2 spools)	£96.90
Aero GT 4500 (2 spools)	£99.90
Spheros 4000F	£81.90
Spheros 5000F	£86.90
SS 3000 (Daiwa)	£175.00
PM 4000H	£85.99
Br 2050 (2 spools)	£69.99
Br 2650 (2 spools)	£74.99

ROD HUTCHINSON
The Ultimate Bivvy Available May	£159.95
One Man Bivvy **NEW** Available May	£139.95

LUGGAGE AND ACCESSORIES
Pukka Rucksack	£99.99
12' High Protection Rod Holdall	£85.99

THE EDGE BRAIDED HOOKLINK
10lb 25 metres	£7.99
15lb 25 metres	£7.99

HOOKS
Kinryu – size 8, 9, 10, 11 (pk 6)	£2.50
Owner Eyed Cutting Points (pk 6)	£4.95

ROD STANDS (K/B)
2 Rod Unit	£61.99
3 Rod Unit	£66.99
3 Rod Special	£71.99
Stalker Unit	£47.99
Intruder Alarm	£40.99

KEVIN NASH
Hooker 12' Deluxe Holdall	£87.99
Hooker 13' Deluxe Holdall	£89.99
Hooker S 11' Standard Holdall	£44.99
Hooker S 12' Standard Holdall	£46.99
Titan Rucksack 90	£98.99
Titan Rucksack 120	£125.99
Oval Umbrella	£97.99

PREMIER BAITS

FISH BASE MIXES
Fish Base Mix	£ 5.20 per Kg
Spiced Fish Base Mix	£ 5.75 per Kg
Marine Mix	£ 5.75 per Kg
Fish Fodder	£ 4.20 per Kg
Supreme Fish Mix	£ 7.50 per Kg

FISH OILS
Fish Feeding Inducing Oil	£ 5.50 per 500ml
Noddoil	£11.00 per 500ml
P.D.F.A. Supplement Oil	£10.00 per 200ml
Liquid Flavours	£ 2.50 per 50ml

SOLAR TACKLE

NEW MIXMASTERS
Golden Plum	£ 4.50 per 100ml
Japanese Squid and Octopus	£ 8.99 per 100ml
White Chocolate	£ 6.60 per 100ml
Esterblend 12	£ 4.99 per 100ml

POWDER ENHANCERS 4oz TUBS
Fresh Fruit	£4.10
White Chocolate	£5.99
Candy Sweetener	£4.55

SAVAY SEED MIXES
Spice, yellow, quench	£ 6.99 per 1Kg
Red	£ 7.45 per 1Kg
Neptune	£ 6.45 per 1Kg

NEW FOR 1992
Sweet Tangerine	£ 8.90 per 100ml
Stainless Pod	£89.95

OPTONICS
Super XL	£77.00
NEW 4 Channel Sounder Box	£69.95
Daiwa MkII Sensitron	£76.99
Bitech Viper	£49.99
Sounder Box (3 rod)	£35.00

KRYSTON PRODUCTS
NEW Magma Liquid Weight in a Tube
NEW Hawser Permanent Stiffener
NEW 'Klin-ik' Fish Care Antiseptic

RODS
AKN 12S 12' 2¼ TC	£210.00
AKN 12SU 12' 2½ TC	£215.00
AKN 12H 12' 2¾ TC	£215.00
WKN 2212 12' 2½ TC	£150.00

SHIMANO
NEW Diaflash Specimen 12' 2½ TC	£178.99
Diaflash Specimen 12' 2¼ TC	£173.99
Twin Power 12' 2½ TC	£123.00
Twin Power 12' 2¼ TC	£117.00
Twin Power 11' 2¼ TC	£112.00
Twin Power 11' 1¾ TC	£101.00

ARMALITE
12' 2¼ TC	£159.10
12' 2½ TC	£162.50
12' 2¾ TC	£166.10
Black Max 13' 3 TC	£217.85

ORDER BY PHONE USING ACCESS/VISA OR SEND CHEQUES/PO's
WE HAVE THREE OR SIX MONTHS INTEREST FREE CREDIT AVAILABLE